SHOT GLASS

One woman's fight to save her kingdom ~ A raw, powerful memoir

ROCHELLE

Rochelle Books

The only person you become is the person you decide to be. - Ralph Waldo Emerson

TABLE OF CONTENTS

2009

Crispy bacon sizzled next to scrambled, golden yolks in a cast iron pan. The billows of cooked egg were neatly piled atop fresh croissants – three hearty breakfast sandwiches for three hungry kids. After the feeding frenzy, my cubs scurried out of the kitchen to brush their teeth. Ah, it was the perfect opportunity to discreetly call the police.

Chief Harold addressed my issue, stating flatly, "Your item is ready, ma'am. Sorry it took so long."

The wait for this item had been tinged with reluctance, so I hadn't minded the delay. "That's all right. I'll pick it up before noon." I went back to washing dishes. Suds whirled and swirled down the drain. Cleaning up everybody's mess was a task I often seemed to do.

"VÁMONOS A LA MINIVAN, kids! We're running late."

Arriving at the soccer field, Connor – the oldest, at eleven – was the first to get out. He waved goodbye with a boyish grin and ran off to practice. Next, I dropped my daughter and youngest son off at a thespian camp.

"Thanks for sewing our costumes, Mom," said Jolie, aged nine, as she exited the van.

"Today, we practice the sword fighting scene," exclaimed five-year-old Nicholas as he drew out an imaginary sword to fight what must have been giant pirates dangerously encircling his sister.

I headed back towards our police station, treating the stop as another ordinary errand. Our Americana town was close-knit, having only one school for grades kindergarten through sixth. It also had a library built in the late 1800s, a dance studio, a third-generation dentist, a single eatery – Athena's Coffee Shop – and Whitehall's Greenhouse. Mr. Whitehall delivered his Christmas trees straight to your living room, with tree-stand attached. Our town developed in the mid-1800s; it's humble lakes were a lure for wealthy city folk. It even boasted a military academy at one point. Woodland areas hugged the outskirts of this mile-by-two-mile gem, while canopies of oak and maple branches arched gracefully over the streets and sidewalks. The compact police station was housed inside a Tudor style municipal building.

Once inside the station, I greeted the chief with a smile that hid my underlying embarrassment. Chief Harold's sincere expression and casual conversation eased my defenses. We engaged in small talk. He inquired, "How are things going?" He really wanted to know if I was safe. This regurgitated the taste of post-traumatic emotions, once laid to rest.

"We're good, thank you."

With a rapid pulse, I wrote out a check for twenty dollars: twenty bucks for a cassette tape, but I'd pay anything to hear his statement about *the incident* one year ago. Pulling into our drive-way, I found that he had already left for work. Once inside, the house felt unusually quiet, as if I was being directed to do nothing but listen to that tape.

I sat focused and poised in a bedroom decorated with a Hawaiian theme. The cassette player rested on a yellow hibiscus-print bedspread purchased when we lived in Hawaii. Our bedroom had Polynesian artwork and a magnificent, hand-carved teak armoire which had taken four strong men to carry up the stairs. Unable to press 'play', I pondered: what would be gained from listening to his version? Maybe I wanted to hear some kind of explanation, or a sense of remorse in his tone about that day. The day I ran from my house, fleeing in a zigzag pattern to lessen my chances of getting shot. Then I hid in a neighbor's yard – crouched against unforgiving branches – my instincts akin to a deer listening for any twig to break underfoot the approaching hunter. Burned into memory, was the image of my husband, emerging from the shadows, with a gun.

BACKSTORY

Preliminary scans: no red flags. My husband and I had been married for eleven years, both working in healthcare. Our grand, colonial house with mint green stucco and white trim was dubbed one of the prettiest in the neighborhood. The rolling backyard opened to a brick patio overlooking a variety of boxwoods, dogwoods, and a massive cherry blossom tree. In late spring, the fallen blooms transformed the bladed grass to pink snow that coated both the gazebo, and a wooden play structure. Tucked off to the side was a raised, in-ground pool surrounded by a brick deck laced with spherical boxwoods and rose bushes that we couldn't quite master. By request, our property had been in the community's charming "Garden and Porch Tour" two years in a row. This home was a far reach from my pleasant, split-level house/early-on trailer park upbringing where "swimming" meant running through the sprinkler. We weren't poor. I would label it as contained cookie-cutter living with muted stimulation.

After college, my spritely wings flew me to Hawaii to begin a new life as an occupational therapist at one of the largest hospitals on the islands. Two other recently transplanted occupational therapists were looking for a third person to share renting a house near Diamond Head. Immediately, I had friends, a home, and an amazing job at a hospital designated as the trauma center for the entire Pacific Basin. Occupational therapists (OTs) are trained to treat clients with disabilities in the fields of physical, mental, and pediatric health; in addition, some OTs specialize in hand rehabilitation. Regardless, we all use daily activities, exercise and therapeutic use-of-self to return our patients back to living as independently as possible. My roommates worked on the mental health side of the hospital. I worked on the medical side, rotating through all the departments: cardiac, orthopedic, pediatric, oncology, neurology, and the saddest, ICU. I heard *Amazing Grace* sung many times by a hopeful family member standing watch over a comatose loved-one with a fresh spinal cord injury or brain bleed. Often, the only movements from these patients came from the hands of a therapist, such as myself, performing range of motion. Working in this hospital had a profound effect on me. I took nothing for granted and kept life's tragedies in perspective.

My roommates had done all the inviting for our house-warming party at which I met my future husband. One of the invited guests was a resident from their department, a blonde-haired man reminiscent of a young Robert Redford, except for the donned earring and a homemade Mickey Mouse vest. I opened the door and he handed me a house warming plant. He was the only one who had thought to do that for us. He drank a lot that night, like many others, but he held it together. I rarely drank, same as my parents; I did not give it much thought. We hit it off at the party, and began dating from there. Socializing within the pack of new friendships and roommates while exploring the islands helped to enhance our relationship. I was twenty-five, and he thirty-one. He played guitar, grew up in Europe, cooked with international flair, read Hemingway, and had won a marathon race. He seemed so worldly—a true Renaissance man. I was in awe. Marriage and kids soon followed, as did a move back to the mainland to be near my family. That house warming plant lasted the entire eight years we lived in Hawaii.

Alcohol had befriended my husband way before we got married. I had come to understand the phrase: *he's got the monkey on his back*. Addiction has power like that of a wild, intelligent, manipulative animal and that beast would have sooner chewed me up than give up its host. In retrospect, it took a while to uncover myself from the feces this animal threw at me. I became educated about alcoholism. I talked to recovered addicts who broke their denial and walked the walk of accountability. Their genuineness helped me to recognize that I was swirling in a sea of denial and chaos, while defeatedly trying to point out someone else's shit. Occasionally, my husband's cover-ups dissipated; nurturing opportunities emerged between us. Our kindness and forgiveness became a salve for the malignancy in his wounded core which festered in Pandora's Box – the holding place for trauma and secrets. Pandora's Box is where evil creeps in and God gets pushed out.

PRESS THE CASSETTE BUTTON. Round and round the small cogwheels pulled through a vast turning point in our lives. I fast forwarded my statement, which came first – it was not why I had asked for the tape. Upon hearing his voice, my heart jumped to my throat, but settled back down on command. Intently, I listened to what my husband had said:

"...We had an argument; there was some confusion... My wife was screaming she was going to take the kids. I did not want her taking the kids from their home. I just wanted to scare her. Yes, I had been drinking... I thought she might get the gun—safer if I had it. Yes, she knows where I keep it. ...target shooting in Hawaii. I never re-registered it. The kids were sleeping; they never even woke up! ...My older son was at a friend's? Yes, right. ...I was by the stairs. ...Oh right, must have been the other room. I showed her the gun. Said something like, 'We're not on the same page' and she walked out. I put the gun away and went back to sleep."

The officer repeated some official data, and the statement ended. The tape continued to spin, much like my head. Static waves filled the air around me. He said, "I walked out?"

I stopped my brain from reeling and seized the moment to summon my analytical mind. Perhaps it was unrealistic to expect total recall after an alcohol-influenced psychotic break—if that's what it was. Naturally, he wanted to avoid the immense shame from exhibiting behavior unbecoming of a spouse. The police did not probe why we had been arguing; certainly, I was not "confused". In my humble opinion, the police interviewers lacked some competence; for example, when my husband's event sequencing did not make sense, the officers filled in the blanks. More importantly, he was never questioned about the most critical detail: "Was the gun loaded?" "Were there bullets in the gun?" *It sure seemed loaded from my end. Did it matter what I thought?*

ALCOHOL CAN BE a dark bridge for the past to cross over into the present. My spouse's habitual drinking pattern was there every day from the beginning, maintaining a low profile. I was able to roll with it for a while, but then I had wanted more from a partner, and kept scratching the surface. My husband tried to make changes, made limited progress, and inevitably, promises were broken.

Whatever personal growth I was supposed to gain from my marriage would never be realized. I was so done, like an exhausted hamster spinning on the wheel of samsara, or, as so eloquently defined by Albert Einstein: "Insanity is doing the same thing over and over, but expecting a different result." That dude was on to something.

Time to let go, but what was the plan? My plan...was to make a plan. Perhaps I could generate some forward momentum by re-examining, with fresh eyes, what had happened one year ago on that August summer night because I was facing, yet again, a turning point. *What would I do?*

2008

Train yourself to let go of everything you fear to lose. ~ Master Yoda

The three of us snuggled in Jolie's bed like an Oreo cookie. My precocious eight-year-old daughter was on one side of me, reading a 'Little Critter' story, and my sleepy, four-year-old Nicholas was listening on the other. As youngsters, both Nicky and Jolie had golden blonde hair and Nordic blue eyes, like their father. Connor, who had inherited my green Irish eyes, beating out my Italian side, was sleeping at a friend's house. What else was new? After story time and goodnight hugs, Nicky and I had gone to his room. There, he was tucked into bed with his favorite pack of stuffed animals, fondly known as *The Stuffies.* My husband preferred to remain downstairs watching TV. Again, what else was new?

The family room was dimly lit by a brass reading lamp and the TV. I sat down on the navy-blue carpet with only the coffee table and a glass of red wine between us. My husband lay on the brown leather sofa with his feet crossed and his head propped up on a throw pillow. He methodically glanced at me, then refocused his attention to the screen across the room.

Our conversation had begun with the phrase every spouse

loves to hear: "We need to talk." My soliloquy was well rehearsed: brutally honest, yet calm and concise. I would merely pin-prick his emotional responses. My goals were to introduce the situation as it stood, make clear expectations, and establish a later date for making a joint decision, thus allowing him time to get on board and not feel ambushed. By design, this conversation was to be a "prep-talk" before the "talk-talk".

My husband's immediate response was to turn off the TV and demonstrate a passive annoyance by folding his hands across his stomach, fixating on the ceiling, and continuing to lie on his back. Wearing my warrior skin, I ventured my request. "It's about your drinking. You have promised over and over to quit, and you haven't. You've put our lives in chaos, and quite frankly, you are abusive—verbally abusive." To this he allowed a dismissive wince. That particular complaint had come from me before, leading to his usual explanation that I did not really know what the word "abusive" meant. He would then further proclaim: "You are not some battered woman in a shelter; you have a problem, with feedback".

Onward I forged. "Here's the bottom line: I cannot live like this anymore. I can't raise our kids in this environment, and be who I am supposed to be. You need to do something different. Take some time to think this over. Leave the house for a couple days. Tomorrow is Wednesday; come back on Friday. We'll talk and make some decisions together."

My husband took a moment. He sat straight up, cocked his head slightly one way, then, looking less annoyed, tilted it the opposite way. He calmly affirmed with a staccato nod, "You are right. I will cut down—quit, if you want." His elbows were resting on his knees, fingertips lightly touching, much like a politician.

"I'm sorry Josh; your word isn't good enough anymore." I reminded my husband of our latest compromise: no "hard stuff". He had told me that hard alcohol was "the start of a slippery slope", but beer and wine were okay. A fine prescription...we had thought.

"Do you want to taste this?" he asked, pushing the stemmed glass in my direction. "It's Merlot."

"I know you're drinking hard liquor."

He gave a firm, straight in the eye, "No, I am not."

"Come on. Is this where we get stuck? I have to prove you're drinking, so that we can address you're drinking?"

"You're crazy!" he said. "I have some wine at dinner, and you want to make it a problem!"

"Okay," I said, pulling my shoulders back. "If I produce a bottle, right now, to prove you're still drinking, can we move to my point? And my point is that you broke your promise, and our family shouldn't have to live like this anymore."

"Sure." Josh stiffened up, effectively smoothing out his purple, Hawaiian marathon T-shirt.

HIS HARLEY MOTORCYCLE was parked out back in a small, attached garage. After digging inside the saddlebags, I retrieved a bottle of Jack and brought it inside. I stood the empty whiskey bottle on the table, next to the now emptied glass of wine. After appearing surprised, my husband regained his composure stating, "That is an old bottle."

"You made this promise over a month ago."

"I do not know exactly how old that bottle is, Jessica. I probably forgot about it. Technically, that bottle is outside the house. Why do you have to be so controlling? Why do you come after me? I work all day and pay the bills. I make myself dinner because you can't cook. I'm sitting here on the sofa, trying to relax, so that I can get up and do the exact same thing tomorrow — and I'm such a bad guy?" His broad sinewy shoulders and neck stretched out toward me.

Stay calm. The plan was to speak concisely, and repeat as needed.

With the intensity of a gentle breeze, I said, "Let's try again.

I know it's hard to see how your drinking affects us, but it does." Josh appeared to ponder this data while maintaining a straight face. He offered no reply. I continued. "If I produce another bottle, can we agree that you're still drinking?"

"What bottle?" as if I was talking about a ghost.

"If I find another bottle of alcohol, can we agree that we have a broken promise?" My husband folded his arms across his chest and entered a state of peculiar stillness which often stood out to me.

Within a few moments he replied, "Sure."

OFF TO THE BASEMENT, where behind a spacious playroom was an unfinished workroom. In recent years, the playroom had doubled as a yoga studio so that I could teach yoga and Pilates classes while staying at home with the kids. Josh had started hiding his alcohol in the workroom about eight months ago, after I confronted him about his failed, three-week attempt to quit drinking. I never told him that I knew about the stash. Keeping it a secret gave me a sense of security that I had a handle on things.

Climbing onto a work table, I reached around the exposed ceiling rafters, grabbed his bottle of Evans whiskey, and rushed back upstairs. Just because I'm five foot four didn't mean I couldn't look up. I placed the half-empty Evans bottle, next to the empty Jack bottle, next to the empty wine glass. *Does he really think I'm clueless? His personality changes when he drinks – that's what rats him out, not my snooping. I snoop to confirm that I'm not crazy.*

Josh lifted his chin, scratched his jaw and articulated, "I know you have concerns. I-I need to get healthy again. Consider it done."

"You tried that, a few times." We were beyond words.

"Tried a few times? Jessica, what are you talking about?" he exclaimed with surprise.

"Josh, we have been in this place before. You are escalating.

You've become physically menacing. This, this...I don't know what to call it— "layer" in you—is bleeding out." I pressed on sarcastically. "But, according to you, I should be thankful for your courteous physical restraint, right?"

My motionless husband's face held a cold, removed expression as he stared at the table. Josh had weaned himself off any acceptance of responsibility towards his actions. But inside me was an incubating quest to make him understand, and stop: stop all of it. I continued like a persistent knock. "You are verbally abusive, and you psychologically twist things. It's absolutely draining."

His jawline snapped to face mine. "I do not call you names, Jessica. I call you out on the things that you do."

"Upgrading from 'stupid fuck-up' to 'twit' is still name calling, and it's equally degrading, coming from you." He had scowled and turned away. Imitating Josh's tone, I mimicked, "'Jess-i-ca, I don't know any other ed-u-cated person who would think the way you do.'" With my hands in the air, I snapped. "That's like smearing dirt on my face, and calling it a facial."

Josh remained a tense statue as I forged deeper. "You tune me out at night like I don't exist. I have to ask you to put your kids to bed so they can have meaningful time with you. On top of that, if I don't ask you in the right tone, you snap about it in front of the kids. Your justification is that I asked in such a 'crabby way'; if I would just 'ask nicely', you wouldn't get 'so mad.' I don't want the job of asking you to be a parent – it's exhausting, and frustrating. Raising a child is a beautiful, loving part of life and you are robbing me of it. And for what? So, you can drink from a bottle that doesn't exist? I don't think so. This is not a request."

"You cannot kick me out of the house, Jessica!"

"I am not kicking you out. I'm asking you to step away for a couple days to grasp the gravity of the situation. I am treating you with respect."

"No. I am not leaving my own house!"

Deciding to play hard ball, I said, "Fine. I will go."

His eyes popped open beneath furled, blonde eyebrows. "Where are you going to go?"

"I'll stay with my dad. He's four minutes away. I can easily drive the kids back and forth to school. Oh, you get that, right? If I go, the kids come with me," I stated matter of factly.

Pounding his fist on the table, "You cannot kidnap the kids!"

"What?" My brain reversed a one-eighty. "I'm not 'kidnapping' the kids! You choose not to get up with them. I handle their care. The choice of the kids having to leave their home is yours."

His eyes flashed like a dog's when you try to take its bone. "You are going to take the kids from their home? From this beautiful house that I work to maintain?" his arms opened wide, waving around in the air. His tone was a steady, rolling boil.

Momma Bear answered through clenched teeth. "No, I am not taking them from their home. You are choosing not to go! If I leave, I'm a package deal. End of story." *Checkmate or stalemate?* I stood up and nodded my goodbye. I climbed up the stairs and closed the bedroom door. I crawled across the bed, made an agitated nest amidst the comforter and crossed my arms tight. *Humph. That went well.*

MUCH TIME PASSED. Safe to say, neither I nor my spouse slept. Then I heard Josh's footsteps on the stairs. He quietly entered our room and climbed into bed. The basic ritual of going to bed together rarely occurred, least of all after an argument. The norm was my husband drank his wine, or whatever, while watching TV and fell asleep on the sofa. According to Dr. Josh, he had exceptionally stressful days at the psych clinic, and this routine was his way of relaxing. Hence, for years, I usually slept alone or snuggled with a kid. Next rarity was to have a make-up conversation after an argument. Typically, I brewed or journaled and Josh read a *New Yorker* or watched TV. The next morning, we would act like the night before never happened, which was not my preference. It left me in a stupor, holding onto words said, and their still-tethered emotions. Under the covers next to me, Josh whispered, "We both got out of hand. I'm sorry. Let's just wake up in the morning and get back to being us." *No can-do, mister.* His attempt to blow this away like a crumpled leaf was not going to fly. Replying with full composure I said, "I appreciate that, Josh. Let me know in the morning what you want to do. One of us needs time to pack." I grabbed my pillows and left the room. I marched straight up to the third floor, which was set up as a comfortable spare room, and made my stay.

FOR OVER AN HOUR I laid in bed, emotionally and physically exhausted, craving for sleep to hit me like a tsunami and over-power my brain waves. I wanted to wake up to a fresh beach of thoughts and know where to place my next set of footprints. For too many nights I had asked myself, "Should we stay together for the sake of the kids?" Most times, that answer had been *yes.* Without roles to play, such as wife or husband, father or mother, Josh and I were good roommates. Overall, he was a better room-mate than me. He was neat, organized, habitual, and motivated. But recently, I had experienced a paradigm shift from asking myself, *What was the best I could do in this relationship?* to *What kind of woman would I be if I were in my ideal relationship?* or *What if, I was in an energizing and uplifting relationship, versus a starving and shielding one?*

My upgraded response: I would be amazing. So, I had shifted some blame and ownership onto myself which helped manifest solutions to appear within my grasp and upheave the mental status quo. I stopped looking at how to stay in this marriage and began searching on how to get out. Many people would have used such a juxtaposition as an excuse to seek an affair. In my opinion, that would have been a medicated way to jump ship and search for the next ticket to ride without bothering to dock the life raft currently in use, and safely let all the other passengers off. For now, I had to hold the tiller and steer this family ashore.

Lying in an attic bed, my consciousness finally gave way. Before drifting off, familiar noises rose from the floors below. First, it was the sound of Josh walking around, then the front door opening and closing. Unable to claw away from desperately needed sleep, I managed a mental note to later check as to why he had exited the front door.

MISSION IMPOSSIBLE

One REM cycle later, I woke up, placing the time to be about 4:30-5:00 in the morning. My gut told me Josh had done something, and I had better figure it out. Quietly descending the attic stairs was no big deal. I peeked into our bedroom: empty bed. The next set of stairs ended by the front door, an obstacle course of fourteen boards that creaked at random. Carefully distributing my weight on each step, and pausing after each creak, I finished the descent by scooting down the bannister. *Whew. Don't think he heard me.*

Sensible thinking led me to investigate outside, but what was I searching for? Guessed I would know when I knew. If Josh had gone outside, it was most likely to do something with the cars, which we kept unlocked with the keys inside for convenience; we trusted our neighborhood. Both vehicles were still in place. I pulled the door handle to the minivan – locked. I checked all the doors on both cars – all locked. No doubt he had taken the keys, so that I could not take a car.

Wanting a complete assessment, I looked around everywhere, even glancing over the backyard. Nothing appeared out of place. I ransacked the Harley saddle bags for hidden keys: no luck. I re-entered the house through the backyard basement door, and ascended the back stairs into the kitchen pantry. I padded through the kitchen to the small, six-foot hallway where we kept the landline. The telephone was there, but the cord had been disconnected and removed. Red flag, but I soon made it pink. He had done this once before after a fight, explaining he did not want me to call a friend and complain. All systems were on alert, but I was not alarmed. I had already learned a new normal.

Moving on, I noticed that resting on the counter was my purse, undisturbed...too undisturbed. I opened it. My driver's license, credit cards in my name and my cell phone were missing. *Uh-huh. He had never done that before.* Well, if his plan was to stop me from leaving before he woke up, then I would remain one step ahead. In order to do that, I needed to find where he had hidden my keys. They were probably near him. I assumed Josh was sleeping in the TV room, which we entered by way of the formal living room through narrow French doors. Never had I thought, we would live in a house with so many rooms.

Through the darkness, I tiptoed across the useless living room. Once at the skinny French doors, I went commando and belly crawled into the TV room until reaching the back of the sofa. Josh's deep, half-snore was unusually loud; he must have really tied one on. From behind the sofa, I rose to my knees and peeked at the situation: Josh was out cold, the bottle of whiskey completely empty. There was no visible sign of my keys, or my cell phone. His front jean pockets appeared empty; checking them was not worth the risk.

Going commando again, I retrieved his work bag from his desk, then crawled back out to the living room. This was the attaché jackpot: Dr. Josh kept everything here. My searching hands found only his keys, his wallet, and his cell phone, all in their usual compartments. *Darn it.* Once again, I crawled across the floor, returned the attaché, then popped up to check his desk. This proved to be a fruitless search of three drawers. I briefly checked other spaces in the room, but my stuff did not turn up. I crawled on all fours past Josh's snoring body. His new, grown-out biker hair splayed around his goatee; it was a far cry from his usual clean-cut attractiveness. I regrouped myself in the living room. Where else would he put them? *Ah, the downstairs workroom.*

IT WAS AN ADMIRABLE, makeshift workroom with tools, bicycle parts, hockey equipment, and the scent of damp cement. No way we could have afforded the house if my husband had not possessed the ability to repair at least half of the ever-arising problems. Leaning against one wall was Josh's homemade wine rack, crafted to hold about forty wine bottles. It currently had about twenty, all empty. My things were not in the workroom. This dead end spawned another idea—a brilliant idea: *I will take his wallet, his keys and his cell phone...an eye for an eye! Then, I shall report this to the police for documented proof.* I visualized a stern police officer requesting right in Josh's face that he give back my keys and my phone. This time, Josh would not be able to deny his behavior, or claim that his wife was being irrational. Finally, someone would have my back, although, that someone was supposed to be my spouse.

One last rummage through his hockey bag...nothing. Before turning out the workroom light, a tiny thought pulsed through me: *check the gun case.* There it was on the shelf. I opened the case; it was empty. There was nothing but grey foam molded to fit a 9mm handgun.

I dismissed this information, deciding that the weapon must be upstairs, under a pile of clothes, on that high shelf in our closet. Josh had gotten the gun for target shooting with one of his friends back in Hawaii. Once that hobby was over, it went by the wayside.

UPSTAIRS, I crawled back into the sleeping lion's den to carry out my plan. Once again, while he snored, I pulled out his work bag, absconded his wallet and keys, and hid them downstairs in the basement inside a cooler. I thought it prudent to keep his cell phone on me. By now, it was 5:30 a.m., so I decided to take a shower before going to the police station. It would be a long day ahead and I was tired; it would help me to trudge forth at my best. During the shower, my morals gave rise with the steam. Thought-provoking words surfaced in my mind from one of our world's greatest teachers, Gandhi, who preached, "An eye for an eye leaves the whole world blind."

Seriously? Fine. I will put his things back. But I am keeping his phone and going to the police station; I will be back here with an officer who will hold my husband accountable!

Once washed and dried, I shuffled down the hall to put my dirty clothes in the laundry room. Here, I put down his cell phone and inadvertently left it. I returned to the bedroom closet to get dressed. A nervousness was forming; my heart pumped with anxiety. I swallowed it back. There was no time for fear...I must rotate to other thoughts. I donned a pair of comfortable blue jeans and a white, V-neck shirt.

Relax, you are a step ahead of him. That thought was comforting up until the moment I opened the closet door and Josh was standing there. I froze. Josh simply turned toward the bed and went under the covers. He enigmatically asked as his head touched the pillow, "Why were you taking a shower?"

Thaw, thaw, blink. Someone could have guessed that I was not the brightest bulb on the tree that evening. I imagined a devastating scenario with the police. "Did you ask your husband to give back your things?" and I would be forced to reply, "No." Then, I imagined the worst. The police would demand I go back home, alone, and ask Josh for my stuff back. "If your husband says 'no', then we will help you." End scene.

Right there, that combined notion of losing my only chance at authoritative backup and going back alone against Josh to justify my reality was something I could not bear. I had gone

Looney Toons trying to figure out and point out reality. I just wanted a cop to say to his face, "Knock it off! Stop! Stop all of it!" That was my mental state. Hence, I revealed my hand and blurted out: "Are you going to give back my car keys?"

Boom! came the audible silence of Josh processing the fact that I knew what he had done. He responded with a deep, solid, "No."

Mic-drop. That was all I needed. "Okay then." I left the room, never expecting, that he would follow.

CAT CHASES MOUSE

We darted down the stairs, Josh an arm's length behind me. Again, I asked about my things. Josh handed out more refusals. He maintained an uncomfortably close distance while we moved down the dark hall. I wanted him to get away from me, so I surprised him by asking, "Do you know where your keys are? And your phone?"

It worked. This caused him to retreat to the TV room to check for his belongings. I made the break to rush downstairs and retrieve his stuff from the cooler. Hardwired in my head was this Gandhi-inspired, action-correction plan which had landlocked my thoughts into thinking I could not go to the police about Josh taking my stuff because I had taken his stuff. First things first. In my panicked state, all I could do was cling to the only invited, sane person in the room, and that was Gandhi!

I arrived at the cooler in time to retrieve his keys and wallet and hide them under my shirt before coming back around the corner. *Bam!* Josh was there, looking perplexed. There was just enough natural light to see each other's baffled expressions.

"What are you doing?" his voice low with annoyance.

"Nothing."

He was blocking the stairs. "Where is my stuff, Jessica?" His arms stiffened as his chest neared me.

"Out of my way," I demanded.

"Where is my stuff?" He grabbed my arms. We were face to face.

"Let go of me." My tone was of equal force, ready to call his bluff. He let go of my arms with a shove and I darted up the stairs, still holding his things under my shirt. I was swift enough to reach his desk and put both his items in a drawer before he entered the room. We collided as I exited the TV room.

"Where did you put my stuff, Jessica?"

"Hmm, I don't know. Maybe it's in your desk."

He walked by, disappearing into the TV room while I left with haste for the kitchen.

Here, in the darkened solitude of my most used space, I did something normal to calm myself down. I got a drink of water from the tap. My hands were shaking, but the cool water down my throat felt good. Guess I could have left then, but his anger, mixed with my persistent desire for him to recognize he was being a jerk, gripped me in place. I had figured that the worse our situation got, the more easily we could point out how messed up it was, and somehow find common ground.

Josh plodded down the hall and stopped across from me at the entrance to the kitchen. A butcher's block was between us. Off to my right were the steps to the basement. Without missing a beat, Josh asked, "Where is my phone?"

Volleying back, "Where's *my* phone?" I brought the water to my lips, finished my drink and placed the empty glass back down to rest.

From a place of both shadow and light, he said gruffly, "I don't think you understand. Give – me – back – my phone."

Subtly shifting my weight from hip to hip, I persisted. "How about, you give back my phone, and I'll give back your phone?"

"I don't think we're on the same page," and my husband pulled out a gun from behind his back. He pointed it at the ceiling and cocked it, immediately registering to me...*the safety is off.* That piercing, haunting gun-cocking sound filled me with absolute terror. My quadriceps pulled off the bone, involuntarily yanking my legs toward the back steps before I thought to run. My body was flying down the stairs before my next breath. Heavy-footed, I heard him enter the stairwell, so I jumped the rest of the stairs, landing hard, and sprang left, towards the door. Commands were going off in my head. *Get out the door before he makes it down.* Josh yelled my name from the staircase. *Slam the door shut and get out of sight.* Swiftly, I slammed the basement door, and bolted towards the quickest route out of the yard. *Get up the pool steps before he opens the door.* Leaping up the brick steps, I ripped open the pool gate before Josh swung open the basement door. *Get out of sight.* Sprinting across the brick patio, my focus was on the pool exit leading to the front yard. He called out my name. I pulled on the latch and kicked open the gate which was much taller than me. It flew wide open to the hopeful avenue of escape. *Run. Run! Don't look back, or you'll never outrun him!*

Bucking it across the lawn, I turned with a short zig, then a quick zag to avoid being a direct target. I started to flee towards Tom's house, the nearest across the street. Tom was a big guy. I caught sight of his daughter's tricycle, and my heart said, *You can't go there.* My eyes teared up at the choice to pass the safety of their home so as not to put Tom's family at risk. I kept running, turning left across the street. I ran, leaving a path of trees behind to block a clear view of me. At the corner was a yard with evergreen bushes the size of ginormous snowballs surrounding the porch. Taking a peripheral glance and seeing no sign of Josh, I jumped into those porch bushes like a rabbit to a hole.

SHRINK. Get small. My lungs, desperate for oxygen, were exploding inside my chest. My ears and senses were on high alert as I crouched down into the dirt, against the branches. I waited and listened for him. Frantically, I searched my back pockets for his cell. Where was his cell phone? *Oh no.* I had left it – in the laundry room.

Ten minutes passed before I dared to telescope up to peer

around. I concluded that it was safe to come out of my foxhole and knock on the door of this refuge. I knocked several times, but Mr. Quinsley did not answer. Bedrooms in these old houses were often two stories up. It was about six in the morning. The streets were quiet and undisturbed, unlike my head swirling in the paradox of being surrounded by friends and neighbors, yet being alone, and hunted.

The house next to this house belonged to Kate and Mike, family friends. They were away on vacation with their girls who often played with Jolie and Nicky. Could they have left any doors open? What if they forgot to lock the back door and I could get inside? Before my hand turned their knob, I knew it would be unlocked. This proved true.

As I began to feel safe inside their house, an equally frightening thought entered my head. What if Josh resolved to harming himself? Surely, he was pacing anxiously over this grave stunt to pull a gun on his wife, and the consequences of such actions. Would he consider ending his life as a way out? If he was willing to harm me, I felt he could truly take that option. My world shifted; I became the safe person. I wanted him safe too, or at least not dead. Pacing in Kate and Mike's kitchen, I called 9-1-1 and reported the situation to the dispatcher, also relaying my location, and my concern that out of deep remorse, my husband might try to commit suicide. Obviously, he had gone over some edge.

OUT OF OUR HANDS

The dispatcher asked, "Are there any children in the house?"

I never thought for a moment that Josh would ever harm our kids, and I knew they were still sleeping. This came off as reassuring to the dispatcher, but it was not a guarantee. I walked with the cordless phone into Mike and Kate's backyard. Coincidently, from their backyard, I had a view of my front yard. The dispatcher said the police were on their way and to stay on the phone until an officer reached me. Within minutes, I saw two patrol cars slowly approach...no sirens. One car pulled up next door to the house with my refuge bushes. The other cop car stopped short of my home, hiding from view by parking next to thick, tall hedges. I hung up from my call with the dispatcher, and met a female officer next door on the porch.

She introduced herself as Diane and asked, "Can you call inside your house?"

"No. He disconnected the phone."

"He disconnected the phone?" raising an eyebrow. "How about a cell phone?"

"He took my cell phone and I left his in the laundry room. I'm sure he won't hear it." Diane repeated this information into her communication device. She asked me to try Josh's phone anyway, but there was no answer.

Another officer approached. They both asked me rapid-fire assessment questions. "Did he do anything else? Has he been drinking? Which room is he in? Would he hurt the kids?"

The apparent gravity of the situation was increasing as at least five more police cars crept onto the scene. Some were designated to blockade the streets as neighborhood morning walkers emerged. Other officers began stalking the perimeter. I overheard on Diane's walkie-talkie that two officers had been dispatched to visit the surrounding neighbors, warning them that there was a man with a gun. They were warned not to come out of their houses, and to keep away from the windows.

Funny story about that... One of those dispatched officers came over to speak with Diane, to tell her that he had just finished warning all the neighbors about a man with a gun. Then he asked how were things going in Mike and Kate's house. Oops —this particular officer mixed up the address of my home with the address from which the 9-1-1 call was made. Hence, Diane deconstructed and reconstructed that this officer had just knocked on the door to my house and warned Josh about Josh.

The expression on the officer's face was priceless. Apparently, Josh had thanked him.

Equally diffusing and amusing was the reaction of seventy-year-old Mr. Quinsley, homeowner of the house where the cops and I congregated as command central. Without warning, Mr. Quinsley came shuffling out of his house with the utmost urgency. Mr. Q was shirtless, wearing red-striped boxers and an untied terry cloth robe flapping back like a cape. Upon reaching the end of his porch, he put up a hand toward an officer as if to ask the obvious question, saw me with two more officers, and without a word, did a straight-legged, one-eighty degree turn like Monty Python's skit of silly walks, marched back into his house and shut the front door, leaving us all pleasantly stunned and without comment.

IN SUMMARY, we had tried calling and got nothing. Josh was not presenting himself. He had a gun and there were two children in the house, presumably sleeping. In addition, Josh could have been suicidal – or at this level of dumbness, should have been. The police presence was spontaneously multiplying. I wandered back to Kate and Mike's backyard to take another peek at the front of my house, and— holy crap— a SWAT team had arrived! Where had they come from? Our county had a SWAT team? It was the full package: black van, black body armor, bulletproof shields, and hand signals going. Surreal had just gotten real.

I rejoined the officers at the porch, who were confirming something over their radios, and suddenly, they all darted straight to my house. No one stayed with me. *Okay.* I decided to reverse dash to Kate and Mike's backyard to check out what was happening in my front yard, and saw approximately five regular police officers positioned behind the SWAT van. Then there were three SWAT guys hiding behind sycamore trees, each holding a huge, curved shield. Another lead SWAT guy, holding a bulletproof shield above his face, was backing away from my front door, which was opening. Josh slowly stepped out of our house and descended the red brick steps with his hands in the air. He was still wearing ratty jeans and his purple marathon t-shirt. His recent biker-look with the grown-out hair and the scrappy goatee made him look like a punk.

A megaphone appeared from behind a tree. "Keep your hands in the air!" The lead, crouching SWAT officer cautiously motioned a hand at Josh to come further down the path towards the flanking sycamore trees. Official black gloves pointed for Josh get down on the ground. As Josh went to his knees and then his hands, another SWAT officer sprung out from behind a sycamore, jamming his knees into the offender's back. Josh's body went flat to the ground. The other officers swarmed over and handcuffed Josh while he laid motionless. I could see the empty expression on Josh's face as it was pressed against the grass he meticulously cut week after week. He had a blank stare, and wore the face of complete surrender. This moment mimicked a wild animal to animal take down with Josh dropping to the ground, exposing his vulnerability, and yielding to the hierarchy of the pack. It was a degrading act that was not easy to witness.

Collapsing to the ground, I started sobbing for many reasons, especially that the ordeal was over. I really had thought that Josh was going to kill himself and had felt a surprising amount of relief that he was not dead. I was glad to know I still genuinely cared about him that much. After the feeling of relief touched shore, all the fear he had put me through flooded out, keeping me on my knees.

Emotions, like the tide, receded and revealed the intact pieces that remained on the shore. Collecting myself, and putting these pieces together mentally gave me renewed energy to take on a now manifesting role in my family. Since I was "okay", tables turned on their own because Josh was no longer "okay". What he had done was over. Instinctively, I moved to sorrow for him because he could no longer protect himself. Had

I not witnessed this *animal takedown*, I may not have been so instantly zapped into protector mode. But much like a lioness, I felt that protecting the cubs and our cave included protecting their father too. Behind the vicious roar of Josh was a very decent man; Lord help me separate the two.

UPON REGAINING MY COMPOSURE, I walked around the corner and approached my home. Diane was coming out of the house carrying my four-year-old son, his legs and arms wrapped around her uniform. This had emotionally broken me. I went racing across the street, lifted my son into my arms, and held him. Diane reassured me that my precious daughter was fine and still asleep in her bed. My husband was already in a squad car. I carried my son back inside to find cops swarming around the house. There was a commotion around finding the gun. *Why were they looking for the gun? Josh had it.*

Apparently, word from my husband had been: "There was no gun."

Excuse me? Is someone friggin' kidding me right now?

It would appear Josh's plan of survival was to deny he ever had a gun. Not only was there no gun, but Josh told the cops, "Jessica is crazy and she's being irrational." *Welcome to my world, officers! That is exactly the crap I'm talking about.*

Josh was ever so willing to sell me out. But here came the kicker, I started to sell myself out. First, I tucked my snuggly son into a blanket in front of the TV to let a good 'ole SpongeBob cartoon transport him to the underwater world of Bikini Bottom. Then, I helped look for the gun in the basement, in the kitchen, in our bedroom...until enough time had passed that I jumped ship and tried to make everything go away. I confabulated to them, "It could have been my son's air-soft gun." Officer Diane was not buying it. Another officer insinuated I must know where the gun was hidden. Swearing I did not, I took them to Connor's bedroom and showed them Connor's hand-held, air-soft gun. "Maybe my husband used this, and not a real gun?"

Diane took Connor's gun, but not before giving me a look of total disbelief. And just like that, it became a piece of evidence. Now I was feeling badly that Connor would be upset. He and his friends would often go into the woods, make teams at the mulch pit, and shoot targets. I could not imagine explaining all this to my son. A competition between panic and stupidity arose within me. Catching up to the officers, I offered some honesty. "Perhaps Josh said there was no gun because he's scared that it's not registered."

A tall male cop offered, "Ma'am, that is the least of his problems."

GLANCING OUT OUR FRONT WINDOWS, I could see the chief of police questioning the handcuffed punk in the squad car. Our town chief was not a man to be played. Yet, there was Josh, still holding on to his version. Unbelievable. Another four or five minutes went by before the chief came inside and headed straight for me. He was broad and stocky. The chief squatted next to me like a quarterback would in a huddle and introduced himself. He talked with his hands as much as his words.

"This is what I told your husband. 'There are kids in the house. I don't think you want one of them finding your gun. I know there's a gun and I am not leaving until I find it. If I have to tear up every board in your house, I will.'"

Chief Harold continued. "Your husband said it's in his work bag. Do you know where that is?"

"Ah, yes. He must have put it there after I left."

I took the chief to the TV room where Nicky remained obliviously curled up on the sofa, smiling at the antics of Sponge-Bob, and Patrick the loyal, dolt Starfish. Leaning against the back of the sofa was Josh's work bag. The chief opened the black bag, removed the gun with a cloth in his hand and vanished from the room, ending the "find-the-weapon" drama. That brevity, compared to the gravity of it all, left me like a zombie. I hugged my son; Nicky squeezed me back, as always.

Chief Harold returned and whispered to me: "Are there any other weapons?"

"No," I said getting up to stand next to him.

"I would never forgive myself if there was another one. I doubt there is, but I am going to have an officer with a trained dog search the house. Is that okay?"

"Yes, I'm fine with that." I knew there were no other guns, but could your sniff-dog find my reality please?

"I appreciate what you're doing. My daughter is still sleeping. Can we try not to wake her up?" I requested. Knowing she was safe from the knowledge of all this was comforting. Unlike Nicky, she was old enough to ask questions about what I could not find words to explain.

"I'll let the officer know. It won't take long. Then I will need you to come down to the station and give a statement. Can you get a sitter?" he politely asked.

"Sure," I said. A rush of emotional gratitude overtook my flat affect. "Thank you for looking out for us."

An officer walked past us with a huge German shepherd. "Mommy, look at that dog!" said my cuddled up blonde bundle.

"Oh yeah, he's big! Looks like a wolf, huh? He sure is pretty." I sounded like Mary Friggin' Poppins trying to prevent the K-9 wolf-dog from stirring my son's curiosity. My kids did not watch a lot of TV, hence, they tranced easily. The dog search concluded no further weapons. Next thing was to find a babysitter. Who do you call at 8:00 in the morning and absurdly ask, "Uh, sorry to wake you, but could you watch the kids while I make a police statement? By the time you get here, the barricade should be gone. Just park behind the SWAT van." For me, that person was my girlfriend, Sara, who arrived in twenty minutes. Sara did not ask a single question, she just showed up. I did not call my mom, dad or Greg, my only sibling. I knew they would have been here for me, but the weight of their concern, or anger at Josh – though justifiable – was added emotional weight I could not bear. Sara, my yogi friend, was a communication artist. She was a natural at maintaining neutral, thoughtful responses. Sara had supplied me with my first hug after this insane, epic event.

POLICE STATION

The station was about eight blocks away. Inside the station's main room were four desks pushed together on one side, and two telephone booth-sized holding cells on the other. Down the back hall were interrogation rooms. When I entered the station, I immediately saw Josh behind the plexiglass, seated on a wooden bench. He was hunched over, leaning on his knees. He noticed me. I expected him to mouth the words, *I'm sorry*, but to my astonishment he lipped, "I won't be able to work." Although I said nothing back, an officer scoffed, "You're not supposed to talk to him!" and pointed to the back hall, shaking his head.

Diane and that same male officer took my statement at a small table where a tape recorder was set up. Both officers reminded me that I was the victim, not him. Sadly, that fact penetrated me to about the depth of a pimple. The officers were a bit cold as they sensed my underlying protection for my husband. They shook their heads when I dismissed a restraining order, and looked at me oddly when I spoke of putting this all behind us. I understood that they were suggesting I let him swim it alone. But what if that man couldn't swim? Their lack of sympathy put my defenses up. Watching Joshua drown would not serve anybody, and saving him would serve many, both personally and professionally. If my end goal was to get back to a sane, loving life and avoid the nightmares and angst my children would face at having their dad in prison, I had to start things rolling.

Upon completion of my statement, I was free to go. The police said they would take their time with Josh, providing me the opportunity to get out of the house before Josh went home to get ready for work. Funny how my life will pick-up right where my self-integrity got off.

As I exited the building, the police chief was just returning from my home. Standing beside his car, we conversed in private about the legal progress that lay ahead. I mentioned not wanting to press charges: we would handle things at home. The chief put it to me straight. His tone was firm, yet gentle. "Ma'am the law changed five years ago. It is not you who presses charges, it's the state. Many victims change their minds. The police go through all the effort of protecting everyone, only to have their hands tied."

"This has to be a mess we can clean up," I pleaded.

"This law was designed to take the pressure off the victim and put it on the perpetrator, where it should be." I felt his sympathy, but it did me no good. This perpetrator was part of my family; that didn't magically change. What happened to him indirectly happened to me and my kids, as well as each of our extended families. I could already see the pain on the faces of Josh's loving parents if their son were to be going to jail.

Swallowing back horror and shock as if it were medicine, I replied: "That makes sense to me, and he does need help. Believe me, he will get it. But he needs to be there when his kids go to bed at night; he needs to help pay for the house. Even if he's not good for our marriage, he helps so many people at his job. I don't want the system to take apart what is working for us. Can you please do what you can for us?"

"I understand," he said, and he walked away to deal with my husband. Alone, feeling ashamed and depleted for having spoken with such desperation, I trudged back to my car like the walking dead. I mustered the courage to validate my actions—I was not stupid. This had been the crucial moment before the chief made his official charges. My hope was that Josh would be granted an opportunity to work through this episode versus being rubbed out by it. Under the circumstances, I had done the best I could.

. . .

DRAINED, I went back home to the kids and my waiting friend, Sara. She didn't ask for details, only, "What do you want me to do?"

"I want to get out of the house. The police said they would take their time so that I could collect myself before Josh is let out."

My daughter, Jolie, was now awake and completely unaware of what had happened while she slept. She was sitting next to Nicky, watching cartoons. Still in pajamas, they were sharing a blanket, and had matching, matted-up blonde hair indicating which side they had each slept on last night.

Sara and I rushed around, gathering items for the day, and hurrying the kids to get dressed. We were in a silent panic mode to be gone quickly. I did not label myself afraid; however, I was overwhelmed with anguish from emotionally carrying Josh. He had been humiliated, and his power taken away, not to mention his best friends—alcohol and ego—had left him high and dry the moment he was pushed face-down in the grass. "Fend for yourself!" yelled ego. "I'll never take the fall!" added alcohol. At that moment, I felt that all he had was me. As Sara and I were leaving, the police called to say my husband was asking if I would bring his checkbook to post bail.

"Are you kidding me?"

Alas, he had no family close by. They were all scattered, living in other countries. Josh had maybe a few friends he could call. At this point, I simply wanted the man to go to work. I sighed, "Yes, I will bring his checkbook."

Here was an off-the-cuff definition of an enabler: someone who denies the seriousness of a situation and sheds the consequences. Sure, at times I played the part of an enabler, a term I did not yet understand. My view was narrowed by Josh, who downplayed his actions and drinking which I bought into, and that co-created the reality we had engaged in. Even if I had disagreed with him, I was still on a playing field created by him, so, my separatist ideas were tethered to his ideology. The legal system was on a different playing field from our reality, and that left Josh and I floundering. Separately, Josh's reality was not holding up well; neither was mine.

Revisiting the police station, I dropped off the checkbook, talking to no one. Josh was in a back room. I drove back home to get something the kids forgot. Returning to Sara's house, I chose a route that allowed a view of the station. From my car, a couple of blocks away, I saw the back of my husband, slowly walking home in the hot morning sun, barefoot. At first glance, I felt intense fear, then disgust, and then, a sense of sadness for him. He may have just altered his life entirely, including whether or not he would have his kids. I saw him take out his phone from his jeans and dial. I pulled out my phone, put it on the seat next to me, and waited. Across the tiny screen flashed, *Josh calling*. I did not answer. Eventually, I listened to his voice mail. He asked how I was, and how the kids were. The message was short, polite, and awkward.

BACK INSIDE SARA'S HOUSE, my girlfriend made us some tea, serving it in her Victorian style parlor. Seated in an antique loveseat, we drank our tea facing one another, with our knees touching, like girlfriends do. I gave her a very condensed version of what happened. Sara quietly listened except for blurting the occasional, "Holy shit!". Embraced by her friendship, Sara's company helped me to rebalance. We agreed to keep a regular day with the kids. I had already promised Sara I would watch her four-year-old son that day. I reassured her that one more kid didn't matter; life as a mom was not about to go on hold. I would still take the kids to the community pool where they could entertain themselves, and the lifeguards would provide me some respite of responsibility. Before escaping to the pool, an urgent task awaited. I excused myself to make a private call.

The chief of police had compassionately given me a pamphlet from the county's Domestic Violence Organization (DVO). The pamphlet provided a definition of what was considered domestic violence, the typical emotions victims experience, and safety guidelines. Naturally, a hotline number was included. Despite what I was suppressing, I logically knew this was a big deal.

DOMESTIC VIOLENCE ORGANIZATION - DVO

The woman on the phone from the DVO was quite empathetic. She asked for basic information to determine if I was in immediate danger, which I was not. Then she said, "Let's make an appointment this week for you to come in and give us a formal intake. From there, we will meet to determine your counselor, and schedule a therapy session with your assigned person for the following week."

I took a deep breath to cool back the lava flow inside me. "What you're telling me is, I should make an appointment, to make an appointment, so that on the following appointment, I can bond with a counselor to discuss what I should do?"

Silence was the reply. Upon drawing another deep breath, I stated, "On the surface, I may sound calm and collected – I'm good at that – but my husband just pulled a gun on me, and I want someone, now. May I suggest doing the intake over the phone today, and determining my therapist—which is probably one of three or four counselors—and then making the next appointment an actual, therapeutic session?" I was holding back a swell of tears and clutched the phone like it had the power of a detonator. *Please don't let this go off. I'm attached.*

"Someone will call you back."

THE DVO WAS VERY ACCOMMODATING. Twenty-five minutes later, a different, friendly and confident counselor called me back. She took my information and we reviewed my immediate plan. In my misery, the counselor was a competent angel. She confirmed it was healthy to return to normal, routine tasks, saying, "It gets the wheels of functioning and strength going again."

I asked if she could recommend a domestic violence couples' therapist for my husband and I. Josh was definitely going to see a therapist, and we were definitely going to have a third person in our relationship—someone I deemed sane, and steadfast. Underneath, I was scared to go back to our relationship alone, not because of him per se: he did not push me underwater, he just set me up to drown. I laid out my request. "I want a therapist who is the ultimate at handling bullshit."

"Oh, I know just the person. She's the best... Has an incredible reputation, and a lot of experience. She developed our county's domestic violence crisis program, the one you are calling. She was the director for many years. She does both couples and individual therapy."

"Hmm. She is going to meet her match with bullshit."

Her perfect reply, "She has also worked in the prison system with offenders. She is very competent with bullshit."

That was the toughness needed for Josh, but to seal the deal for myself I asked, "Is her heart in her therapy as well?"

Her answer came out smooth as silk. "Dr. Rachel Phoenix is phenomenal."

"What's her number?"

Those were the crucial first steps towards feeling saved: immediately grabbing threads of sanity to weave myself a lifeline. I knew I had to be strong enough to tow my family and my husband along because of what the police chief said about the law of domestic violence situations. The state was pressing the charges.

SARA HELPED me gather my kids so we could all go home and grab our things for the pool. Josh would be at work. Later, Sara would drop her son off at the pool. As I pulled into our driveway, I noticed my husband's Jeep was still there. *Hmm, guess he took his motorcycle to work... Not unusual.* Full of excitement, Jolie and Nicky ran into the house ahead of me. I was tired, and moving pretty slowly. Walking through the door, I found the kids hugging their dad. My mouth opened to speak, and got...nothing. Everything inside me had stopped working.

Josh looked at me with soft eyes, then bowed his head. Something about him was different; something was missing. The kids chattered about the pool, and he stooped down to give them better attention. *Ah ha! That's what's missing: his arrogance.* His pedestal, his ego, his throne – gone. All it took to lock up his ego was a SWAT team, and being handcuffed for an hour.

"Hey kids," I said, "please go upstairs and put bathing suits on. You guys can play up there until I come get you."

"Okay Mom!" And two pairs of feet raced up the stairs.

I immediately led us into the kitchen where we each settled into a standing position on opposite sides of the butcher's block. The smooth birchwood surface provided enough of a barrier between us.

"Why aren't you at work?"

"I was going to go, but I couldn't. I'm too shaken up. I called in sick. I didn't think I could see patients today. I can't really focus." Josh appeared weary, the total opposite of hours before in this very room. He asked, "How are you?"

"Been better, I gotta say," leaning back against the kitchen counter.

Josh placed his forearms onto the butcher's block. "I'm sorry."

"What were you thinking?" I started rubbing my temple.

"I thought you were going to take the kids from me," his eyes welling up.

"Taking them to my dad's," I reaffirmed.

He said nothing to that, then continued, "I thought you were taking the family apart. I thought that if I could scare you, you would snap out of it and be rational." He stood straight up with a hand resting on the block between us.

"You took my car keys," my eyebrows wrinkling with inquisitiveness.

"I thought when I woke up, the kids would be gone," his voice breaking. "I took your cell phone and credit cards because I was mad. I thought: well, I pay for them. I'll show you."

Not exactly true, we both paid on the cards, but that was beside the point. My interest was building. "And the phone? You disconnected it. That did not help the situation, especially with the police."

He sighed; his chest caved down. "I thought you would call a friend."

"It's helpful to get a picture of where you were coming from." Disarming someone was more powerful than arming oneself.

Josh offered to the conversation, "The police said they could smell alcohol on my breath. I know I drank too much. I don't mean it as an excuse, but I want you to know, I'm admitting... I know I did." He slumped his shoulders down, his blonde-covered forearms rested again on the wood's surface. Greasy blonde hair hung into his small blue eyes.

"Here's the hardest thing for me," my throat constricted as I felt my heart breaking. I could barely say the words. "You cocked the gun." Josh didn't say anything. Tears filled the space beneath his lashes. His face was blank, and sad. "Did you put bullets in the gun?" I pressed.

His eyes went dry. His arms extended and locked still. "No."

My chin drifted down; my eyebrows arched up. I leaned in a little closer, my lips poised to articulate each word inches from his face. "Why would you cock a gun, if there were no bullets in it?"

Josh's posture went fully erect. He spoke with a tone that resonated education. "A gun will make the same sound when it is empty. I grew up where farmers had guns, and kids had BBs. We would see it in movies. If someone pulled a gun to be threatening, they also cocked it. I don't know, it's just one motion. I know that sounds stupid, but I've been around guns." We maintained eye contact.

Josh came from more outback country, and his dad was military so it was true, his environment was integrated with guns. Josh's childhood best friend had always been an avid gun collector, even as a teenager. This was not a hobby of my husband's: fixing up cars was his thing. Nevertheless, his explanation—that using guns was more common in his upbringing—was valid to me.

"I would never hurt you," he said.

No other words were exchanged. The well of truth had dried up. Inside, my core was receding from the light as if a window shade was being drawn down. Weary of standing, I leaned back into the counter edge behind me. I informed Josh of my expectation that he would stay at a hotel. His eyes popped open, like peas shooting from a pod. "You want me to go?" He teared up, then blinked them away.

His surprise was unbelievable to me. He was like a duck swimming in a pond of accountability: every behavior, every action beaded right off—no doubt a clinical symptom. "Yes Josh, I want you to leave. I'm not really comfortable around you right now." My words were flat-lined.

Joshua took a deep breath, and with a nod, offered a bloodless ounce of accountability. "Guess I should have done that in the first place."

POOL GOSSIP

We arrived at the town pool without any social commotion. While the kids splashed around, I managed to rest in the healing warmth of the sun on an uncomfortable lounge chair, my hand getting caught in the web of plastic slots with every position change. After a nice, but too short a nap, I sat up and peeked around. I spied my friend Chelsea. Tall, blonde, and beautiful, she was hard to miss. Our sons were the upcoming sixth graders on the block; they had been friends since first grade, and Chelsea had been an active member in our town for over a decade. Thankfully, Connor had stayed at Chelsea's house last night. I couldn't wait to see him. I caught up with him by the diving board, making sure to limit my display of public hugging in front of his friends. As always, my son was happy to see me, and then he ran back to the diving board to perform more daring flips. Chelsea waved me over to join her at one of the many umbrella tables. That's when I got a pulse on the story infiltrating the town. Chelsea was not a woman to mince words. "Honey, are you okay?"

"I guess you heard."

"Listen, Jessie — you don't need to tell me anything, and people are going to say what they say. If people ask me anything, I got nothing to say to them. It's your personal business. I don't have a problem telling folks how it is. You know me." Chelsea's feminine swag brought a smile to my face, until she dropped the rumor bomb—a rumor being spread by kids.

"Beware, Jess... Earlier, that Bunky kid came running over to my older son and his friends. Connor wasn't around. Bunky said that your husband had a gun to your head and that your house was swarming with police and SWAT cars."

"Oh my God!" I replied. "Yes, something happened, but that did not happen."

"Oh my God, honey, I'm so glad!" I told those boys if I catch them saying anything, especially to your son, it isn't gonna be pretty. And they looked at me like, ya know, and then Bunky said, 'How could he do that to her? She's so nice.' It just breaks your heart." Chelsea was able to carry both parts of a conversation.

Upon hugging Chelsea goodbye, I retreated back to my private sunning spot and called Dr. Rachel Phoenix. Her voice message revealed a thick New York accent which I found refreshing. I didn't want a Jungian type therapist using a slow process of self-realization. I wanted brilliant insights swooned out of me, and blocks of self-actualization stacked up quick. I left Dr. Phoenix a message. My next idea was to feel normal. Dialing...

"Hello, Franny's Hair Salon. How can we help you?" Oh, to hear those words. Please someone else take the wheel... "Can you make it here in forty-five minutes?"

"Absolutely," I said. "Kids! Let's go!" I took the kids home, Sara's son still in tow, and informed Josh of my hair appointment, explaining I needed some time to myself. Naturally, he was amenable to watching the kids and also offered to make dinner for everyone.

When I dropped off Sara's son, we spoke for a bit. Sara listened as I told her about the rumors *Bunky* was spreading among some kids. Sara let out a long sigh and said, "I didn't want to tell you this, but earlier this morning, I heard Bunky's father talking about the incident in the coffee shop. He was telling folks the same thing. He lives up your street; think he overheard police talking. I didn't say anything to him. He comes into the shop a lot. He is always one to sit and gossip." Sara worked at Athena's coffee shop part time.

What the heck? I was pissed. Show me where I could find Mr. Bunky, and I'd show you a fine example of anger transference. But this was the nature of rumor. I could give it energy, allowing it to chip away at my intentions, or as I resolved to do, I could face it or ignore it as it came, thus reserving my strength to focus moment to moment.

HAIR SALON

Pulling into the gravel driveway of Franny's Hair Salon, I reassured myself that this was a good place to escape. Once inside, I was escorted to the shampoo sinks. Flopping into a red leather recliner, the smell of tropics in the air, a sense of relief washed over me. I was here to be cared for, and be responsible for no one.

A pretty, young woman dressed in a fitted black outfit whispered, "Lean back. Just relax." She draped a soft towel over my shoulders. I arched back, my auburn hair cascading into the bowl below. A firm spray of warm water coated my scalp leaving my hair wet and flat. The woman tenderly began to scrub, her fingernails giving extra attention right above the ears and temples. The air was infused with scents of lavender and jasmine as her hands worked an immense lather. Her dexterous fingers rubbed the back of my scalp in broad circular motions. Then, again with a squeeze, tepid water caressed through my hair, rinsing out the foamy lather. Finally, with a swift pull and a twist, she wrung out the excess water, bringing the experience to a happy ending.

In magazines, where they show the before and after makeover transformations, I could have qualified as the 'before' girl. I had an earthy, casual look, an average to petite frame, and usually wore supportive shoes—the kind most health professionals wear. I was comfortable with or without makeup, and had a consistently pleasant mood. I got compliments here and there, occasionally turning a head. The haircut turned out pretty, and I had left the salon feeling better.

AFTER OUR FAMILY DINNER, Josh packed his bag, leaving with his head up and his tail down. I did not mention his departure to the kids; they wouldn't notice and it avoided questions. Tucking all three kids into their separate beds felt sweet, and sadly tedious. They remained unaware of the day's events. Nicky did not even mention the K-9 wolf-dog. The night was welcome. Exhaustion was hitting like a disorienting twister; my home had no ceiling or floor. Then, the landline rang.

FAMILY CALLS

"Hey, uh, are you okay?" My brother tried to downplay his intensity.

"Yes," I answered. Then came mutual silence.

"Are you sure?" Greg asked. "Is Josh there?"

"Yeah, I'm fine and no, he is not."

Sounding slightly perplexed, "Did something happen over there?"

I sighed, "How are you hearing about this?"

"Did-did Josh have a gun? My friend called and said he heard on his police scanner possibly your address: 'a domestic situation with a gun.' Is he there? Did this just happen?"

"Greg, I'm fine. Yes, there was a big deal. It was earlier. Josh is at a hotel."

"It's true! Jessie I'm coming over!"

"Greg, it's fine. It's been such a long day. The kids just went to sleep; I can't take anymore."

"Jessica you're my sister; I'm coming over! I'll be there in ten minutes!" And with that, he hung up. I started pacing in an effort to stay calm. I did not want to feel responsible for anyone else's emotions. I was so tired. Then, the phone rang again.

"Hello?"

"Honey, are you okay?" Popular question.

"Yes, Dad. I'm fine. How come you're calling?"

"Your brother called me. Is Josh there?"

"No. He's —"

"I'm coming over." Click.

"—not here." *Where had everybody been all those times they could have told Josh to stop treating me like a piece of crap?*

Suddenly I understood why, after someone got attacked or mugged or worse, she (or he) did not want to talk about it for a while. You needed it to stop; you needed to get some distance from it. Because my family could not wait to see me, I had to keep running on the same tank of gas, and it was on fumes. If they could have waited until the next day, I would have had time to switch to another tank.

MY DAD and Greg arrived about the same time. Once again in the kitchen, I relived an accurate, but condensed version of what happened. My unwanted tears came like enemies, held back by surface tension. I wanted privacy, yet I did want my family. I provided Josh's explanation, which seemed to have some crazy validity. "Josh said, 'he was afraid I was taking the kids away and breaking up the family'," I recounted. My dad and Greg were both pretty silent and pent up, either shaking their heads or erratically shifting around while they stood listening. Finally, my turn was over.

"I don't care what he was thinking," said Greg. "Pulling a gun is no solution. How about working on your drinking problem as a solution!" Greg was pacing. My dad was vicariously in pace-mode by watching Greg. My dad always tried an old school, gentlemanly approach first, before flipping out.

"Did Josh give you any trouble as he was leaving?" asked my father.

"No. Not at all." My dad rubbed his clean-shaven chin.

"Well, that's good." The telephone rang yet again. *I should have left it disconnected.*

"Jess-i-ca-a-a... Are you okay-y-y?" An elegant reprisal of the night's hymn.

I chose to flip my response. "Hey, Mom. How are you?" I said, as chipper as could be.

"Uh huh. Is-s-s your Dad there?" Mom asked.

"Yes. Yes, he is. He's right here," I replied, looking at my dad who was already finding this play on my mom amusing. My parents had a friendly, divorced relationship.

"Is your brother there too-o?" she asked with confusion in her voice.

"Uh, yes. He is here too. We are all having a visit," I said with cheer. My Dad was smiling. He alleviated pain with humor almost as much as I did.

"I should get back to them, Mom. Can I call you back tomorrow?"

"Uh huh. Okay-y-y. I will see you tomorrow. Good night, Jessica." My mom had made that too easy for me. She was aware that something was up and didn't want to step on Dad's or Greg's toes. Her phone call helped defuse the tension and concern brewing in the kitchen. Greg began to insist that the kids and I should stay at his house, fearing that Josh might return.

"Josh is not coming back. He has the fear of both losing his career, and jail looming over him. Josh is a tad more logical about things right now." Greg conceded his idea once my Dad agreed to stay at my house overnight. As it turned out, I did not mind one bit. *Thanks, Dad.*

GETTING A THERAPIST

My appointment with the Domestic Violence Office (DVO) took place in a nondescript, two story building next to an Applebee's. The deliberate absence of an office sign was meant to protect the clients they served. Empathy swelled in my heart for women in more difficult situations. The need for this underground world of safety developed because so many men got away with abusing their partners or their kids. For a woman to utilize this underground system, she had to have the wherewithal to seek it out.

My advisor, Heather, sat behind her desk in a clean, tidy office with no windows. After pleasantries, a history intake, and the incident description, Heather got right into it. "You know, there are many forms of abuse. Abuse is not just physical."

"Okay," I said, "but that topic—*abuse*—still feels too foreign to me. That is not my situation...not really."

Heather stated, "Fair enough. But allow me to give you the

full definition of what constitutes abuse. There is verbal abuse, emotional abuse, financial abuse, and physical abuse. Demeaning and degrading words about you as a person, as a mother, or as a woman, or how you look or act is abuse. Instilling fear, anger, discord in your family, threatening to withhold finances, limiting or denying access to mutual funds or funds for basic needs, or threatening to take away items necessary to livelihood, such as a car or food, is abuse. Threatening to cut off communication, or to stop children from attending school are threats used to instill fear. It is abusive to threaten; it is abusive to cause physical harm. There is also sexual abuse." She continued, **"Women have the right to be free from all of it. This treatment is not something to be welcomed in any woman's home or life."**

Heather's delivery of information was disarming. She did not speak to me as if I was less than her, or any other woman. As Heather spoke, I felt safe to discern in my mind, and question if those behaviors were in my home, my marriage, or my private life. Had I built up muscles to form a resistance to abuse, hence blinding myself to the abuse going on? But if I resisted abuse, or didn't believe what my husband said, was I truly being abused?

Is that what we women think? If we can take it, then it's nothing? How far do we let them go before determining enough is enough? Heck, we'll go all the way. But all the way to where, and at what cost? I needed to get out of my own head. Even though I usually blew off the belittling things Josh said, I had to deal with him saying them and waste energy protecting myself, or guarding my reality. I had to concede: someone must truly be a victim when she doesn't even know it. One of the hardest things at that time was mourning the loss of not having the kind of partner I had envisioned.

Heather asked objectively, "Can you be your best, true self at this time or in the near future with the way things are?"

"No. But we both made sacrifices. Josh compromising to remain a married man, if he found out that that didn't suit him, was I guess his big sacrifice; but he seems to take that out on me."

Heather replied: "Abusers 'take out' things on their victims that which have nothing to do with them. How about the woman raped in a parking lot by a stranger? He woke up a predator, and was going to turn someone into prey no matter what. That's an extreme example. In your case, a marriage is a partnership where roles, responsibilities, and behaviors should be agreed upon."

I concurred with Heather, then said, "I remember him saying one time, 'I can't hurt you physically' and he slammed his fist into his hand, 'but I can hurt you financially.' Then he went on to list some things he wouldn't assist to pay. It didn't faze me too much because I have quite a bit of financial autonomy. But those comments definitely were abusive comments."

"They weren't 'comments', they were threats," Heather asserted. The root of his intent was to hold you down and keep you down." I let that sink in. It was interesting to label what was abusive, because everything in our relationship felt absurdly difficult. Heather was providing a validation that was proportional to the incline of the hamster wheel I was treading.

"Yes, he has been verbally and emotionally abusive. He gets agitated, though he doesn't cross some kind of line. However, hands down, the most difficult aspect of living with my husband is dealing with his manipulations of the truth. Woven into his truths are strands of grandiose exaggerations. It is hard to discern where the facts end and the fiction begins which means I am battling in a fictional world. You cannot win a battle of fiction, ever, because pay dirt is a piece of reality the size of a grain of sand resting on a sink hole of reality that will not come to the surface by design. Yet there I go, standing in a Lord of the Rings circus field, confronting Ancalagon the Black dragon with one arm reaching way above my head holding out a grain of sand in my mighty palm against his raging, Kelvin scaled flames."

"At best you'll reach a stalemate," Heather said at the edge of her seat, "with some charring."

"At times, Josh will admit his problems, but then he thinks the solution is keeping to himself which in turn leads us to another big problem: we get ignored. We seem to exist as an extension of him."

"He ignores all of you?" Heather clarifies.

"Well, yes, but he's not that insensitive. He is more aloof." Wanting to explain, "You wouldn't wake up and wonder, 'What is the weather like in Japan today?' It doesn't cross your mind. However, if I said Japan was hit with a tsunami, you would be very concerned and genuinely interested for a while. You might even initiate doing something like donating money or clothes, until you stop thinking of Japan again. At that point, someone has to remind you that we still need to do things for the people of Japan."

Then came my familiar sigh as I continued, "The kids are like Japan. I feel as though I'm turning on his awareness to his family, because he is a constant foreigner. Josh wants to be helpful; he does care very deeply. However, he doesn't understand what to do as a parent, and the innate value isn't there to make it stick... Basic thoughts and actions you would assume are there, are not."

"I understand," Heather said warmly. "He sounds like a...well, never mind."

"A narcissist? You have no idea how many times I have read over the symptoms of narcissism in the DSM. The killer is that telling the person does not help. That's what stops me from hanging a DSM description page on the fridge, in his car, or heck—as a rolled-up message in a bottle. Got plenty of bottles..."

"That would not go over well."

"What pisses me off is the fake *this-is-who-I-am* resume he handed me. But then, I still hired him, right? For the job of husband and father..." I notice her nod. I take a breather and collect myself. "I want to get strong enough to move this entire family in a better direction. Blaming him won't me get me there, but changing *me* will. Therapy is to get me on track. I'm slacking somewhere."

Heather probed, "How are you so centered? There is a certain calmness about you not often seen in these rooms."

The feeling of truth had brought out my smile. I noticed her dark eyelashes and chocolate eyes as I conveyed, "For my entire life, I have never felt alone. I was always connected to some kind of loving, vast energy."

"I can see that," she said.

County funds covered the cost of seeing Heather for crisis counseling. Due to the specific severity of my case, I also qualified for state funding to cover individual therapy. As much as I liked conversing with Heather, I did not need two therapists, nor did I have the time. Also, I did not want to deplete resources from the crisis center needed for others, especially since I had already chosen an anti-bullshit specialist who could see both Josh and I. Since my individual session appointment with Dr. Phoenix was next week, Heather was in agreement to discontinue further sessions here at the DVO. "Besides," added Heather, "you're in good hands with Dr. Rachel."

TOWN REINTEGRATION

No one from town approached me about the incident, therefore, I reached out to some of them to remove a level of awkwardness for us all. First neighbor I visited was Mr. Quinsley. He deserved an explanation as to why we had all been congregating on his front porch.

Mr. Q immediately invited me inside. He was wearing a maroon sweater with khakis and emulated nothing but concern and an interest to listen. We stood in his antique-styled parlor room while I initiated the conversation by saying, "Well, thought you'd want to know my family is okay. Sorry I kind of brought things to your front door. I'm unaware of what details you know."

Mr. Q replied as we both took a seat on his Queen Anne sofa, "I have basic information from a neighbor across the street. She could see police activity from her third story window. We all felt concerned for you." His living room seemed quite regal with the gold framed paintings and a tiffany lamp ceiling fan.

"It's a tough call knowing what to say in this type of situation."

He nodded. "How is Josh? Is he in the house?"

"No. I told him to leave. He is staying at a hotel. He has a big legal problem now."

Gently Mr. Q asked, "What happened?"

"Well, he threatened me with a weapon, and I ran...actually..." my throat started clamping. "Ugh, uh...I ran and hid in your bushes like a rabbit." He smiled so warmly at me. "Wait 'til I tell Kate I broke into their house to call the police. Actually, I didn't break in; they left the back door unlocked."

"Why didn't you knock? You could have come in here," Mr. Q said earnestly.

"I rapped on your door for a moment; I wasn't about to go banging on it. Plus, I didn't want anyone else at risk. I went where I could go very quickly."

Mr. Q leaned back into an overstuffed throw pillow with gold tassels. "How are the kids?"

Sighing with relief, "They don't know anything. Two of them were asleep. Luckily, Connor was staying at a friend's."

Mr. Q leaned forward, with his knees wide, elbows resting on his thighs like he was about to catch a heavy ball. "My dad was an alcoholic. He was physically abusive. One day, my mom had enough and she called the cops on him. I remember them hand-cuffing my dad on the front lawn. I will never forget it. They dragged him away in a police car. It was a hard thing to watch as a kid. I remember the angst of my mom having to make that decision, but my dad was not a nice guy."

"Did he ever come back?"

"No, she kicked him out. It was tough on her. There were five of us, but I had a couple of grown siblings by then. You know, I missed my father and we stayed in contact with him, but I can understand the decision she had to make."

Interesting... Of all the stories anyone could have told me, I walked into that one.

OBTAINING A LAWYER

More than our worst mistake. In 2008, the United States had the highest number of incarcerated people in the world, with 2,300,000 people in jail. Sadly, one out of three black men were expected to be incarcerated. Was sitting in jail always the right answer? Was society better when we shunned? Reverend Michael Bernard Beck asked: How many of those 2,300,000 individuals, if given the chance, would be kind? Make amends? Keep to themselves, hope for love, return home, and make it up to their parents?

After the incident, Josh spent his immediate days securing a lawyer. His first lawyer, a guy from town, went to the county courthouse to investigate the charges filed. Apparently, he was not expecting any of them to be felony charges, but the gun had not been re-registered. The case was out of his league and his connections. The recommendation from that lawyer: get another lawyer.

Josh told me with an unsettling voice, "He said this involves serious jail time. It probably won't even stay in the county court system. He flat out said, 'Get Franklin. He's the lawyer you want. If I were in your shoes, I would pick him.'"

"Wow."

"Franklin also lives in our town. He will cost a lot, but apparently, he can swim with the sharks."

"I guess there are a lot of big fish in our little town."

"He has an Asian last name I didn't recognize. Apparently, he is well respected."

"Hey wait," I recalled. "I think I know who Mr. Shark Swimmer is, well, not him actually but his wife. She is a cute, petite woman—the only Asian woman in town."

"You know her?" he asked, still in his overall daze of late.

"I know her to say, 'hi'. We stand outside the school yard together, waiting for our kids to come out. She has a fun personality, always laughing with her friends. Let's hope that's a good sign."

MR. SHARK quickly got to work on Josh's case. His first efforts would be to reduce the charges for a lower court hearing. This path would hopefully protect Josh's professional license, which was a huge concern. Next, Mr. Shark told Josh of a program for first offenders. The end result was expungement of charges after a certain amount of time passed without further offenses. That program sounded promising.

"The last critical item the lawyer mentioned was," Josh spoke without manipulation, guilt, or a sense of expectation, "that almost everything will rest on your sole testimony." That was the reality.

JOSH CONTINUED to come back from the hotel each day to get fresh clothes. We had dinner together with the kids, as if all was normal. He asked about coming back home. What I needed was day-to-day peace in my house. Josh was in a forced state of peace with his ego banished, and his drinking abstained. I started thinking...it was costing us eighty bucks a night for the hotel. Perhaps that was my Achilles heel: having enough money. I saw money towards a hotel room as money that should be directed toward a lawyer. Josh had no family nearby, otherwise kicking him to his family would be an absolute. As far as anyone in town, I assumed no one wanted a man who had just pulled a gun to stay at their house.

Certainly, I was not leaving the house. I was not going to cram the kids into my dad's house and make day-to-day life more difficult. A few days was one thing; an infinite amount of time was another. My kids were bound to notice eventually that their dad was staying elsewhere at night. Josh could not stay with my family: they were pissed, and not speaking to him. None of them went to confront him, which surprised me. I would have if it were my daughter or sister, but then I cannot tell them what to do any more than they could tell me.

Josh and I decided to handle this as adults. I had been living with Josh as a drunk and a jerk for a long time. The current situation dictated he was neither. I could deal with that for a change. Josh said he could not even look at alcohol right now. We agreed he would come back home once he made his therapy appointment with Dr. Phoenix. Regarding sleeping arrangements, he had preferred for years to fall asleep on the sofa watching TV. No need to change the status quo.

THERAPY

Her office was part of a no-frills business complex. The waiting room had a common sitting area with four chairs and three doors. Exactly at my appointment time, the middle door opened and there, wearing shoes as spikey as her hair, was Dr. Rachel Phoenix.

"Hello! You must be Jessica," she said warmly, extending her arm from underneath a beautiful scarf. "Come-awn in." Ah, a hint of New Yorker.

A welcoming black leather sofa accented with gold and jewel tone pillows was pressed against the far wall, and flanked by floor plants of varying heights. The sofa triangulated with an overstuffed, hunter green chair and a high, wingback vermillion chair for Dr. Phoenix. The vibe was a tasteful East meets West. We each sat in a chair. A tatami lamp glowed from the corner behind me. The mere gesture of her full attention put me at ease. She wore layers of patterns beginning with red-speckled eyeglass frames, a shawl with watercolor dots of pinks, reds, and magenta that flowed over a muted grey dress, and finished with a pair of zebra print pumps. Dr. Phoenix settled into her chair, tilted her legs to one side, and waited.

I took the bait, and started. "Well, I am not sure where to begin. I'm glad to be here. I like the room. It has a Zen vibe to it." I preferred to let her set the groove.

"Thank you," said Dr. Phoenix. "I'm glad you like it. We can start with *how are you?* I'd like to get a sense of how you're feeling," she said in earnest.

Chuckling out an answer, "Overwhelmed—like everything is over the top, and I can't quite get my feet on the ground... Or worse, I'm standing on the ground, but it's like fake dirt. I'm not really sure where I should be standing right now... That's where you come in, I suppose."

"You would like me to help you get your footing – is that right?"

"Yes."

"And the 'ground' you are standing on and maybe have been standing on for—let's say, a while—feels fake to you: you said like 'fake dirt'."

"Yes, that is correct. I thought that was a nicer way of saying, *I'm wading through bullshit.*"

Ah, the Phoenix laughed at that one. She even gave it a clap with her hands. "Let's call bullshit 'bullshit', shall we?"

"Hmm, okay," I said smiling, but warned her, "you better bring boots instead of heels if you're going to open that barn door."

She leaned back as if on a throne. "Please...these shoes can walk through anything. Don't worry about me." The Phoenix nodded, "What exactly is the bullshit part?"

"Umm - well, living with a man who drinks all the time and ignores his family; raising kids with someone who puts me down half the time, and doesn't seem to enjoy...anything related to our life. If we head towards a divorce, I am not out to get him, or make things worse or complicated. I just want to call a spade a spade, and then make a solution based on the fact that oil and water do not mix."

"So, you and he are completely different, like oil and water?"

"No. I mean, Josh wants to avoid his family, be miserable, drink and keep to himself, and yet, he enjoys us some of the time. Hence, when he joins us, it's like he is oil trying to be in water. Being a married, family man doesn't penetrate his own skin." I add in frustration, "Why is it so hard for him to give himself permission to leave, and go do what he wants to do? Let's call a spade, a spade."

"Jessica, you want Joshua to admit that he is probably a drunk; that he is a lousy father, or at least, an uninvolved father, as well as admit that he is an incompetent husband and that he should leave his big, stately home so that everyone else is better off? And you are wondering why is that such a big deal?"

Ah, who let all that in here? "I suppose that is one way of looking at it," I said while crossing my legs. Dr. Phoenix appeared to be a combination of an all-knowing Shirley MacLaine and a fully-assured Catherine Bates rolled into one. Her dark brown hair was shaved up the sides and outcropped on top, hanging into long bangs. Her thick bangs had strands that blended into deep red tips. A chunk of these hair spikes came down and swooped over one eye.

"I am merely stating that the skill of parenting is not my husband's forte, and even with that, he need not crawl away with his tail between his legs."

"Jessica, it doesn't matter how you say it. What I said is probably how he is going to hear it, because − if we are calling out bullshit − it is probably true. When you start chipping away at the 'everything's normal persona' he's got going on, it is a big deal. Even if that persona is false, he spent a lot of time building that up. Calling a spade a spade may be a big deal to him, and that may mean danger for you." Dr. Rachel Phoenix folded her hands in her lap.

I uncrossed my legs. "Well, I am not living under this fake spade anymore. I don't like chipping away at him, but he admits to some things one day, then denies them another day. When he goes back to denying, I feel set up to point out stuff just to get back to reality. Constantly pointing out stuff isn't the kind of wife or person I want to be. What I intend as feedback usually goes straight to causing him shame." Ah, I had revealed the hamster wheel.

The Phoenix tilted her head. "Speaking of denial, are you skipping over the part where he put you in danger? I understand your frustration in trying to have a rational conversation with him..."

"Yes, it is extremely frustrating!" I interjected.

"I bet. But you keep circumventing around how to get through to him, how to handle his feelings, and how you are willing to bend over backwards to accommodate his sensitivities, wondering why can't he just surrender?" Phoenix waited, undoubtedly taking note of my ghostly expression. She continued, "You are not stating the harm he has caused, nor the extra burden you carry to create and hold up a marriage with a child-raising environment. You are also not stating that you are worth more than the devaluing circumstances you currently live under."

Mulling that over, "It sucks and I want it changed. I want it stopped."

"You do not speak of holding him accountable for his end. Are you holding him accountable for his direct actions?"

"I-I asked him; I have told him, in the past, to stop drinking."

"And did he?"

"No. I mean, he tried."

"Did he? Did he really try?"

"He stopped for a while. He cut back on being a jerk, which he isn't all the time. Quite frankly, I don't think a wife should have to be a babysitter to the actions of a grown-ass man."

"How long did he completely stop drinking?" Dr. Phoenix asked.

"Um, I guess the longest has been like two or three weeks," I answered.

"Weeks? Two or three weeks! Like ever? Like the whole time you've known him, he has not drunk any alcohol for two, maybe three weeks?" She seemed to be in some kind of shock.

"Uh, yeah. I mean, he would say 'longer' but that's because beer and wine are not really drinking."

She looked at me like...I had two heads? I was serious. I was so serious. Oh my God, I was serious! Like, only two weeks serious. Like if he only had a few beers and that's it for a few days in a row that is "not drinking." I totally believed that was not drinking. I started to laugh. I mean, I had to...at myself...this was pretty stupid brainwashing. But I hadn't known about the lifestyle of a heavy drinker. Growing up, I was never around drinkers.

I sunk back into the sofa. "Sheesh. There's some tunnel vision."

"Ya think?" Dr. Rachel smiled. "And that is okay with raising three kids, three young kids. You have to focus and run your micro world. Marriage is full of compromises and evolving roles that each partner plays, but causing harm, threatening harm, evoking fear, spewing belittlement and bouts of rage or guilt or depression or destabilizing anxiety is not a compromise. That is one- sided. And you cannot help someone if you try to own it for him. That person will always try to manipulate the truth, and will always have an escape plan until that person owns his consequences, and makes the connection to his behaviors."

"Sounds like a lot of work."

"A lot of work for whom?"

"A lot of work for – *don't say me* – him," speaking as her star pupil.

"Good answer!" Dr. Phoenix looked at me like I had one head, which was reassuring. The session continued. We never talked about the gun. I did not bring it up, preferring not to look that direction. The incident was something traumatic wrapped in a gummy-numby coating. Why would I disturb it? Dr. Phoenix left it alone...for now. We set some therapy goals for me: separate my behavior from his behavior, and define which behaviors were reasonable to accept.

Opening her appointment book, Dr. Phoenix said, "I would like to see you in two days. Can you come in the evening?" her pen was at the ready.

"Two days? Uh, yeah. I will have to get a sitter, but that's the case anytime, unless they're in school. What time?"

"Is six o'clock okay for you?"

"Yes. But is it too late for you?" I was afraid she was squeezing me in after her usual hours, which she didn't have to do. I was fine.

"No, not all. I will see you at six o'clock." She closed up the appointment book, her client book, her book of clients— domestic violence clients... Some of them...I meant us; we...I meant me: I had become a domestic violence therapy client. I did not look the part: I did not have bruises, and wasn't in a shelter, although I could have ended up in a morgue if there had been bullets in the gun. I didn't mean to minimize; I was trying to keep things in perspective...keep a level head. Maybe I was conning myself. I was not too sure where my solid spiritual beliefs ended and my denial and myopic tunnel vision began. I wanted Dr. Rachel Phoenix to help me open what yogis refer to as "the third eye".

EXPLORING THERAPY

Arriving a few minutes late, from the waiting room I could see Dr. Rachel in her office beyond a half-closed door. She appeared to be catching up with notes or something clerical. No secretary here—Dr. Rachel Phoenix does it all, which included getting me to talk about the...

"...and that's when I called the police from a friend's house... after I felt safe to come out of the bushes." Sitting on the leather couch, I ended my accurate retelling of the entire incident.

"I have to say you seem pretty calm revisiting the whole thing," Dr. Phoenix said sincerely.

"It's not like he held a gun to my head."

"Is it really that different?" she asked with interest. I stared at her; I didn't know what to do with that comment.

"That seems like the wrong question," I responded. "The instant I heard the gun cock, I was out of there. My legs were moving while the rest of me was still registering the threat. Whatever his intent might have been, he never got to carry it out. I never endured his full intent. I don't believe he wants his children to have a dead mom, nor do I think he wants to go to jail and lose everything. If you give anyone a chance to back up from a crazy stupid moment or event, it's important to reflect on whether he or she would do it differently. Long before I was a victim, I believed that someone should not be branded for life over a moment in time, especially if you have an understanding of that person's perception. It would be hypocritical to change my view. I think we need to look at our criminal system before someone is put behind bars. All that said, I still have to deal with the original problems in our marriage," I admitted, slumping back against the sofa. "Am I making any sense?" *There, my guts were on the table.*

"Do you feel like you are making sense?" She was the one not blinking.

This had made me laugh. "I think where I am coming from

makes sense. I try to think what God would do, what Jesus would do, what Gandhi would say, or what Mother Teresa would say. What would the Buddha's contemplative advice be after eating a serious amount of nuts and seeds while sitting under a Bodhi tree?"

Answering my own question, "'Ah,' the Buddha would say, 'You are what you eat...NUTS!' Ha! Get it?" All I got was a raised eyebrow.

"Jessica, when folks have their belief system challenged, they often become hypocritical. They do not pause to try and reflect in some moral 'high ground' above the situation. But if someone allows herself the grace to pause, then a person can search for clarity and decide on a response based on consulting with a 'dream team'. I admire your effort to do that. Many people react from their ego or unchecked emotions, and they miss adding empathy and compassion. Empathy and compassion are truly healing. Those are strong character traits you possess; however, they can be tough to emulate with boundaries."

Dr. Phoenix went on. "I have worked in prison systems; I can tell you a few things. One is that kids usually want their parents back. Even if the mom or dad harmed them, children want their mom and their dad. Next, many offenders never had the second chance, nor the support that would change their life around. Society often dehumanizes an offender. Not everyone deserves that, and jail time is not always the quick fix solution. It takes much in terms of a capacity for forgiveness and healing for someone to see a broader perspective, and show empathy. Again, I admire your efforts to do that." I nodded in appreciation of feeling heard, and understood. We seemed to have connected on a common belief system: offering relationships a chance to heal ultimately serves humanity.

Not lost on me was Dr. Phoenix's message to keep myself in check. I responded, "It's fair to say I have trouble with the boundary part of things; I'm probably clumsy in the 'setting boundaries' department."

"I would say that both you and Josh have trouble with boundaries, and closure. He probably feels you are head crashing him, but that is because he wants an awful lot of distance. That is what alcohol does—it can help make closing the distance easier."

Exasperated I said, "But he's a mental health doctor, for crying out loud!"

Dr. Rachel shifted, and sat on top of one leg. She proceeded with her insight. "A client-therapist relationship is full of boundaries. You can get very close and personal, but it is not intimate." She gestured a swirling arm in the space between us. "This space is always here between us. It is always safe, so yes, he can cross over with lots of empathy and caring and he probably is very genuine. That safe space allows it."

I jumped in to confirm, "He is very good at it. I've heard ideas he has come up with for his patients that stem from empathy. He is also very good at diagnosing. He said he is very thorough about chart reviews and diagnostic testing. We used to work at the same hospital together. His supervisors were always impressed with his insights and the speed with which he could complete complicated reports. More than once he has figured out a diagnosis another could not. He was taking on more cases than his supervisors. Josh always cared about making his clients better. I admired his professional work, and his ability to be self-sufficient."

Dr. Phoenix said in a matter of fact way, "So, he is good at his profession. He gets to be an intellectual and be admired. He is successful in a clinically interpersonal, safe space. That works for him. Marriage may be an entirely different animal to him. When you start having kids, things change. Issues get triggered that may have lain dormant and suddenly, he is not competent anymore. Narcissists, for example, are very fragile inside. That is why there is a lot of overcompensating or putting other people down – it diverts the focus from themselves. Sometimes tearing others apart is a method to keep others off, or away. They are usually avoiding shame."

"You nailed it! I totally feel torn apart at times," almost jumping out of my seat. "The worst is the splitting between relationships. It doesn't matter who the parties are, just so long as they never collaborate with each other. Then there's these elaborate stories my husband tells. Sometimes, the focus of the tall tale is to make him look better, other times it is to make someone else look worse – a complete chop at the knees." Becoming a bit more animated, waving my arms and pointing in imitation, I add: "Josh cannot watch the TV at night without insulting somebody. The focus could be as trivial as somebody's tie. For example, if a good-looking actor with a skinny black tie comes on the screen, Josh would say, 'Look at that guy! Doesn't he have any fashion sense? What was he thinking? Does he still think it's the eighties? Look at his tie! Jessica, do you see his tie?!' This could be the only thing Josh says to me if I choose to watch TV with him, on the only TV in the house. He monologues at me."

"What is that like for you?" she asked.

"It's like I am watching a show inside a show. It's weird; sometimes it's amusing, though not so much anymore. Josh will never ask what I think, or turn off the TV and have a conversation with me, or suggest we do something. Quite frankly, I feel like part of me got put in a coffin long ago. If I didn't need that part of me anymore, then I would be fine. Can't say I never got angry over that, even super pissed. I morphed my desires so not all of them had to be fulfilled by him. I think that is a pitfall in marriages anyway. You expect the other person to finish what you can't about yourself. After I saw a therapist in Hawaii, I decided to share a lot of the child raising with friends, and I joined a mom babysitting co-op group. I'm physically active with the kids. I read books by developmental experts about raising children as my consult. I changed what I expected from Josh, and tried to appreciate what Josh does do. He is more an action guy than a word guy, according to him."

"It makes me sad to hear you say, 'you put yourself in a coffin.' That is a sad and lonely place to be, especially if that is where you're watching your life. You are a lively and vivacious person!" She was looking right at me. She continued to notice me. My eyes got wide; I looked around the room. Another moment went by. Yup, she was still holding that caring gaze right at me...right through the coffin boards until there was a crack. My composure slipped under the weight of heavy sorrow.

Reaching for a tissue on the wooden coffee table I said, "It totally sucks. This was not what I intended for myself. It feels like a sad waste. I accept I made that choice, but sometimes, I feel robbed. That's what I get most angry about. I feel robbed of what life could bring me in an opposite situation. I thought that when you married someone, the goal was to engage in your life's purpose, and experience joys and challenges together. But for Josh, it seems like getting married was on his society checklist, just to appear normal and successful—though I know he definitely wanted children. He adores his kids, and kids in general, even if he cannot parent them."

"Did you have some of these conversations with him?"

"Yes, to a fairly insightful degree, and he either says the perfect thing, or he puts down what I say. But all that aside, we're good roommates. We don't cheat on each other. We truly wanted kids. He is happy to fix things around the house and is typically generous with money. We enjoy good food and a beautiful yard. A perk of his personality is that he doesn't try to micromanage my parenting. There is a lot of fun that goes on, even if we exist in parallel universes. But, ugh...too much of me is spent defending and deflecting. And I am so angry at him for the exhaustion I feel. Every night, he is that guy with a drink in his hand and I am repeating the same thing I said the night before, and even the year before. Every day, Josh wakes up to a shower and a cup of coffee and manages only himself. He's out the door in twenty-five minutes, primped and ready to go. I manage myself and three kids, hold a professional job, and provide back up to his routines. Sometimes, I would like some back up too! I am not the most organized or time efficient person. It would be nice if Josh handled a ball I couldn't quite juggle." I grabbed a throw pillow to squeeze. "Don't worry. I didn't forget the coffin thing. Yeah, it sucks."

"It is okay to be pissed off. There is a lot to be pissed off about. I like how you explained feeling robbed: it touches on viewing your life through your own eyes. Often, you're cautious about what you say, and filter your thoughts through Josh. You measure out every thought process. It's crazy."

"It is a full-time job! I rehearse and rehearse in my head. I even rehearse not rehearsing. It wouldn't be so bad if he initiated a conversation, or shared an interest. I have to put the interest out there. He doesn't know who the kids' teachers are. I bet he would get their ages wrong. There's one dad at school who jokes I am not really married because he never sees Josh at school functions, or weekend birthday parties. There I am, managing three kids by myself, watching couples work together; watching other men be dads."

Dr. Phoenix asked, "What about you two together, without the kids?"

"I took a painting class one time. When I would walk into the TV room with a canvas in my hand, he didn't even ask what was on the canvas."

"What would he be doing?"

"Reading in his chair. He would look up at me and smile and say hi. That would be it. The first week, I jumped in front of him and showed him what I did and talked about the class and he listened. But after that I thought, what if I wait to see what he does? I got a genuine hello, but zero interest. I get that in the morning, if I see him. A genuine good-bye, and he is out the door."

"You don't have breakfast together?" she asked assumingly.

"No. He doesn't eat breakfast. He gets up right after the kids are gone, which means he didn't bother to see them in the morning, connect with them, or take them to school. He makes a coffee, showers, gets dressed, and grabs his work bag. If I am nearby, he gives a kiss goodbye— usually on the top of my head on my hair; sometimes my cheek—then, he's out the door. Uninterrupted. Pleasant. Solitary."

"That is interesting. And he doesn't get up to see the kids?"

"Nope. We've already had that argument."

She asked, "What about lunchtime on weekends?"

"He doesn't eat lunch either," I slumped back. "Don't get me wrong...he loves and enjoys the kids; but quite often, I give him a cue to 'cross over'. It's like he prefers to do it through the looking glass. For example, tending to the yard while the kids play somewhere. If our son has a soccer game, he will show up to the game separate from us, of course, because he prefers to drive his sporty, two-seater car. He'll watch the game, talking with other dads, or if he sits with me and our other kids, he usually insults the playing skills for the entire game. If our son does well, he yells out. If he doesn't, he'll slander our child, calling him '*lazy*', or '*he doesn't care*' or '*the coach doesn't know anything*.'"

"Sounds exhausting for you," Phoenix exclaimed.

"Bingo! Being exhausted pisses me off! Then, I feel additionally robbed of what I thought we clearly agreed upon, which was to raise a family. And then that broken agreement pisses me off! I was so naïve: I didn't realize the only version I got of Josh is the one who drinks. The first few years, our jobs merged; we lived with roommates for three years, which filled gaps I didn't know were there. On the flip side, I look at the things I don't have to complain about. Like the fact that we have a good lifestyle, etc., and soon enough, I go about my day and it all kind of balances out."

"Clearly, it balances out," stated Dr. Phoenix, clasping her hands together. Her fingers wiggled in a rhythmical order that lingered. I noticed the metallic blue polish on her fingernails.

We wrapped our session up neat and clean. I thought from then on that Dr. Phoenix would schedule me once a week.

"No. You're coming twice."

LEGAL PATH

A task of the "first offenders' path" was to obtain at least twenty personal reference letters speaking on Josh's behalf. For obvious reasons, my family had little interest, and since his family members were in other countries, I was not sure their letters would count for much. Hence, I decided to invite about ten to twelve of our friends from town over for a short meeting regarding our current dilemma.

In the end, everyone I invited came; curiosity alone secured that. They all gathered in my living room, and right off the bat, I explained our basic legal situation and summed up the incident as 'an evening that got out of hand, and we wish we could turn back time.' I gave almost no detail, citing it was a case pending, but offered that what had happened was a problem for Josh and I to solve, and that incarceration would not serve either of us. We were asking and hoped for a character reference from each of them in a basic and honest manner, e.g. Josh was a soccer coach one year, our families have kids that play together, etc. Our goal was to reduce the legal issues to manageable consequences. I also mentioned that we were going to counseling.

"Shouldn't Josh be at this meeting?" Mike asked.

"Yes, yes, he should. But he is embarrassed and not coping well. Protecting him protects my family. If you decide to write a letter, turn it in to me within a week. One page, or a paragraph or two is fine. If not, you don't owe me an explanation; no hard feelings." I handed everyone a copy of a 'to whom the letter should be addressed'. No one asked any further questions; no one pried.

After a long inner debate, I moved forth to ask my mom, dad, and brother to consider writing a letter. All three were reluctant; however, each agreed that Josh being in jail was not the cure, stating such an outcome would be devastating for the kids. My family thoughtfully expressed that it would not be fair for me to be left completely holding the bag. They agreed on the condition of meeting with Josh beforehand. My mother and brother each met with Josh separately. My dad felt he could not keep his composure, and took the longest. Emotional discussions were a challenge for my dad. I remember that as a kid, we would take a car ride for any "serious conversations". Driving while he spoke helped my dad.

Josh listened to everything my family had to say and answered all their questions. Both sides reported back to me feeling satisfied. Josh said he thought their conversations were fair, appropriate, and to his pleasant surprise, supportive. Personally, I was embarrassed Josh did not man up and seek each of them out with an apology.

WITHIN A COUPLE OF WEEKS, eleven letters arrived. One friend, Nora, painstaking declined. She did not believe writing on Josh's behalf was the right thing to do, and she hoped it would not cost our friendship. On the contrary, I respected her decision.

Josh obtained the other six letters to meet our quota. Initially, he was mad when he learned I had a living room town meeting that discussed his situation; he felt it embarrassing. I educated him on the scope of what the town already knew and that his initial actions were the problem. He conceded. Josh received a letter from his father, Caleb, who basically wrote of his 'shock over the whole situation and that his son has a commendable history'.

Josh told his dad. Informing his family about what he did was another condition of mine that Josh had to meet to return home. His family consisted of two brothers, and his bitterly divorced parents. In my mind, telling his family was a step of accountability. Josh admitting to his family how screwed up he had become might help him return back to being the son/brother they saw him as, and the guy Josh wanted to be. I drew a boundary line – they're his family; he should tell them. The letter from his dad was my proof he had in fact told them. That said, none of them called to check on me. Our phone calls were rare anyway, but we were certainly close from long visits over the years. If my son had acted the way Josh had, I would have called my daughter-in-law to get a better handle on the situation, and I would have wanted to apologize on behalf of my child for his actions. I quizzed Josh about what their reactions were so I could believe he had really called them. Basically, he said that they were "disappointed".

BUILDING A DEFENSE CASE

Time had come for my deposition, and to speak with Sharky for the first time. His office was in a neighborhood of residential homes turned commercial. These charming, private law offices were all within walking distance of the county courthouse, a place I had never been. Sharky's homestead had dark green cedar shingles, a dark grey porch, and modern hanging lanterns. Beyond the double oak front doors, weary clients with deep pockets entered a grand foyer adorned with a fireplace, a Persian rug, and oversized landscape paintings.

A legal assistant escorted me to what was probably once a formal dining room. Crystal chandelier lights bounced off the gleaming, oval, mahogany table. Sharky greeted me with a warm smile and a handshake before introducing me to Meghan, a mature woman with blonde hair obviously styled with hot rollers. Meghan was the tallest among us. Sharky explained that Meghan was a hired third-party person whose role was to make certain that no coercion occurred. Meghan was for my protection, and signified a stand-up approach on Josh's behalf. I found her presence reassuring.

They sat across from me, a tape recorder between us on the polished mahogany. Sharky formally explained the testimony procedure, and stated that he was representing only Josh in this case. First, he wanted to review my side of the story and, if I felt ready, he would then record an official statement. Sharky invited me to start from the beginning; I readily complied.

He listened attentively as I unfolded the story with hand-picked words, careful omissions, and minimized, emotional reactions. Occasionally, Sharky asked for further clarification. I dutifully re-explained, adding my empathetic understanding of the confusion that Josh must have been enduring during our tepid discussion. My report was simple, calm, and emphasized Josh's misunderstanding that I was taking the kids. I mentioned that merely hours later, I got my hair done while Josh watched the kids, and that he cooked dinner for us that same day. I took it upon myself to mention those details because I had secretly overheard Josh say to Sharky on the phone that those things had happened. Of course, Josh was saying them to downplay the effects of his actions. In that spirit, I described that I went to the pool and salon as if I were unaffected. I expressed that Josh left our home at my request to stay at a hotel for a few days, and I shared that we were seeing a therapist who specialized in domestic violence. Concluding, for the record, I reiterated feeling safe, and hoped this could all be resolved in the best way possible for my family to move forward.

During my statement preview, I absorbed the importance of moments when Sharky emphasized certain questions, such as, "You didn't get a restraining order: why?" Obviously, that was because I felt my husband was not a threat. I never brought up the phone cord, or the credit cards, or the cat and mouse chases through the house. How I felt when he cocked the gun never came up because cocking the gun never came up.

Sharky seemed quite satisfied with my run through. Nodding that I was ready, Sharky pressed the tape record button and we proceeded with the formal testimony. During this second and final retelling, I was even more concise, articulate, and avoidant of any aspects of my fear while again empathizing Josh's "confusion and fear" that I was taking the kids away, which lead to his break in judgment. I altered phrases like "running for my life and hiding in the bushes" to "I ran to a neighbor's house and called the police". I served Sharky his case on a fucking silver platter. The tape went off. By his expression, Sharky seemed professionally impressed and was about to thank me for my time when I interrupted him with an off-the-cuff question.

"If Josh moves out of the house, would that hurt his case?"

Sharky appeared taken back. He and Meghan exchanged surprised glances before he expressed, "Uh, it is...most likely better for his case that he is living at home."

I had to ask again, "Do you think Josh living at home is an influential factor?"

"It is, uh, certainly a plus for him, but you are free to do what feels comfortable for you." He appeared stunned and concerned at the same time. Perhaps he fully believed my Meryl Streep deposition. I bravely sought more answers.

"The letters we are getting—the first offender route—that gives him the best chance to keep his job, yes? Josh doesn't want to lose his career, which I can understand. I would not want to lose my profession either."

Sharky answered with trepidation as my pleasantries dissipated. "It is worth pursuing the first offender route and I thank you for obtaining letters on his behalf. You can turn them in once you get them all. Are you almost done?"

Clasping my hands together tightly, "I got eleven from the community, so Josh could be seen in many facets, plus my family changed their mind. Three will be coming from them, which is a big deal. Josh is getting the rest."

"Wow, you work fast. They will definitely help." Sharky kept still. His body movements did not rush me, and he never lost eye contact with me. He was courteous and professionally abrupt; however, I wanted him to briefly connect with the face behind the mask sitting across from him. As I spoke, Meghan deepened her gaze towards me.

"I carefully chose details to assist this case, and help you sleep at night in doing so," standing up to add more girth like another ring on a tree. My strained voice continued, "but Josh is a very difficult man to live with and he is not presenting his full character to you. I recognize I need to sell myself out so Josh can be seen with every strand of good light possible. I am willing to do that, and I will see Josh's case through – you can count on me. But you have been spared what lies underneath. I will have to handle that separately." That tree ring was proof I was not stupid. I was so much more. Stronger is the woman who lifts others higher than herself.

SCARECROW IN THE FIELD

Normal routines began to steady our lives while therapies and lawyers guided the direction. One rather carefree evening, Josh and I engaged in a private conversation in the TV room. He was somber, sober, and low key – had been for quite a while. The jail time looming over his head for an undeniable wrongdoing had shaken his reality. He had not been drinking for several weeks and had settled into a more vulnerable state of being. Cutting back on alcohol did not seem to be noticeably difficult; he had just stopped. I didn't think he was drinking beer or wine. There was a refreshing softness about him, and myself as well.

I said to Josh, "I received all the letters. My family was not going to write any, but they each changed their mind." He was sitting beside me on the leather sofa.

"Really?" he replied looking at me. "I wasn't expecting that. I don't deserve that."

"They are looking at what is best for the kids and trying to go from there. It's just a drop in the bucket, but a good drop."

"You are really doing a lot for me. Thank you. I appreciate what you are doing." His hands were either resting on his lap or he was gently rubbing them. His subtle movements were free from frustration or tension. He frequently turned to look at me during our conversation.

"You're welcome," I said with lighthearted reassurance. "At this point, we both need to be part of the solution. I am going in a direction that fixes problems, not creates them." He smiled at me, looked at the floor or perhaps some sincere drishti he created within his visual mind. A *drishti* was a term often used in yoga, referring to a focal point created out of physical reach that draws the attention outward, allowing meditative focus inward. It is the 'nothing' you "look at" during yoga poses.

"Hey," he said, "I want to tell you something." Josh sat up a bit straighter, a gust of wind in his sails. "I am really sorry. I know I scared you. I know I acted stupidly. I know I should not have been drinking and that is not an excuse. I am only saying that so you know that I know – because I often deny it to you, and ah," sounding throaty, his sail losing its bellow, "I do not expect you to forgive me. I will try to make it up to you —at least start by treating you better." He maintained his composure, intent on conveying his deep sincerity. Indeed, we were meeting on peaceful ground. Prepared to say something else, Joshua strained at his articulation. "I understand if you want out of the marriage. I understand. I won't stand in the way of things, if you want out." He gasped a deep breath, folded his hands together, and moored against the sofa, sails down.

Who was this guy? A rare honesty perfumed the air. Josh breathed in accountability and ownership, and exhaled the truth with zero threat, or manipulation. The space around us became neutral without a play on an advantage of power. For me, there was no satisfaction in being righteous or punitive or mistrustful. It was appropriate for him to say what he had said, and for me to listen. An incoming breeze from far beyond lifted my sails.

"Hey Josh," he was focused on keeping his composure. "Josh." He turned his head. Taking hold of his hands, I said, "I forgive you." His blue eyes went red and wet. Placed on an arrow's piercing tip, I sent those words again, "I forgive you."

Eros' arrow broke his shell. Josh appeared illuminated from within; he seemed younger and humbled. "Jess, I wasn't looking for that," he said. "I wasn't trying to..."

I cut him off. "I know Josh. We can move forward. I don't wish to hold you prisoner of your past actions." His breathing got louder, mine went deeper. There was a coolness of peace in the air. He seemed lighter, less sullen. Then he began to smile and brighten.

"Oh no," I brought my words up like a shield, "that doesn't mean a divorce isn't the right thing for us. We are not handling our marriage well," I stated. "The point of a divorce is to make things better. We'll still be a family. Maybe we could even be a role model for other divorced couples."

"Don't even say the 'D' word," and he did a quick body shake, as if removing the chills. "I get it," he said crossing his arms. "I get it. It hurts to hear the words."

"It's not easy saying them," organizing my thoughts. "Let's set aside getting a divorce, and get everything else squared away. It's not a bad thing to hit the pause button for a moment."

"Thank you," he sighed, "I would like that." We smiled, not really at each other, but at the palpable relief of cutting out navigating a divorce. We sat in comfortable silence for a bit. Then, an urge to feel like a woman again overcame me. The strength to nurture ignited a light within me. I found myself turned on by this space that held no judgments, nor labels, nor fear; no boundaries. Moving closer, I reached out my hand to touch his neck and caress a shoulder. Josh didn't respond. I pressed both hands across his chest and leaned in to kiss his cheek, kiss his neck. Josh, a bit taken back, chuckled. He was not relaxed. I placed gentle kisses on his collarbone, detecting our spring scented laundry detergent on his shirt. My roving hand started to slide down his shirt. He whispered, "No", but sounded lighthearted.

"Uh huh," I playfully said back as my hand reached the

frayed denim of his belt line. He cupped my hand and held it. Then he took my other hand and held them both the way a child would hold the corner of a blanket. Then, my husband started to cry. I did not understand why. The depth of his cry grew; his body started heaving individual sobs. *Whoa! Who let this freight train in my living room?*

Joshua started chanting some kind of mantra. "I don't want to be like them. I don't want to be like them. I don't want...to be...like...them." His eyelids squeezed shut, he continued. "I wasn't strong enough. I wasn't...strong enough."

Startled, I asked, "Who are you talking about? What are you talking about?" Joshua moved to lay horizontally on the sofa like a patient on a therapist couch, or coincidently, like a corpse on a morgue table. I sat near his feet, which he placed over my lap. My hands rested gently on the jean-covered shins. Josh's eyes were still shut tight.

His words came out in whispers. "My brother and my dad— they were so much stronger than me. I tried to fight them, but I couldn't. And my dad would hit my mom. He would hit my mom and he would hit us. Sometimes, she was protecting us. He would use his belt or his fist and he wouldn't stop. And my mom, she would...she would say," his whisper went into a higher pitch, "Caleb, stop! Caleb, stop!"

Josh paused and regulated his breath, the windows to his soul still closed tight. "Dad was so mean, but my brother was sadistic. He would choke me and choke me so hard and wait 'til I had one breath left before he would let me go. I couldn't get him off me. And he would tell me, 'Stop crying faggot!' They would both say it. If I cried, it got worse. When he'd hit my mom, she would say, 'Caleb, stop!' Sometimes she would get mad at us and she would dig her nails into my arm," he began to rub his forearm with annoyance.

I was unaware of this past. There had never been even a hint of violence from his family, although I guess there were clues. The level of animosity between his parents never seemed fully explained. His mom, Ingrid, had commented to me once, "Things were not good when Caleb wasn't happy. Not good at all."

Josh's whispering style changed a bit, and became less broken. He revealed, "That's why I don't like turtlenecks, or tight shirts. I don't want anything heavy around my neck or my chest. I have to get it off! Or any sudden hand movements... If you put your hands on me, I think, 'Oh no. No, not me!' So, you can't be angry at me and use your hands, okay? You can't."

"Okay, gestures are bad: bad triggers." I was unaware that my hands did that, but coming from a line of Italians, I probably talked with my hands. Whenever Josh got a new T-shirt, he always pulled the neckline way out of shape. It had seemed like a quirk to me.

Josh continued in the same tone. "You could not get away from him. My dad would come home from being at the bar and come into my room while I was asleep. I could hear him take his belt off. I would pretend to be sleeping." Josh's breathing ramped up. "My mom would say, 'You just wait 'til your father comes home!' And we would think, 'No! He's crazy! Mom, you don't know!'"

Josh took a few deep breaths that gave way to a calmer breathing pattern, the flow of his angst subsiding as he lay motionless in an aura of profound sadness. I imagined this must have been what it was like to lie in his bed as a child—a child pretending to be a dead man floating in a pool of silent tears as a means to survive. No doubt these were moments in his childhood development where a shadow was cast over any possible sign of an all loving God.

Managing to stumble past my shock, horror, and sadness, I offered, "Josh, I had no idea. Your whole family gives off no hint of this although...your mom has mentioned some controlling things about your dad, like he did not want her to drive, or that he would look for something 'not right' so he could blow up about it. She told me he blew up one time because the laundry was not folded right, and then he stormed out of the house. She said it made no sense."

Josh chimed in, "She neglected to add that he would leave the house and go to the bar. Sometimes he would come back; other times, he would be gone for days. When he came back, things would be fine for a while."

Behind the scenes of our conversation, I was piecing together bits of information in my head which I knew to be true. His parents could not be in the same room together. When I had asked Ingrid if she dated much, she oddly told me, "I will never have any man control me like that again. I am very happy having my own house." Josh's older brother had mentioned trying to protect his mom when they were young. The first time I brought Ingrid's name up to Caleb, he immediately gave me the indication Ingrid was crazy. Caleb blurted out to me, "Whoa ho-ho! She's a crazy one!" which ended further questioning from me because I knew Ingrid was not crazy.

Josh picked up where he had left off. His voice sounded calmer and older...more matter-of-fact. His eyes were still closed. "He broke my arm. My dad kicked me while wearing his boots. I went flying across the room and my arm got broken. I had to wear a cast."

"I saw a picture of you with an arm cast. You told me your dad accidentally broke your arm while you guys were wrestling. This makes more sense."

Josh gave the faintest acknowledging nod that he had told me a tale, then continued. "Dad felt really bad, really bad. He took me to the hospital. He told me, 'Now remember, it was an accident. Tell the nurses that we were wrestling and it was an accident.'" Straining his voice, Josh added, "When I was alone with the nurse, I wanted to tell her: 'He-is-right-out-there! He's – right there!' I could not do it at first; I was too scared. But then, I slipped-up on purpose and told the nurse 'He did it.' I told her flat out, and looked at her. But then she asked my dad, right in front of me, if that was true! My dad said, 'No ho-ho! My son fell off my back while we were wrestling. It was an accident. We were horsing around!' He even laughed. I could not do anything. When we got home, we didn't tell my mom the truth. I wasn't sure if she could tell." Thinking that a mom couldn't tell made my head spin.

Josh revived himself, and came back to life. He opened his tired eyes and sat up on his end of the sofa. "Guess I should have told you."

"Um, yeah. Explains quite a bit." There was Josh, offering the largest amount of validation I may ever get. "Seems your entire family kept things under the rug. How do you still have a relationship with your dad, for starters?"

Josh replied, "As soon as I finished high school, I was out of the house. I was mad at him for years. At the same time, my mom was divorcing him and he was drinking a lot. He was a mess. At one point, he came to live with me. Can you imagine! That was such a wreck! I felt sorry for him, yet hated him at the same time. But to answer your question, I don't know... We moved on. I had therapy, and that helped a lot. I see my parents as people now; my mom was a victim too, and rather young. That is why I went into mental health: people understand physical disabilities, but I felt that I understood emotional disabilities and mental pain. I wanted to make all I went through worth something."

Josh released a big sigh. "Let's go to bed. I feel drained."

"I bet. I'll get the lights."

WE WENT UPSTAIRS and uneventfully got ready for bed. He had been sleeping on the sofa, but tonight, that boundary didn't matter. Josh settled in before me. The outline of his body was faintly visible due to the street lights seeping in through the blinds. My husband was lying on his stomach underneath the hibiscus print bedspread, his head turned away. I slid under the covers and laid next to him. The only touch was my hand on his arm. As I nestled my head on a pillow, Josh's head popped up. He gave me a quick glance before facing his pillow again. Surprisingly, he said, "We weren't even safe after we went to bed. I'd pretend to be asleep, but it didn't matter." There came the voice of the living child corpse.

Say something. My whispered words slid out like sharpened skate blades gliding over ice with smooth crossover turns, "I understand. Thank you for sharing all this with me. It was very brave."

Josh lifted his head off the pillow. "I do not feel brave."

My reply was select, but heartfelt. "Josh, you have become a remarkable man. That is how I see you."

A pleasant "hmmm," resonated from his throat. My husband revisited his pillow, this time facing me. He grabbed my hand, gave it a kiss and said, "Thank you. Good night."

"Good night."

My eyes did not close that night, at least, not from the inside.

THE NEXT DAY I woke feeling a slow, rolling boil of anger towards Josh's parents. As the saying goes, *good people do bad things.* Not exactly fair to bring up my present-day ballistic emotions to his family when they all dealt with this years ago. Interestingly, I felt more anger towards his mom than his dad, which was not a balance of justice. I mean, why do perpetrators get off so easy and moms get all the blame? Perhaps on some level, I accepted his dad to be sick, granting him a pass, or maybe, and more likely, I could not fully believe what seemed undeniable. But his mom should have protected Josh; should have protected them all! How does something so chronic keep happening? I wanted to shake her, blame her, and mostly have her bear Josh's cross instead of him. Did she ever own any of it?

Josh talking while lying on the sofa with his body frozen, I began to piece together his past, his belittling defense mechanisms, and his silences which probably spoke as much truth as his words. In clinical readings about narcissists, I surmised that they internally feel the near opposite of what they convey outwardly. Beneath all those pompadour layers was someone with low self-esteem and feelings of being a piece of shit. Josh appeared to be speaking from behind those built-up layers. I found real-life psychology intriguing, and believed that understanding the development of a personality fostered a sense of relatability. In the end, we were all human.

The discussion with Josh evolved because he was the driver, or more likely, the work horse pulling the cart. He must have felt safe, and free from shame to be able to go where he needed to go. No doubt my arrow of forgiveness and freedom from judgment had cracked open the lid of Pandora's box. The voices and stories trapped inside got some air, and an audience member who cared and believed. That's the added pain with abuse, someone else not believing it.

OVER THE NEXT day or so, Josh did not bring up anything else, nor act differently. Of course, as a sober guy, he was rarely animated. Post-revelation day two, I casually mentioned to Josh that he had brought up some really big topics, and that perhaps, knowing some of this before now would have been helpful. He nodded and said, "Probably." I wanted more from him, and asked how could he carry all that around. He explained that it was old stuff his family had dealt with a long time ago. "Times were different then," he said. "You accepted that parents hit their kids. I guess it all gets stuffed down."

I asked, "Do you think maybe it contributes to your uh...drinking habits?"

He chuckled as he talked. "Hmmm, maybe. I started drinking when I was thirteen." Then point blank, he asked, "Why? Do you think so?"

"Uh, duh! It was a rhetorical question."

Josh let out a little laugh, but said nothing. Guess he was agreeing by not disagreeing. Conversing with Josh often felt like getting shot with a tranquilizer dart: it left me too stunned and numb to elicit a full, normal reaction. I was counting the days until my next therapy session.

ANOTHER ROUND THERAPY PLEASE

Dr. Phoenix was dressed in layers of black. Her sweater was black, her draping scarf was black, and her pants – black. Her slingback mules, however, had something to say. They mimicked a tuxedo shirt. The front foot portion was covered in folded bands of white rayon with three hot pink buttons on top. The sides were black leather, as were the bowties resting above the four-inch silver heels. Her soles were fire engine red.

Filled with a bright expression, and poised in her high wingback chair, the Phoenix was at the ready, ascertaining how to begin the session... Dive right in? Or perhaps do some coaxing, or a wee bit of probing...

"Oh, we are going there today! You are not going to believe this!" I blurted from the edge of her coal-colored sofa.

"You never disappoint," she laughed. "I mean that in a good way. Despite the chaos, you have a humorous filter." Dr. Phoenix never used a notebook during the session, hence her red fingernails fluttered with anticipation. She continued, "Don't get me wrong – I would love for Josh to bore us and do nothing besides what's expected, but usually, that is not the case."

"Not by a long shot!" I proceeded to take Phoenix on the roller coaster ride of Josh coming to me with no walls, and apologizing for everything; that he had owned his actions and left no claw marks behind. I revealed that in the breath of that peace, I came to forgive him.

She stopped me and asked, "How did that moment of forgiveness feel?"

Reflective, I said: "It was not so much a feeling—more like an opportunity to behave in the highest way. It was an action, an exercise. If anything, it released feelings...for both of us. Right afterwards, a certain knowing came over me: a knowing that true forgiveness means it is done. It is an agreement that on my part, I will not make him feel that low in shame—over that issue—again. I cannot drag him back, no matter what future crap he may pull. It is a bound contract between me, and the integrity of forgiveness."

Phoenix: "Do you also mean he is free from accountability?"

This made me smirk. "No, not at all. It means he can hold his head up and be accountable, versus hang his head in shame and be accountable. It also means I choose the high road, and it is my responsibility to stay the course."

"Forgiveness allows victims to write a new contract for themselves, and forgiveness opens a positive door for the other party as well. I like it!" the Phoenix exclaimed as her hands went up in the field goal position. "That is wonderful news. I am sure that was good for both of you. Moving forward you still..."

I interrupted her. "Sorry to cut you off, but that was not the big news. That is not why you should strap on a seat belt, and big girl therapist pants. By the way, nice shoes. I usually fashion orthopedic loafers, a rehab therapist's trademark."

"Consider me strapped in tight. And thanks...these shoes are just for sitting."

Slowing things down, I gave her the details of Josh's emotional break, describing his body movements, his voice...his story. It was not easy to tell. It was not easy to hear. It deserved to be believed and perhaps, at least by me, to be understood. There was no more joking in the room and for a moment, we were not a therapist and a client. We were two women, two mothers, absolutely horrified and heartbroken that yet another one of our own, a child, went unprotected – a pain that holds you motionless.

Breaking our heavy silence, I said, "He became the scarecrow from the Wizard of Oz, pulled apart all over the field, bits and pieces everywhere, an absolute mess of what used to be a whole person."

Phoenix gave a sniff and stated, "I am sure that is what it felt like to him, only more confusing. There is no rhyme or reason for what happened to him. There is no organization of abuse patterns. Victims are targeted and meant to take the blame, no matter how they respond. And it is more psychologically and manipulatively confusing for a child to be betrayed by those meant to protect him and provide for him. I have worked on many child abuse cases...this a common way it plays out. The victim is not believed as a child, and then again, often not believed as an adult."

Running fingers through my hair in frustration, "I want to scream 'how can this be?', yet bits and pieces about his family I collected or observed over the years are coming together and it makes sense." I leaned back into the sofa cushions for the first time since I had started speaking.

"It would not be surprising if Josh's father was abused as well. It is a vicious cycle."

"Caleb's current longtime partner, Jacques, is someone who knew Caleb from childhood. She said that Caleb had it rough, and that because of things Josh's brothers said to her, she believed Caleb used to hit Ingrid. At the time Jacques told me that, I only imagined it to be once or twice."

"Rarity does not make it any less wrong. And as a child or a spouse, if you are thinking it could happen anytime, then you are always under that mental anguish. And look, you are getting the filtered down version no matter who you are talking to about it. Do you know what kind of drinker Caleb was back then? Does he still drink?"

"Caleb being an alcoholic was also a news flash. He was in the military. I got the impression he went out to the bar a lot. I believe Josh thinks he is not like his father since he does not drink at a bar—he is home, watching TV; he is approachable.

And Josh never wants to harm the kids. Josh will have temper tantrums around them; we just kind of watch."

"Josh cannot handle disciplining at all, or let's say, setting parental boundaries," Dr. Phoenix further clarified.

"No, he cannot. He will talk about it in the third person, like, 'This is what I tell my clients to do, Jessica' as if he is the expert. Towards the end of last soccer season, Connor wanted to quit. He grew tired of the constant butt kicking because they lost every game. There were only a few games left and the team had no substitute players. I made him stay on the team, because at that point in the season, you show up for the team, not yourself. I suggested he further practice his soccer skills as an alternative to quitting, which he did not do. When Connor continued to give me a hard time, I said to my son, 'Tell your coach, face to face, you want to quit. That is how someone maturely handles these situations.' Connor was not willing to quit to his coach's face and wanted me to do it for him. I did not. All that said, once a game started, Connor always did his best, and afterward, he asked to play with a friend, acting like losing the game was no big deal. And things would be completely fine until an hour before the next game. So, this one time, I insisted Josh handle it. Maybe an alpha male thing was the trick to get Connor in the car—fine by me. Guess what Dr. Josh does?"

"I don't think I can."

"He paid Connor! Paid him twenty bucks to get in the car and go!"

"Twenty is a lot, even to me."

"Friggin' easy way out instead of character building... I explained to Josh that paying Connor undermined me, undermined the purpose of being part of a team, and conveyed it was okay that his friends lost, but Connor was entitled to better. I told Josh that paying his son was the opposite of practicing soccer with his son. Josh responded by saying that I wanted him to clean up my mess, and that it wasn't fair to expect Dr. Josh to come in and fix what I was not doing right. And Josh added that yelling at Connor would hurt their relationship." I grabbed a throw pillow and plopped it on my lap.

"It is not surprising that Josh fears that setting a boundary with his son would hurt their relationship. There are times when your kids are not going to like you. As a parent, you need to have tough walls because kids are going to try to knock them down. It is part of being curious, autonomous, and learning through experience. It is natural. That is why tough love is tough. It is hard to know where the perfect boundary should be and hard to keep it there as well as difficult to admit when you get it wrong. However, when an adult admits wrongdoing, kids pick up on how to apologize, be accountable, and learn humility."

"I don't know if Josh ever received any apologies. Josh genuinely gets along now with his parents and his brothers. They all live far apart from one another. The animosity is between Ingrid and Caleb."

"Regarding Josh and parenting, Josh is like a broken vase. He is always going to be broken. What you want is for Josh to be able to hold water. My approach is not to over analyze, but to place pieces together and go back to holding water again. If you are expecting Josh to become unbroken, that is not going to happen. And if he is expected to hold more than he can, or more than he lets on is really possible, then those pieces are going to come undone."

"That would be an example of decompensation: a leak in the vase."

"We all decompensate. How bad it gets depends on how many cracks were already there. I'm sure he has been using alcohol as glue, or as an escape for a very long time, but it is not permanent. Alcohol and other drugs provide an illusion or a numbness that gives the quick fix. Alcoholism, as a disease, will eventually have someone living his or her life from quick fix to quick fix with lessening value for anything else in the way."

Aware of our time ending, I surmised, "I guess I will adjust my expectations to be more realistic for Josh, then I won't keep going down a dead-end street."

Dr. Phoenix responded with a different mindset. "How about you work on expectations for yourself, and what you consider as fair expectations in a marriage and as parenting partners, as well as what you are going to do when those expectations are not met. There is a saying by Lao Tzu, 'When I let go of what I am, I become what I might be.' Think about that. I will see you next week." Dr. Phoenix stood up with a smile.

"Sounds good. Shall I only come once next week?" I asked Dr. Phoenix as she reached for the door. I assumed my progress was evident by now.

"Nope." She spun around with extra flare. "We remain at two," and she wiggled two magenta-colored fingertips at me.

THE PROSECUTORS ARE COMING

A turning point phone call occurred one afternoon. Curious about the incoming restricted number, I took the call outside, away from the kids, thinking I would add a stroll around the pool and boxwood gardens. Since boxwoods do not drop leaves, the yard always had a lush and serene fairy garden atmosphere. This lush lifestyle was a far cry from my trailer park beginnings where I used to dig holes in the dirt with a spoon. My grandma said if the hole got deep enough, I would reach China. I had wondered... Would land in China by dropping from the sky, or pushing up through a manhole cover? Either option was fine by my childhood daydream standard. Walking toward the pool, I politely asked, "Who is this?"

"My name is Cherice. I am with the county prosecutor's office. Attorney Wendy Miller will be handling your case." Right, because I was the star witness for both the prosecutor and the defense teams. "We are calling to prep you to testify for superior court. Is there a time you can come into our office next week?"

Bereft, I cut her off. "Wait. I'm sorry. Did you say 'superior court'? Because I was under the impression this will be heard at the county level."

"These charges are at superior court level, ma'am. We are calling to set a meeting to prepare you for testifying." She was very matter of fact, with no room for error.

Politely, I redirected my friend...my enemy... Was Cherice my frenemy? "Okay, Cherice, let me explain where I am coming from. My husband is planning to qualify for the First Offender Program. I believe it's nicknamed 'one and done'. His lawyer is in the process of doing that now."

Cherice responded, "Ma'am, I know that program and he does not meet that criterion. He has charges that include an unregistered weapon. Felony charges are not in that program. This is going to superior court, ma'am."

Air – I needed air. I was already outside. Either she was speaking fast, or I was processing reluctant information as slowly as molasses. I sat down on the pool's diving board. "Who is the attorney you are calling for again?" I mustered.

"I am calling on behalf of Wendy Miller. I am her assistant and will also be working on this case.

"Didn't you guys speak with Josh's attorney?"

"No, ma'am. We have not heard from them. We are calling to connect with you." The molasses began to crystallize. I got up from the diving board and paced around the pool.

"Okay Cherice, first – please call me Jessica. We are on the same team. Next, I'm surprised you haven't heard from my husband's attorney. Josh and I are on very amicable terms. He has been diligent in meeting requests by his attorney. We are both seeing a therapist who specializes in this area doing both individual and couples' therapy. Josh has stopped drinking, completely, and we are still living in the same house, raising our three kids. I am sorry and embarrassed our marital problems have spilled over into a legal mess that is bigger than our reality."

Cherice sounded surprised. "You are still living together?"

"Yes, we are."

"And you are both going to therapy, and he is going to therapy?"

"Yes. Believe me, do you think I'd have him in this house if I did not understand what was going on with him?" I stated with blunt honesty.

"See here, that is the question of the day isn't it? We need to get to the bottom of things. This is not ordinary behavior." Cherice sounded like the outraged girlfriend sharing drinks at a bar, calling out for justice.

"You do not need to tell me this was crazy, and that he acted dangerously. We are both in health care—we see crazy all the time!" Josh and I had both worked on lockdown units.

Grass roots honesty was on a roll. "Cherice, honestly, when this man leaves the house, he helps people. There are patients he treats that he truly helps every day. And when Josh comes home, we mostly do our own thing. I am not locked in some house in an abusive situation; I would appreciate these efforts if I was. Clearly, I am in a marriage that is not working, and Josh needs some kind of professional help. I requested the best of the best for our therapy. Jail time is not the solution; jail time is not going to help me, or my family." I was urgent to open some kind of window: something that created a different future. "Has your office received a copy of my testimony from Josh's lawyer?" I inquired.

"No. We have not received anything yet," Cherice swiftly answered. *What the heck? Then this conversation is their first impression!*

Wanting to sound reasonable and secure, as well as push our conversation a baby step in the right direction, I suggested, "Cherice, on my behalf, would you ask Ms. Miller to hold off moving forward until she receives my statement, and speaks with Josh's lawyer?" Pressing on before she answered, "Is Wendy a reasonable person?"

Cherice responded with a downgraded tone, "Yes, she is a

reasonable person and she is very good at what she does. I understand what you are trying to convey, Jessica."

A tiny swell of relief washed onto my shoulders. "I appreciate that, and I definitely feel heard. I hope my request is reasonable?" The air felt so thin, reminding me of hiking in the Colorado Rockies.

Cherice let out a heavy sigh on the other end. "I will present to Wendy the details of our conversation, and your request to hold further action until we hear from Josh's attorney."

Yes! Jessica and Cherice climbed the mountain and reached the summit! I restrained my outward excitement and said with much relief, "Thank you. That is very fair. I will contact Josh's attorney and make sure he reaches out to you."

Cherice concluded, "It was nice talking to you, Jessica. We will be in touch." The prosecutor's connection faded away.

WHAT JUST HAPPENED? Seriously—what... just...happened? It had fallen in my lap! It – It – What *was* the "it"? *It was Josh's destiny!* For a moment, his destiny was in my hands. *Why me?* Maybe, because Josh would screw it up. Or perhaps, because I had the skill set and Josh did not. This call was a big deal, that's for damn sure. My fingers started scrolling my contacts to find Sharky's number; however, they paused and trembled upon the name, 'Phoenix'. My heart dialed her number instead. It went to her voicemail; I left a message. Then, I called Josh's lawyer. Sharky's secretary answered the phone with a friendly disposition. I had not called to play.

"This is Jessica, Josh's wife. Is your boss around?"

"No, I'm sorry. He's in court right now. Is there something I can help you with?"

"Will he be back soon?" asking with determination.

"He is not due back for a couple hours. I can leave him a message." I imagined a pen and a little yellow sticky note all ready to go on the other end. This was not yellow sticky note.

"Okay. You'll need to give me a minute to explain what just happened so that you can convey the urgency of my call-to-action from to your boss. Please understand, I am a little overwhelmed right now."

"It's okay." She gave a pleasant laugh. "Go ahead."

"Wendy Miller's office just called. Their plan is to handle Josh's case in superior court and I'm their girl. They wanted to schedule a meeting with me to get the prosecution ball rolling."

"Okay, I will let him know Wendy Miller's office contacted you."

"That is not my message. My message is that they have not heard from you guys. They said lower court is not an option. They had zero information as to why there would be any reason to pause, or negotiate this case. They never received my testimony. Talking to me a few minutes ago was their very first impression of this case. Recognizing that, I started to turn a ship around that was full steam ahead to superior court island. Do you hear what I am saying?"

"I can see why you are upset," she spoke with kind reassurance.

"I got their office to see Josh as a person: a non-crazy, let's not send-to-jail kind of person. I got them to consider, based on my on the spot character referencing, that they should wait to hear from you guys because my family depends on it. I am pissed off right now because I was not the person paid a $5000 retainer to handle this! Please inform your boss that the time has come to handle this! *That* is my message."

"I hear everything you are saying, and the urgency you want conveyed."

Well, didn't she put my runaway panic attack on a neat little serving tray? Taken aback, I said, "Thank you. You are saying the right thing at the right time." Sensing our mutual resolution, I asked, "Why has he not reached out to her office yet?"

"I believe he was waiting for all the letters to come in, and to make sure he has everything."

"Josh got the remaining letters; we have them here. I will hand-deliver them to your office today."

"That is fine. Is there anything else?" Dang, she was polite, which was forcing me to calm down.

"Thank you for listening to my rant."

A SOOTHING CUP of Chai tea was calling my name. I gathered Chai, letters, and kids for a quick field trip. Walking out the front door, the cell phone rang. Dr. Phoenix was calling me back. I could ignore the call and rush to take care of Josh by dropping off these letters, or sit in the sun, drink my tea, watch the kids run around the yard, and talk with my therapist. I chose myself.

After spilling the tea with Dr. Phoenix, I said, "Because I was talking with someone who could make a pivotal difference in Josh's case, it felt serendipitous. Maybe Ms. Miller indirectly hearing my voice through Cherice, is the better way. Maybe I wouldn't have gotten through to Ms. Miller; maybe it had to be through Cherice. I hope I turned things around."

"Oh, I absolutely think you did. First of all, you have a way of disarming people. Next, you got the prosecuting side to see that you are not a whack-a-doo, and that Josh is a productive, safe citizen, which is especially critical in these situations."

"Do you think they consider all factors in these matters, or is it cut and dry no matter what?"

"I think everything matters. When I used to examine cases, we would consider everything."

"I forgot that you also have a law degree."

"I have so many degrees, it's ridiculous," Phoenix stated dismissively. "Look, I do not think Josh needs to be in jail. And I think you are smart to realize that if Josh goes down, it doesn't serve you, or the kids. Josh needs to man up, and learn how to go about that."

"You have your work cut out for you if he continues therapy," I exclaimed.

"It is Josh who needs to do the work," Phoenix stressed, "and he can drop off his own letters."

"I know, but this is not that battle. Josh would certainly drop them off later, but I want it done ASAP. Besides, it feels therapeutic. There isn't much more I can do; it will symbolize letting go."

"Letting go is okay," Dr. Phoenix echoed

EVERYTHING IS FINE

After the kids went to bed, I explained the day's scenario to Josh one final time. We were sitting on the sofa together, much like a couple on a park bench. The TV was off and his reading lamp gave a soft illumination next to us. Typically, whenever I talked with Josh, he did not validate my fears or feelings nor say much, but this time, he thanked me.

"You really stuck up for me. I probably don't deserve it." He still had this humbled aura about him. His words were nice, yet I was disappointed that he was not telling me how amazingly well I handled the situation, or validate how scary it must have been to talk with someone from the prosecutor's office. Then, I thought about the topic. For Josh, this was about facing serious jail time. My wanting a gold star was a bit over the top.

The jail time was serious. We had already received an unbelievable stream of letters from unheard of lawyers offering to take his case. Guess there was a name registry or something for lawyers to access potential clients. Many of those legal representation letters mentioned that Josh could be facing up to seventeen years in jail; a couple of lawyers quoted twenty years as a maximum penalty. Josh never saw these letters—I hid them. Reality was already in Josh's face, and no doubt Sharky had already had these conversations with him. Venturing uncharted waters, I asked, "How are you doing without a drink?"

"I'm fine," he sighed. "I don't even think about it until I walk in the front door and I automatically go to get a glass of wine. I

think, *Nope. Not having any*. And I move on to the next thing."
He smiled, putting his hand on my knee.

"I know you don't like water – 'fish piss in it' you always say."

"Hmm, true. I have been drinking a lot of seltzer water. Do
you mind keeping that on hand? Having other options to drink
that have flavor is helpful."

"Consider it done. I will get a variety of seltzer flavors for
you." I was the one who did most of the food shopping.

Josh leaned back a bit and scratched his head, rapidly, almost
like he was getting rid of fleas. "I started having really vivid
dreams; dreams that bother me. I think when I drank, it helped
me stay in a deeper sleep. Now, I remember some of them. It
makes me very on edge."

"Anything particular stand out?" I turned and angled myself
to face him more.

"No, not really," Josh replied. "I am always trapped. Sometimes, I might be in water. One time, I was standing in a river
fly-fishing, but I had nowhere to go. I couldn't leave my spot. I
could see the shoreline, but I could not move towards it." He sat
back, scratching his head again with both hands. "I'm going to
watch some TV; it helps me go to sleep."

"That's fine," I said. "I'm tired. I'm going upstairs." We gave
each other a quick kiss goodnight – nothing special – except it
was familiar, uncomplicated, and conveyed we were not out to
get each other.

"I'll be up in a bit," he said out of polite habit, like one does
when hanging up the phone, but I knew he wouldn't be and
poof! – my thoughts were triggered back to old crap. Moving
forward always seems to involve going two steps back.

———

THE DAYS MOVED on but with less drama as Josh's case became a
lawyer-to-lawyer battle behind closed doors. I began to focus on
happier things. Nicky's fifth birthday was around the corner,

and then soon after, Jolie would turn nine. Since Nicky's birthday was near Halloween, we always had a costume party. This year's party included the entire kindergarten class of twenty-two kids. The party activities included: a pumpkin decorating craft that artistically used everything from glitter to googly eyes, trampoline games (I got one second-hand on Craigslist), and tractor rides. "Tractor" meant a John Deere riding mower towing a trailer worthy of hauling an eight-kid cargo. I drove giggling princesses and superheroes around green paths that circled mulched islands of boxwoods, rhododendrons, and azaleas. Then we rode out onto the street, turning around in the neighbor's circular driveway. The party finished with a homemade spider web cake. Martha Stewart's holiday magazine taught me how to make the web design. I admired Martha. She built an empire on the belief that homemaking was of value.

BEST FRIENDS

In high school, I had a small group of three male friends. We loved and identified with the *Seinfeld* show. My friend Bradley was most like the *Jerry* character. We met when we were twelve and working for my dad. My father owned a pizza store and hired Greg and I as well as Brad and his brothers to deliver circulars that advertised the pizza business. Brad was so cute and funny and energetic; he was instantly my first crush. Subsequently, we attended the same junior/senior high school. Over the years, we grew close as friends, took turns "liking each other" and ya know...but we never seriously dated.

Our friend, Peter, was the "George" character in Seinfeld, but without the yelling. Peter moved to Alaska after high school and became a part-time radio DJ. I lost touch with him after the three of them flew out to Hawaii for my wedding.

Then, there was our beloved "Kramer" character, Tom, whom we fondly called Moss. Moss and I became best friends after high school when Brad went off to boot camp. Brad, Moss, and I have built a friendship made to last a lifetime.

Now, Moss could talk to anyone about anything. His memory retains an immeasurable amount of movie quotes and song lyrics from all genres. He was a knower of obscure facts and loved to see live concerts. His left thigh bore a tattoo of the iconic portrait of Jerry Garcia wearing sunglasses. He proclaimed himself to be "queer as a three-dollar bill" despite being a devoted heterosexual-husband to his incredibly talented, *female* wife; so yes, he was on the bisexual continuum. One final detail —he had a slight learning disability. Not that it mattered, except that after twenty years, he still could not spell my name correctly. He would spell out Jessica with either a double "c" or one "s", or use every vowel except an "e" – all of which I found endearing.

Brad, on the other hand, was the youngest of four in his family. He was most beloved, and the one most picked on by siblings. He had a summer birthday, hence he was one of the shortest and most 'baby faced' boys throughout high school. But his boyish cuteness turned to killer good-looks after boot camp and beyond. His blonde hair was so thick that we teased him that it felt like hemp, because it did. Brad and I spent many a high school evening on a park bench kissing each other's neck and ear lobes, avoiding each other's lips. This was our way of not cheating on the other people we were dating. We always had special feelings for one another, but if I tried to write a check with those feelings, it would bounce. Brad and I worked at keeping our friendship solid. He moved to Colorado after serving in the Navy. Neither Moss nor Brad had children; Brad has yet to marry. Eventually, I got over my embarrassment and wanted to tell Brad and Moss about what was happening in my marriage.

A CONFERENCE CALL SEEMED BEST. It took a while before the

two of them would shut up long enough for me to tell my story. I wanted them to bring out the old version of myself. Once they took me seriously, Brad and Moss were disheartened by the news.

Brad responded first. "That sucks, Jess. I use to be jealous thinking you had such a great catch. Now I'm thinking I wasn't so bad."

Moss: "Way to think of yourself, Brad. Go back to thinking you're cursed with women."

Brad: "I just mean that Jessica deserves better. That guy's a fool; he doesn't know what he's got."

Moss: "Jess, I am so sorry you had to go through that. If I was there, you know I would give you a big squeeze. I wouldn't even 'cop a feel'."

"That means a lot, Moss. And Brad, I know what you meant. I'm lucky there weren't bullets in the gun. It could have been worse."

"A lot worse," added Moss.

Brad, who spent six years in the military asked, "How do you know there weren't bullets in the gun?"

Taken aback by this novel question, I answered honestly, "Because Josh told me."

Laughter burst from both of them over the phone. Brad blurted out, "Are you kidding me? Who intends to pull a gun and threaten someone without putting bullets in it?"

"Really, Brad? Didn't your girlfriend say you shoot blanks?" Moss guffawed at his own joke.

"That's not what your wife told me! Ah-ha-ha!" Brad's laughter had a contagious quality despite the often-absurd content.

"Hey douchebags... I asked Josh *point blank* if there were bullets in the gun, and he said 'No'. And then I questioned him about my hearing him cock the gun—which sent panic through me. He said that if there had been bullets in the gun, there would be a bullet in the chamber. He said if I checked the gun, I would not find a bullet in the chamber."

Brad: "Holy Swiss cheese, Jessica. If that's his proof, don't you think he would have just pulled the bullet out of the chamber before you checked the gun?"

"What?" I asked in confusion, as I felt walls begin to crumble.

Moss: "Why did he cock the gun?"

Perplexed, I responded: "I asked that too. Josh said it was all one motion, one thought. It's what you do, I guess. I never fired a gun. How would I know? I only knew that if the safety is off — run! I was flying!"

Brad cut through the lightheartedness. "Jessica, did you ever think that Josh could have taken the bullet out of the chamber and put it back in the cartridge so it looked like it was never there?" We observed a moment of silence. "You can remove a bullet from the chamber without discharging a gun; it's not stuck there. It's basic gun handling."

"I just knew the safety was off. I never thought about a chamber. Josh added the chamber part to demonstrate how there were no bullets. I think I started the whole thing by wondering if bullets were in there. It never came up with the police." Finding this detail out late in the game may have been the only way I would have stayed the course. A course where forgiveness served better than condemning. A course that the universe seems to have supported me to follow in perhaps the only way possible.

"You did the right thing, Jess. The safety was off; you needed to get out of there," Brad said, trying to sound reassuring.

Moss: "Did the police report say anything?"

I had to ask him to repeat his question. "What did you say?" I could hear Moss, but inside, my mind was turning to quicksand.

"Wouldn't the police report have those details when listing items at the scene?" insisted Moss.

"I read two reports from two responding officers. The gun was only mentioned in their description of the situation. I never read anywhere that it was loaded, but then, only the chief grabbed it. Certainly, I was better off not knowing this right away. Josh and I don't want any of this mess in our lives, nor the path leading up to it. I don't know how much his drinking was a factor."

Moss, "How much does he drink?"

Jess, "I don't know—a lot."

Brad: "I have two or three beers, and then I'm done...unless I want to get wasted. Then I'll make sure I'm not the driver. Usually my friends are wasted, and I'm the driver."

Moss: "That's because you drive people crazy: they need to be wasted to tolerate you. Occasionally, I like to have one cocktail and sleep like a baby. My wife says I snore, but she's making it up."

Brad: "Dude, you rock the house with your snoring."

I chimed in. "To answer your question about Josh, he drinks two beers like it's a glass of water. He will easily drink a six pack and a couple glasses of wine, and not seem fazed at all."

Brad: "In a day?"

"In an evening... Over the course of a weekend, add a bottle of vodka or whiskey to the mix."

Moss: "Wow – that's up to four bottles of vodka a month! I don't drink that in four years."

"Josh brushes away the magnitude. He hangs out with other big drinkers. How could a 'norm' be a problem?" Feeling validated, I seeped out more robust detail. "My husband does not buy beer by the six pack. It's by the case. Second, the wine is usually a merlot - double bottle size. When he pours the wine into his glass, he immediately drinks half, then refills it to the top. That is one glass. Lastly, vodka is sometimes bought by the liter. When I say bottle, it could mean jug. I don't drink any of it, nor does anyone else around here. I do not buy it, and I do not pour it. That's what I think an enabler would do."

Brad: "Holy shit! I would puke my guts up!"

"My husband never seems drunk. Well, sometimes he does. I never lived with people who got drunk, so I don't know."

Moss: "Is he drinking during the day?"

Me: "No. Not unless it is the weekend. Then he has like, two or three beers while working in the yard. It's just the evenings, but all evening long. Of course, this is when I spend most of my time with him. He usually watches TV or reads, but I feel like he is a different person in the evenings."

Moss: "I bet. Aww Jessie, please keep yourself safe. If you need me to back you up, I can't. I bruise like a peach. But I can hold you, and make you laugh." Moss was a lover, not a fighter.

"I will stay safe, promise."

"I trust your judgment," said Brad. "Men screw up all the time. If you can make Josh a better dad for your kids by the way you handle this, then it's worth the effort. You said he stopped drinking, right?"

I responded with relief, "Yes. It's like the edge of a knife is gone. He is a little more genuine too. Anyway, it was good to talk with you guys."

Moss replied, "It was good talking to you too, honey. Brad – I would have hung up on you a long time ago, but I didn't want to seem rude."

SEEKING ANSWERS

I took the conversation with my friends to heart. An act of ignorance was one thing; remaining ignorant was another. My mind kept replaying Josh's new behavior of going into the kitchen during the evenings with the lights off. The first time he did it, I almost bumped into him as he came around the corner from the back pantry. He did not have a glass in his hand. He said he was looking for a snack.

Why look for snacks in the dark, in the pantry, where we don't keep snacks? I explored the nagging feelings I was suppressing and searched the pantry. Once again, my spouse thought I'd never look up. There it was high on a shelf: a bottle of vodka, two-thirds full. Josh was obviously sneaking direct swigs. *He fooled me.* It was an easy decision not to say anything. He wasn't going to stop, and he'd only create another hiding spot which I would then have to find. Knowledge of his secret stash meant I was able to keep my finger on the pulse of the situation.

Checking the levels in his bottle quickly became a daily obsession of mine. His stash soon grew to a bottle, plus a back-up. Sometimes he switched to white wine, perhaps as a measure of restraint. Proof of his drinking conjured up a weird mix of feelings for me: validation, alarm, exhaustion, obsession, and deep loss. My job should be watching over myself and my kids, not engaging in a dark act of benign curiosity mixed with power that came from knowing someone's secret. Josh and I had so much to learn about alcoholism. We weren't even using the term "alcoholic". I thought he could simply stop whenever he wanted; that was how he presented it to me. At one point, that probably had some truth in it—like two decades ago. Using the label "alcoholic" now would start a domino effect. I did not understand that asking Josh to quit was equivalent to asking someone to unravel. Josh could not articulate that; he could only react from shame, fear and defeat.

THIS SECRET KNOWLEDGE, as well as the task of creating a safety net for my family were distractions from pursuing a necessary truth. I needed a face to face with the one man who could give me a straight answer. That moment came while driving near the police station. I got a sudden knot in my pelvis, the location of the root chakra which harnesses survival energy. The location was lower than the feeling of having butterflies in your stomach, and did not feel the same. Determined to show up for myself, I parked at the station and pushed the buzzer. Serendipitously alone at the station, Chief Harold answered the door. We chatted briefly, then I got right to the point of my visit. The chief was sitting across from me, at his desk.

"Do you mind if I ask you something about that day at our house?"

He swerved back and forth in his chair before answering. "Sure, go ahead."

"When you found the gun... Were there bullets in the gun?"

Chief Harold folded his hands, slid them across his desk pad, and calmly stated the facts. "Yes, ma'am. The gun was loaded. It had a full cartridge."

"Thank you for your time." I shook his hand, and left.

This information, which I decided to keep to myself, went straight into my Pandora's box. If knowledge was power, then quiet knowledge was fuel. This knowledge required time and contemplation. If I gave Josh a new ultimatum, with no ability to back it up, then I had no plan. I decided to wait until emotions and fear would not drive my actions. In the immediate, I had a therapist in my corner to prevent overreacting on my part—or worse—under reacting.

CHEMICAL REACTION WAITING TO HAPPEN

Fall was turning colder and darker. Josh and I started having small arguments in the evening. I would snap over minor things, secretly pissed about the gun and the drinking. And Josh, who was slowly increasing his alcohol intake, was less restrained in his comments. Together, we were heavily charged particles about to make lightening.

I pointed out to Josh that he was putting the dog downstairs too early. Josh did not feel like dealing with the dog... Out of sight, out of responsibility. We had a 3 x 3 open pen downstairs that Josh had recently got so that Willie would not have an accident during the night in the main rooms. Spending all night in a six-foot fenced area was not fair to the dog, especially as the night got pushed back to start at 7:30/8:00 p.m. That was twelve hours of being penned.

"Josh, I did not want to get a dog because I knew I would end up taking care of it. It is not fair to keep him downstairs for so long," I said, very annoyed as I met up with him on the screened porch off the living room.

"He is fine. Some people leave their dogs outside all night; some get left in a cage. He is in an open pen. Besides, I take him out." Josh tried to brush it off.

"No, you don't. And big deal if you do for five minutes. He's a Border Collie, for crying out loud. I wake up extra early in the morning to let him out."

"You just like pissing me off! I try to avoid you and you still come after me! I work my ass off all day and it's still not enough," Josh said while pacing, then marched off the porch toward the TV room.

Following him, "This is about the dog! I don't care who else puts their dog in a pen. You don't feel like dealing with him and now, I have a fourth kid to look after. If this keeps happening, and I hear Willie whining in the basement, you are going to hear the sound of my car running over that stupid pen!" My turn to leave the room, purposefully heading to the kitchen so he cannot hit up his hidden baby bottle of vodka.

Josh walked out the front door to take a walk. I checked on the kids, and then washed dishes as usual. Josh came back about ten minutes later. He came over to me and said with strained calmness, "I know what this is, Jessica. It's your friends," referring to my town girlfriends, some divorced, some not. "I don't know who is influencing you, or who is telling you to get a divorce, but you are just looking for reasons."

My jaw could not drop quick enough. "Are you kidding me? Do you think I have to make up a reason! What are you talking about?"

"This is not your thinking, Jessica. Somehow your friends, or who knows who— maybe it is mostly you— but you have been baiting me to try and push me over the edge so that you can get a divorce. I don't know why you would listen to them, Jessica! There is a culture here that I do not fit into."

"Hold up. Are you kidding me? Are you seriously claiming there is some kind of conspiracy to get you?"

"I am not saying I haven't done things, but this thinking...I don't think it's just you." He put his hands up to gesture he meant no harm, backed away several paces, and exasperated, said: "I will deal with it, Jessica. Don't worry about me." He stormed out to watch TV.

YO, ANOTHER SESSION

Dr. Phoenix's eyeballs almost popped out of both sockets. "A conspiracy theory! Are you fucking kidding me? What did you do then?"

"Searched the kitchen floor, found my lower jaw, went to search his car, and found another bottle of vodka. Josh drank away all his humility; this saddens me. It takes away his commitment to us and to putting his family first. It undermines his apology, and that he owned his actions. I forgave him and he's working to annul it all," I said pacing in her office and waving my arms. "On top of that, he assumes me so stupid and naïve that I would let my friends decide for me as to whether I should end my marriage of ten years. My friends are mature enough that they would not try to answer that for me. In fact, they are such good friends that they stand by my side while I stay with a man who pulled a gun on me." *Thud* went the leather as I plopped onto the sofa, and cradled my head in my hands.

Dr. Phoenix appeared amused and perhaps a little proud. She asked, "Now what? Do you take your forgiveness back?"

Placing my fists firmly on my lap, I exclaimed, "Hell no! Do you think that monkey on his back gets to change me too? Do you think I can't pass a test? Forgiveness is a gift. You give it away, and you don't take it back. It is up to the other person to reap it or not. Josh did for a while, and it was incredible. But now, Josh has made a choice that leads to this crap. I feel like I am making up rules in my head to some kind of a game."

Dr. Phoenix asked with full interest: "So, what are the rules now?"

"Move forward," I said as I took a deep breath. "When it comes to making decisions, Josh does not get a seat at the table anymore."

Phoenix smiled, nodded her head, and said, "Good answer, kid. Good answer."

SANITY PLAN

Riding my retro-styled, mauve bike around town with the kids one day, I noticed an "Apartment for Rent" sign in front of a large, three-story house about three blocks away from our home. Our town was full of large beautiful properties; it was hard to distinguish which were rentals. This house had a porch, a small backyard, and lots of detailed woodwork. I called the number that day. The landlord gave me the basics: second floor for rent: two bedrooms, a full bathroom, full kitchen, spacious living room, and a small bonus room—$1100 a month. The sign had just gone up that day. The owners were waiting to see what sort of local response they got before advertising in the paper. I made an appointment to see it right away.

Crunching the numbers, I needed to make – wait for it – more money. Recently, I had picked up a few private, early intervention cases from our local school. Meanwhile, I was teaching yoga, and occasionally filling in at a sub-acute rehab center. This piecemeal combo would not do. Yoga had to go, and I would have to trade up for hours working as an OT. If I finished my professional work by the time my kids got home from school, I could be both a dedicated mother and a therapist. During my job searches, I had learned that OT school jobs paid more than those at physical rehab centers. Even better, if I worked for a contract company – without benefits – I could make top dollar at a per diem rate.

A HEALTHCARE AGENCY that staffed both schools and sub-acute rehab centers hired me on the spot, thrilled that I had both skill sets. They placed me in a school contract right away. School therapy had changed over the last ten years: there were now more self-contained classrooms, and more children with autism spectrum disorder. Putting more effort into my career was a solid decision to help make a difference both in the world outside, and within my micro-bubble.

The apartment landlords agreed to a six-month lease, and I signed for an apartment in my name only. The apartment was literally eleven houses from my primary residence. I told no one...not my mom, not my best friends; not even my therapist. This choice was made with the universe's blessing and an inner trust that I had to save myself. I could not pinpoint exactly what I was saving myself from until I entered my empty apartment.

When I walked inside, it felt like a sanctuary. My energy kept rising as I went from room to room, brainstorming about the future. There was no clutter and no big ass TV. Lying down on the bare carpet, staring up at the twelve-foot ceiling, I made the connection and realized why I hadn't wanted to tell anyone: I needed to escape, and be saved from *influence*. I was running from influence—influence from Josh, from society, from the legal system, influence from the chaos of addiction, from all the roles I played...wife, mother, daughter, friend. I was saving myself from the centrifuge of influence. This sacred space would be my chrysalis of peace. Even if I only came here at night, after I put the kids to bed, it was an act of passive resistance to being ignored and belittled. I needed to be in and at peace.

Painting, decorating and shopping at secondhand furniture stores for the apartment was both fun and liberating. Using Feng

Shui principles, I tried to develop a style. While decorating, I listened to Deepak Chopra and Wayne Dyer, my new comrades. Their sage philosophies empowered me, and in turn, my wings grew stronger. Eventually, after a few weeks of secret visits to my apartment an hour or two at a time, I decided to tell my therapist.

REGAL in her high back chair, wearing a floor-length, chocolate colored dress and a pair of cheetah print pumps, Dr. Phoenix crossed her ankles and emoted sincere interest as I spoke of my apartment sanctuary. As I overflowed with explanation, Dr. Phoenix appeared to freeze a polite smile onto her face while her mind perhaps did a series of Cirque du Soleil reactions. She asked some questions including, "When you are not decorating, what do you do there?"

Spoken with all sincerity, "I... I just...exist. Literally lying on the floor next to the fireplace, I just try to 'be': *be* without chaos, *be* without interruption, *be* without a set-up or a judgement or a responsibility. *Be* in a place where I don't have to clean up after others. *Be* in a place that has a beginning instead of an end. Underneath all the craziness, I am in a marriage that is ending. I feel badly for the kids, because I didn't deliver something. They deserved to be raised in a home with parents who are in love. But I also can't handle sweeping everything under the rug. There's a new pile all the time, or worse, the same pile I swept up last time."

Dr. Phoenix offered, "There is a vicious cycle that goes with alcoholism. They talk about it at Al-Anon meetings. You meet people who have not only walked your steps, but have gone beyond what you have achieved. It is not a meeting that bashes the alcoholic—it is for all the other people closely involved with alcoholics to heal themselves. In that sense, it is not about the alcoholic, it is about you."

"I suppose I could prioritize going to a meeting even though I hate carving out more time due to Josh's addiction."

"You can choose to look at it that way if you want, but sometimes you just do what you need to do." Pausing to raise a deep purple fingernail into the air, she said: "I can see why you got the apartment. I think you have a healing plan that can work." Hesitating for a moment, she continued. "Have you figured out how you are going to tell Josh?"

"Oh yes... That is well thought out to handle after the holidays. Josh has a trip planned to California for a work conference; I'm driving him to the airport. Would you like to know the details?"

"Please," planting her cheetah pumps on the floor. Dr. Phoenix brushed her bangs aside, folded her hands neatly on her lap, and said, "Indulge me."

THE CHRISTMAS HOLIDAY came and went with regular flair. At random times, I visited my sanctuary, painting the kitchen and hanging artwork. I wanted it to feel inviting, and fun for the kids. My head was wrapping around the idea that Josh and I could get divorced, and I could feasibly stay at the apartment until my two oldest kids finished high school. Since I was the one leaving, Josh could keep his ego and wallet intact. Before signing any papers, we could figure out all the visitation logistics that normally stall and trip up divorces. Yes, this plan might work.

Good-bye 2008.

2009 - CONTINUED

Stop wearing your wishbone where your backbone ought to be. -
Elizabeth Gilbert

An early dinner crowd had formed at the 'Fish for Chips' eatery. Settling into our booth, Josh and I perused the menus while our waitress hurried off to fetch our glasses of water. Josh, seated across from me, glanced at his menu, made his decision and then searched around the room for something or someone of interest. Sitting across from him, I had decided that French fries were the best choice for my eat and orate agenda. Upon folding my menu, I played that familiar game in my head of how long could I sit in silence, waiting for my husband to ask me something, before I broke and asked about him.

It was less than a minute before he muttered, "I hope my flight is on time. It's already going to be a long day for me." He noticed the waitress swiftly heading our way.

"Are you ready to order?" she politely asked. On her neck, peeking out from her flipped up collar was a first rate, high school, back-seat hickey. *Good to see someone's getting some action.* Josh gave a nod for me to order first.

"I'll have fries with Old Bay seasoning." I handed her the menu.

"That is all you're having?" Josh asked.

"That's all I need right now," grinning back.

"I love Old Bay," said our chipper waitress with a ponytail colored more crimson than her love bite. "I like anything spicy. I'll put it on the side for you."

"Sounds great; thank you."

"I will have the fried calamari and a coffee – black please."

"No problem, sir. I can take your menus...thank you. I will be back when your order is up," and her joyful, maraschino ponytail bounced away. We talked about his upcoming trip for a while, then came the opportunistic lull. Clasping my nervous hands together, I swallowed any anxiety, anchored both forearms on the table and summoned up my voice. He was as unfazed as a dung pie yet to attract a fly.

"Josh, I want to let you know, before you get on your plane, that I got an apartment. When you come back, I will have another place to live. That doesn't mean I am leaving our house...a house that also has my name on the title. It means that I no longer want to sleep in a home where my spouse continues to drink behind my back, ignores my contributions, and some-times, even my very existence. I'll have a second place to go where I can exist in peace." I leaned back with folded hands resting on my stomach. "I'll take any questions you have."

Josh's expression went flat, tortilla flat. Eventually tortilla face spoke. "You are going to stay at a friend's house? Or someone you consider as a friend..."

"My friends do not even know I have an apartment," I said in the murky nebula between us. "News flash: I make my own deci-sions, and they're based upon your actions. You started drinking again, and right along with that came accusations that I conspired to create this mess we're in. To me, that signals no accountability from you, which means you are not going to change."

"Would you keep your voice down," he commanded through a tightened jaw. I don't believe I raised my voice, but alright. Using the word "drinking" had probably got him. My lips tightened; I had no intention of embarrassing him.

His tone changed. "Are you seeing somebody?"

"Here are your spicy fries! A fried calamari here...and one coffee, black."

My fascination with the hickey served as a mental anchor. I marveled at its creation, such intense portions of eggplant color. Someone was sucking *pretty* hard last night, or...ooh—maybe this morning.

"Thank you," Josh said, fixating on his coffee, a hand resting on either side of his crispy seafood ringlets. I chewed on a couple of fries and over-examined the architecture of my potato stick-stack. Josh sipped his coffee. "I noticed you are not answering my question," he said.

"Oh... That's because it's ridiculous and absurd and doesn't deserve an answer. Between loads of laundry, and therapy sessions, when would I have the time? But to answer for the record, no. I am not seeing someone."

Josh's voice grew louder. "Do you want to ruin this family? Do you know how hard I work every day to live in that house, and be in a town where nobody gets me? And you want to throw it all away!" His flat eyes were hard cut, and his open fingers pressed into the table.

"How about you keep your voice down," I said, trying to clamp a lid over us.

"My voice?" Josh said as his stare locked in place. "Why don't you start saying something that makes sense!" He brought his fists to his lap. It seemed as if he was drawing power from the potential of others hearing this; that somehow, a crowd would join him and point at my scarlet letter.

Ignore and de-escalate. Ignore and de-escalate. Slowly, I floated a single fry up to my mouth and munched. Josh remained a tense, frozen knot. Again, with deliberate pacing, another fry levitated to my mouth and I began to chew and chew and chew. His shoulders melted, but the intimidating stare remained. I rotated the next potato stick in lots of Old Bay seasoning. This one was worth savoring – even closing my eyes. Umm, so good. Mr. Tortilla face forcibly drew in a sip of steaming coffee.

Upon dabbing my lips clean and replacing the napkin to my lap, I resumed my civil conversation. "I spoke with the chief of police recently about the night of our incident. You set a low bar for yourself that evening, lower than I initially could fathom. However, you gave me an all-in apology, and I forgave you. I freed you of a burden. But now, it feels like my forgiveness is being tested."

"You are not making any sense."

"Chief Harold told me the gun was loaded; it's in the evidence. Don't worry, my forgiveness remains, even though there were bullets in the gun, even though you have started drinking again; even though you are making up conspiracy theories." Josh gently spun his coffee mug around on the table. "You are not dragging me to a place where I treat you like you treated me." At this, his eyebrows crinkled in towards the middle and his mouth dropped open ever so slightly. *He does have soft, well-defined lips. I'll give him that.*

Without pumping the brakes, I rolled onward. "If I kick you out of the house, it doesn't help your legal case, so I got an apartment three blocks away. Every morning, I will arrive home to wake up the kids. We will have our regular days until I put them to bed, then I will leave the house to sleep in an apartment where I exist; where I matter, and where no one belittles me. No one else lives there; I am paying for it myself. I get a safe space, and you get to save face."

Red-tail reappeared at our table. "Hey folks! Can I get you two anything else?"

"Yes please," I answered, "the check. We're done."

"I see, okay. Do you want anything wrapped?"

Josh had transformed into a weathered, Greek statue who no

longer bore distinguishable features or glory. Responding to the waitress, I replied, "Yes, wrap everything, and here, use my credit card. He has a plane to catch. We don't want to miss it."

"Right away." She took my card and our plates, and vanished as quickly as she had come.

Josh put his head down, then looked up at me. "I don't know what to say."

"That's fine. It's not about what you say, it's about what you do."

I led the way out of the restaurant to embark on our quiet ride to the airport. Approaching the airline drop-off, Josh complained that he didn't feel well. "I think I might be having a panic attack." Through our mucky pond of silence, Josh got out at curbside, swallowed hard, and mustered back a soft "good-bye." My clenched fists remained on the steering wheel. I had nothing else to say.

APARTMENT SHOWING

In Joshua's world, Sharky worked on scheduling a key meeting with the prosecuting team. My world involved decorating at a new level. The living room, with twelve-foot ceilings and thick crown molding, had taken on an African, tribal vibe. The walls came to life with a Ralph Lauren faux-suede textual paint. The mocha color was a rich backdrop to the second-hand Norwegian sofa bed, black as squid ink, found on Craigslist. The sofa sat on a Persian rug the color of Kauai's red-dirt. In each far room corner was a majestic palm in a metal urn, elevating their fronds to eight feet in the air. There were thick-braided baskets for storage, black and tan bamboo sticks for wall ornaments, a warrior mask, and an African print of tribal women dancing in colorful saris. Guarding all who entered, was a three-foot, wooden statue of a female water bearer. A graceful arm was carved in position to hold a vessel, steadfast, upon her head.

The spacious bedroom was soft and feminine, with light pink

paint on the walls. Centered in the room was a queen-sized bed covered by a beautiful white afghan. I had repainted an old school desk black and gold and given it rose pink knobs. A dressing area was created with a three-panel black and white screen of the Eiffel Tower. A rosewood chest of drawers brought from the house added an earthy warmth. Upon it rested gold and white framed pictures I had taken of my kids and garden flowers.The finishing touch was a personal item from Hawaii: my solid, blue lapis Buddha statue about the size of a softball. The plump, happy version sat on a Koa wood stand. My oasis was show ready... Time to invite the kids.

MY KIDS HAD BEEN CLUED in that I had a surprise place to show them. Walking single file up the double-wide staircase, I told my inquisitive children, "Mommy got an artist studio for the hobbies I do. Some people go to an office; others a private place." Connor, Jolie, and Nicky held their excitement while I turned the key. "Ready, set, go!" All three scrambled inside. The boys went left to the tribal living room and Jolie went straight into the wide-open kitchen.

"Whoa!" said Connor, touching almost everything he saw.

"This is so cool!" said Nicky as he turned in circles, mouth agape. "Connor! There's bamboo sticks up there," pointing to the crisscross configuration of three.

"We can have sword fights!" shouted Connor.

"No, you will not," handing out an immediate downer. "Those sticks were a nightmare to get up there."

"Mom, you already have food in here!" yelled Jolie from the kitchen.

"Yup. See if you can find the cookies." Whoosh! The boys went running to join the hunt.

"Holy cannoli! There must be twenty cabinets in here!" Connor was using both hands to open all the lower doors twice as fast as his siblings. Jolie climbed up onto the counter and was methodically searching all the upper cabinets. Poor Nicky was left to check and see if Connor missed anything in his haste.

Leaning in the doorway to watch the show, I shared, "There are twenty-four oak cabinets to be exact. I know because I changed every disgusting handle to a brushed nickel knob."

"I like them, Mom. I like the yellow in here too. Did you paint it?" asked Jolie.

"Yes, I did. I picked and painted all the colors; decorated it too. Told you I needed a creative space."

Connor climbed up on the counter and relooked in the top cabinets with Jolie. He demanded, "Give us a hint. I don't see any cookies."

Nicky asked, "Mom-m-m, did you eat them?" I knelt down to Nicky's level and whispered loud enough for the other two to hear, "I never said they were in the cabinets." I let Nicky watch my eyes scan toward the stove.

"They're in the oven!" Nicky yelled, making a mad dash, while Connor leaped off the counter, landing frog style behind Nicky's trail. Jolie dropped to her bottom and pushed off the counter, landing on her feet right behind Nicky who was already opening the oven door. United in revelation, the children cried out, "Double Stuff Oreo-o-o-s!"

"Jolie, climb back up on the counter and grab some cups. Connor, you get the milk." I placed napkins down on my little table-made-for-four and sat on the side with a bench. Nicky sat next to me. Connor and Jolie joined us, each sitting on a wooden stool. In no time, our milk was loaded with chocolate crumbs, and our tummies were gratified.

"Listen kids, you know how sometimes you play with a friend for a long time and then suddenly, you stop hanging out with them for a while?" I asked.

"No," said Nicky.

"Kind of," said Connor.

"Okay—what I am trying to say is that sometimes you play

with the kids across the street for like three days in a row, and then you don't play with them again for like, two weeks. You take a break from playing with them. Nobody did anything wrong; you are all still friends, but you need to do things that they don't. You take a break in your friendship."

"I get that," said Jolie. "Sometimes I don't want to see anybody. I would rather draw."

"Yes, and that is fine, peanut. And Connor, if you needed to expand your creativity or your ideas, you might build a Lego town. And Nicky, you would play with Thomas the Train, or your Stuffies and enjoy time in your room by yourself. Well, Mommy needs a fun, creative, quiet space too," proceeding with caution.

"This is your She-cave! And you can see therapy clients here, or your yoga people," said Jolie. Connor added, "Or do your photography hobby."

"Yes, though I would not see therapy clients here. You guys get what I am saying. I also want to add that it is necessary for me to take a break... get a little space...from your dad."

"Are you guys getting a divorce?" blurted Connor. Cookies were put down; all eyes were on me. *That went according to plan.*

"No. No we are not. That is a big step and a huge legal process. This is something else. I am not feeling healthy in our marriage, which is a separate relationship from you guys and started before you guys were born. I need to be able to step out of that and get back to my own thoughts and do my thing. Your dad knows I got this place, and he understands. I'll admit it's weird to him, but that's okay."

"Can we hang out here too?" asked Connor.

"Of course. I made it so I could include you guys. The big yellow house stays the same. I will be there every day and we will do our usual thing. In the evening, we will read our stories, I'll tuck you in bed, and after that I will sleep here. You guys will know exactly where I am. Eventually, it would be nice to have you guys sleep here. You didn't even see the other rooms yet."

"But Dad won't sleep here right?" asked Nicky.

"No. That would be weird for him. This is my place, and I even pay for it. I can work more hours now that you guys are a little older," smiling at each of them.

"Dad wouldn't like this place. There's no big TV," said Jolie.

"And you can pay for it yourself?" asked Connor.

"Yes, and everything in it. The furniture was half the usual price at the Habitat for Humanity Store, and the money goes towards building homes for others who need it. That's the store where I got all the nickel handles for the kitchen. They were a dollar a piece – usually they're four bucks a pop. I drilled the holes myself to put them all in."

"You're Super mommy!" Nicky leaned in to hug me from the side. Stretching out my mama bear arms, "I could use a hug from each of you. It was a little scary to do all this." Connor immediately came in, hugging me from the right, and said, "I love you, Mom." Jolie dove onto Nicky's lap, hugging me from the front and exclaiming, "I love you too, Mom. This place is awesome!" Wrapping my arms around these lovable cookie monsters, I had everything I needed.

SHARKY HAS THE MEETING

Josh and I anxiously awaited the decision regarding his charges. Dr. Phoenix said prosecutors were tired of putting women back into unsafe situations; they tried to avoid it. Hence, when Sharky finally had his big meeting with the prosecutor's office, it led to an unprecedented second meeting. According to Sharky, this was one of the longest deliberations they had experienced in this kind of circumstance. He said the prosecutors weighed heavily on my testimony, as well as Josh's professional reputation.

Sharky called Josh as soon as the second deliberation was over. Josh took the call in private, then delivered the news to me in the kitchen. The decision had been made to lessen the charges, and the case would go before a county court judge.

Cost, sentencing, professional license...everything was affected in the best way possible. Josh was visibly relieved.

"My lawyer said it was your testimony that really did it. Thank you. I really mean that, thank you. You probably saved my life. And I am sorry again for everything – the drinking, that night...everything. I do respect you, and you are a great mom." Josh looked at me while he spoke, slumped back against the counter. There was a lightness about him, and a genuine sense of gratitude and surprise that the powers of the universe did protect him this time. His sincerity was forefront.

"You're welcome. By the grace of God, I chose the high road, which means staying afloat is not at the cost of someone else being dragged down. If we get divorced, it's because that's better for our relationship and raising the kids; otherwise, why bother?"

"Don't say divorce. I don't even like hearing it, but I understand, Jess." Joshua shrugged and shook his head and arms much like animals do when they want something off their skin. "Hey, I am going to try and quit drinking, at least the hard stuff. No more! It really does me in, but I like wine; I like beer. I actually enjoy the taste. I think when I try to completely stop, I get mad I can't have anything to drink, and then I go overboard. You can even pour the wine for me if you like, so you know how much I am drinking." He was so earnest, like a kid willing to stay after school for extra credit.

"I do not want to babysit your portions, Josh. You are the one who told me that drinking affects your behavior. Once you clued me in, I saw how it affected a lot of things. I don't know what makes sense. Should you try going to AA meetings?" I asked.

"People there are not therapists; it is all voluntary support. My dad went a long time ago. I think he used to pick up women." Josh went to get a drink of water from the sink, a nice novelty.

I was not aware that Caleb went to Twelve Step meetings. This means Josh knew his dad had a serious problem. Josh had kept that from me too. Why didn't my mother-in-law tell me? Boy, his family let nothing unravel. Ignoring Josh's attempt to minimize the support meetings, I probed further. "Did AA seem to help your dad?"

Josh let out a small laugh. "I guess it helped a little. My mom's father flew out once to talk with my dad. I guess my grandfather was trying to protect us. He told my dad he better shape up. I think that helped for a while. My dad would be great for so long, then it would all go to shit. He would be gone for days at a time. It was a strange rollercoaster. I think if it was always bad, it would have made more sense. Sometimes, I think he may have had bipolar disorder. I'm not sure."

"Didn't your mom do more to protect you guys?"

"Aw, she was a victim too. At one time, she was on a military base in a foreign country with three little kids. She didn't drive and had few friends. Plus, my dad was a well-liked guy, right? She was not in a position to get much help. By the time I was eight, we moved back to our hometown near my mom's family. Being close to my Zeta helped stabilize things. That's when I met my best friend, Henrik. I'd go over his house a lot—practically lived there. No surprise we were each other's best man at our weddings."

"I love Henrik. I don't know if I would have married you without meeting Henrik," I said, mildly teasing. "Having a friend like him rounded you out. Of course, that ended up being no help since we never see him." Henrik lives in another part of the world.

"Hmm, I miss him. I should give him a call. It always helps to talk to him when I am feeling depressed." Josh gave me a big hug and kissed the top of my head. He changed into Dickie work pants and walked out into the yard. I watched him pick up fallen branches while the sun dipped down on another day.

ALL RISE

Spring arrived as did Josh's big day in court. He and I showed up separately since Josh was meeting Sharky beforehand. This was my first time ever in a courtroom or court lobby. The lobby had way more action than I expected. I thought we would be the only case, like you see on TV. We were one of a multitude of cases, all waiting to be heard in the same courtroom, one right after the other. There were probably thirty different cases, some with lawyers, some without. It seemed like a cattle call.

Somehow Sharky found me, wandering lost amongst the crowd, and briefly informed me that the prosecution had a court advocate. She needed to converse with me before our case could proceed. I did not really get what that meant; apparently, she was there for me. He then bid me goodbye with a gentle reminder: "It was all a misunderstanding," and with a sense of urgency, he walked away.

Sharky did not need to remind me of my testimony. This journey was full of serendipitous connections, many people took the time to see the good in us. Heck, my therapist was seeing me without any payment from the state funds allocated to cover her services. It did not escape me that I, a white person, was trusting the justice system. It was impossible to only think of myself. I sent a prayer that all judges decide with fairness and heart for everyone, everywhere.

Squeezed into a grey, pinstriped suit was a most serious-faced, rotund woman headed my direction. She had straight, shiny brown hair and rounded cheeks that would probably look cute, if she were smiling. She was honing in on me, navigating the lobby of frenzied fish in a tank. Sharky must have pointed me out.

Extending her hand, "You must be Jessica. My name is Sherry Hubbell. I work with the courts as an advocate for women in domestic violence situations."

Firmly shaking her hand, "Hi Sherry. Pleased to meet you."

"Come with me to one of the conference rooms so we can talk privately." She led me to a room that should be called a closet; it barely fit four folding chairs. "Have a seat." Sherry hit the ground running.

"Have you been approached by Josh, or his attorney today?"

"Josh and I live together, so we got ready together. He left for court earlier than me. We did not have much to say about today. Josh's attorney gave me a polite greeting. Other than that, I've been standing around."

Sherry was taken aback. "You two live together?"

My polite response: "I see him every day, and we have dinner with our kids every night."

"Have you felt coerced in any way about today's proceedings?"

"No. I do my own thinking, but thanks for asking."

Sherry paused, giving a slight lift of the brow. "You stated that you and Josh still live together?"

"Yes."

"Is he still drinking?"

"No. He stopped."

"Is he getting counseling, or any type of services?"

"Honestly, I demanded it right off the bat. We go individually as well as together, although, by choice, I go more often." I'm glad she did not ask how many times Josh technically went. That answer would fit on one hand, with fingers to spare.

Sherry further inquired, "How are the children?" There was an ounce of warmth to her tone.

"They're fine, thank you," feeling a bit disarmed. "They have been sheltered from a lot of the details. Life is pretty normal to them."

Sherry pulled her hair to one side, over her shoulder. "The judge may ask some questions while you guys are up there, but he will already have our recommendations—like probation, and mandatory rehab. I am not sure what else."

"We were hoping to protect his professional license. Our

marriage life may be screwed up, but he certainly is helpful in his line of work."

Sherry responded, "I see all walks of life here. Profession does not matter in domestic violence. It is everywhere, and in all forms. Often you cannot see the scars, but they are there. I need to get back. Do you have any questions for me?"

"No, I don't think so. Thanks for taking the time to meet with me."

"You're welcome."

I MET up with Josh in time to enter the courtroom along with the rest of the crowd. We sat together, both of us pretty nervous and holding hands. I informed Josh that things were still looking pretty harsh for him, but that my conversation with Sherry was on the positive side.

"She mentioned rehab, mandatory rehab."

"What did you say?"

"Nothing really," whispering back. "It surprised me. I didn't know mandatory rehab was a thing." The proceedings were about to start when out of the blue, Sherry briskly walked up the aisle. As she passed, I saw her side glance directly at us. I'm sure she caught us holding hands.

Josh whispered, "Regarding rehab, I would rather handle that on my own, then be forced to do something. I feel I would respond better to that."

"Guess that's up to the judge," who had entered the room and had my full attention.

When it was finally Josh's turn, he went up to the stand with Sharky, who did most of the talking. It appeared to me that many of the details had already been worked out by the way the judge was looking over papers of recommendations. I guess Sharky and the prosecutor, whom I had never met, had already come to some agreements. For example, Josh's charges were already lessened to "physical menacing". The judge ordered that

if no other occurrences happened within a year's time of probation, then the charges would be dropped. That meant Sharky
could work on getting them expunged.

In an effort to keep Josh working to support his family, the
judge did not mandate any rehab; however, he stressed the need
for a continuation of his current counseling services. Josh only
went if I had made the appointment, so I stopped making his
appointments and accepted a harsh reality: it was not my job to
set the bar my husband should strive to reach. Josh was also
ordered to pay a relatively minor fine. The judge never asked me
anything. The gavel came down. Next case.

"I believe I pay the fine now, and then I am going to work.
I'll see you at home." Josh gave my hand a squeeze and headed
out the same side door where Sharky had exited the courtroom.
I walked alone out of the judicial building, through the cool
cement parking garage and sat in my car, taking note of how
little emotion I felt. I did not feel like a winner or a loser, or
even lucky. I only felt...raw.

"Raw" is what it has felt like relieving this past year.

HAMSTER WHEEL 2009

I sat focused and poised in my bedroom decorated with a
Hawaiian theme. I tucked away the cassette tape of our statements, feeling the same level of quandary as before the incident.
Did we get through it all only to end up in the same spot? That
couldn't be. Certainly, I was wiser. The previous year had been
about the pitfalls of trying to change my husband. Now, I sat
inside proof that it did not work. My husband never walked into
my office and said, "Please fix me." I had clients for that; I
impacted their lives. But "fix me" was not in our marital agreement. "Influence" maybe, but not fix.

I treated tucking away the police tapes as a symbolic gesture
to tuck away some judgements of both Josh and I. In other
words, it was a paradigm shift from thinking what was *bad* or

good to a more functional standpoint of *which conditions work for me* and *which do not*. One obstacle in my current situation stood out: I needed more education about the legalities of the divorce process.

ONCE I SPARKED that idea out to the universe, opportunity presented itself. A friend of mine, Ashley, had recently filed for divorce. She and her husband, Derek, were either fighting a lot or not communicating at all. Derek was often condescending, and not overly involved with their two girls. The moment their separation began, Derek took all their files and hid them at his work. He opened a separate bank account, and oddly demanded to see the girls more often, including when he was at work, which meant Derek's parents were actually watching the girls.

Ashley had been forever stalled in a limbo period controlled by lawyers, but now their court date was set for the next month, although they remained without a resolute settlement agreement. Ashley had been crash-course learning about the divorce process, hence my opportunity to be a good friend, and acquire knowledge. Ashley's number one complaint about Derek was that he would not compromise on anything.

HANGING out in Ashley's three-bedroom house, I asked my frustrated friend, "What is the big deal about letting a judge decide what you and Derek cannot agree upon? I mean, let's assume the judge will opt for what's best and fair for the kids. Why fear that?"

"I don't friggin' know," Ashley shouts while flipping open a pizza box. "I do what my lawyer tells me! And of course, Derek is asking to have more overnights with the girls, but he doesn't follow their routine and the girls end up being tired at school every time they go to his house. It pisses me off!" Ashley opens another beer and grabs a slice of cold pizza.

I asked her, "Why does Derek want the kids so much? He wasn't the most involved father in the first place." Not to put Derek down, but Ashley simply handled most things with the girls.

"Money, that's why – friggin' bastard! Derek won't have to pay as much child support if he has them overnight more often. Suddenly, he has changed from two nights, which we agreed upon, to wanting four overnights per week with some weird rotation shit!" Alice puts the slice in the microwave and slams the door shut so hard it pops back open. "Piece of shit appliance! I can't wait to sell this house. Derek can take everything in it as far as I'm concerned. We already have two people interested in the house. No offers yet, but I am already looking for apart-ments in town. Hopefully, I don't have to live with my parents." Ashley chugs a third of her beer. I'm milking mine, as usual.

"I can't imagine Josh and I fighting about overnights. The kids would stay with me, and he can see them whenever he wants. Simple." I sip to that.

"Ha! You have no idea, Jessica. Every last detail has to be figured out, like who gets the kids for each holiday, birthday, vacation time, school breaks...you even pick the time you drop off and pick up the kids from each other." Ashley ravaged hunger damage on her pizza slice.

"I don't think we could ever be that organized," she sput-tered between bites. "Neither of us are planners. I suppose all the structure will help in the end. Then there's the issue of custody —joint custody—which everybody does. This means that every big decision concerning the kids cannot be unilateral. Derek and I consult each other anyway, except when he is being an ass. Half the time, Derek wouldn't even know what was going on with the kids because he drinks at his mom's house and gets wasted over there. But in the future, I will have to notify him of everything; otherwise, he will try to take the kids more nights because I am not in compliance or something... I know he will. He will use anything just to be a prick!"

Ashley tossed a leftover pizza crust over the table, aiming for the trash can, but instead, the whirling breadstick bounced off the rim and landed in the dog's water bowl. Bongo, her chocolate lab, darted out from under the table, bit down on the crust and scampered around the corner, vanishing from view.

"Friggin' Bongo! She will eat anything she can get her jaw around. She ate two Jell-O cups yesterday. I put them out on the counter for the girls and yelled out the door for them to come inside. By the time I turned back around, Bongo had eaten them both. She ate the plastic cups. She ate the foil lids. Friggin' lime flavored Jell-O..."

"Don't you think you are being a little paranoid? I mean, Derek cares about the girls. Once everything is settled, don't you think you guys will get into your routines and make the best of it? Joint custody means everything gets shared equally, doesn't it?" trying to imagine a glass half full.

Ashley finished her beer, gently put the can on the table and picked at the tab a moment before answering. "First, I am not being paranoid. Money changes people, especially men. Before we even got lawyers, he took all our files, bank statements, and retirement papers out of the house and to his office where I cannot get to them. He says he'll give them back to me when he is 'finished with them'. I have no doubt he is hiding money somewhere. I don't know how much he has in his retirement fund. I don't have a retirement account, and now it's supposed to be okay that he gets retirement money and I don't? Sorry, I didn't ask my seven-year-old kid to make a 401 K contribution every time I read a bedtime story. I dedicated myself to being a parent, and he got to dedicate himself to being a nurse and moved up to be supervisor. We both contributed to the family pot. Just because we have to pull out of the marriage early, it's still fair to balance things out, and respect each other." Ashley stood up and crushed her can by stomping on it. "Hey man, you want another beer?"

"No, I'm good."

"Second thing I want to tell you Jessica is that "joint custody" is not the same as "parent of primary residence". That is the parent who has them most of the time, and gets most of the money to support them. Derek is focused and worried about the math of it all. He works a night shift rotation, yet he wants credit for his mom watching them so he can get money deducted. I am fighting to have my own girls stay with me instead of Derek's mom, never mind asking the girls what they want." Ashley places her knuckles to her head and pulls her eyebrows back in angst before tugging on her own golden hair. She plops back into her chair and sighs, "I'm sorry. I sound like a raging bitch. I'm just scared and I feel like everything is out of my control."

I reached my hand out in comfort. "It's okay. This *is* a night-mare. You have every right to blow off steam." Ashley reached across the table, giving my hand a squeeze. "Ashley, my exhausted friend, I am going to head home. Thank you for the tutorial. It has been enlightening."

We hugged goodbye. While exiting the front door, I noticed Bongo nuzzle over to Ashley, who dropped down on one knee and pursed her lips together. Bongo licked Ashley's face until Ashley lowered her head and rubbed it against Bongo's furry chest. Bongo wagged her tail with the whipped speed of a wind-shield wiper combating a thunderstorm.

DATING

Josh and I had settled into being a separated couple. Since things were at a lull, I decided to peek into the dating world: find a little distraction, get a taste for being unmarried. It was not quite the time to be dating, but I wanted to think and feel like a fully functioning person. I was not looking to enter another relationship – I just wanted to fire up old neurons and give myself some energy... the energy of possibility. While looking for a chair on Craigslist, I decided to poke around their dating category, "Women looking for Men." Very few men had any photos posted, and of those that did, half were simply a body part, like a flexed bicep. One dude posted a photo of his junk. Why would that be appealing? As if women are like some kind of dog in heat, responding to a boner.

During my search, one gentleman stood out as normal and articulate. I wrote him a note, my only note. After finding the whole male section disheartening and unhygienic, I perused over to "Women seeking Women". Women seemed much more appealing at this point. The female postings were considerably less profane than those on the men's site. In fact, there were many married women seeking to have a "girlfriend with benefits" on the side. I had dabbled in dating a woman before—nothing serious. It felt more awkward than natural. I think women are beautiful, and to please a woman is like creating art. It is easy to rouse a man and then some. In contrast, passionately arousing a woman to ecstasy feels like you have made the world a better place, and that you are a champion!

A particular female-post intrigued my senses. She demonstrated articulate writing with humor as well as intelligence. There was no photo, but she described herself as attractive and seeking a similar match. Heh, I decided to write to her too. There, I had done it: one guy and one girl – an attempt to remember that I might be an attractive, interesting, passionate woman capable of intimacy and joy. That said, there would be no sex. None. Sleeping around would not be appropriate at this time. Josh and I had not agreed on, nor discussed having other relationships. The investment of a kiss was all the value I needed, and all I was willing to back up. To me, kissing is the destination where words run out, touch conveys truth, and the magic of intimacy tickles you from the inside out. All too often, the making out stops when the sex begins. I've learned I'm worth the investment, and so is my time.

WITHIN A WEEK, I heard back from both of them. The guy was immediately interested in receiving a picture and immediately sent one of himself. Dressed in a suit, he was a nice looking, tall, Italian man about seven years younger than me. I was reluctant to send him a picture; however, I managed to do the selfie thing everyone was buzzing about. We decided to meet for sushi.

In person, he was handsome, polite, and again, wearing a suit. I had donned a new V-neck, button up blouse and had freshly painted my nails. He didn't compliment me when we met. I don't know if he was supposed to hold back, or maybe he was being honest. Our conversation over lunch went okay. I ate more than him, which felt like a faux pas, but those rice rolls are small. He paid for the meal and our goodbye was a mutual hug by my car. Immediately, his texting dropped to near nothing, and within four days, we texted a final goodbye and good-luck. At least it went safely and I could wear the blouse again. Or—hmm, did I leave the tags attached?

Meanwhile, the Craigslist woman and I had been emailing back and forth, displaying our wit like peacock feathers. Per her report, she was blonde, ten years younger than me, and single. We neither discussed our professions, nor sent photos; instead, we conversed on the phone. She was funny and quick with the questions. We discussed our town of residence. Turned out, she lived in my dad's town, on my dad's street! I drove past her house all the time. This awareness happens to freak her out a bit. She had not planned on divulging her address. She wanted to be extra protective because no one at her job knew she was gay. I, on the other hand, felt more comfortable having seen her house. A nice home in a nice town hopefully raised the odds of her being a stable and sane person.

This expedites our decision to meet. I asked Camila to join

me at a local theatre to see a play, and provided her with some background. "My father is the president of the board of directors at the theater. It's a historic building that used to be a school house. The theater only seats ninety-nine people. It looks like a grammar school stage because technically, it was a grammar school stage."

Camila responds, "Can we not sit in the front row? I hate when the actors can see down my shirt."

"No problem. I prefer sitting further back as well. Since I know where you live, I'll pick you up. Ooh - a heads up, the ticket holders are often a median age of seventy. A couple of assisted living places offer shuttle rides to the theater."

"What you're saying is, I should bring a defibrillator. Got it. See you Friday at 7:00. Adios."

Sweet peaches, I hoped she was attractive. There was something intriguing about Camila; it stemmed from her cut to the chase conversation style. Camila did not know that I had kids. For one night, I wanted to keep that private, which meant the sexy minivan might give me away. I called my friend, Natasha and asked to borrow her sporty car. I explained why, but left out the fact that the date was with a woman. Natasha was thrilled I was going out, and cleaned up her Rave Rover. Josh was aware of the play which gave me the night off. He did not ask any questions. A few years before, I had started going to the movies by myself since he and I never went, hence, my outing was not surprising.

WHEN FRIDAY ARRIVED, I debated heavily...skirt or pants? I went for the skirt. My goal was to look, feel, and smell pretty. After switching cars, I picked Camila up in front of her house. She had dark blonde hair about medium length, with soft waves. She had gone light on the make-up, and oh - she had a stunning smile, and cocoa brown eyes. Camila was wearing a gold, scoop-neck blouse, dark blue jeans, and black heeled boots. Hmm, I'd never had anyone wear high heeled shoes for me before. I found this weird and cool at the same time. Camila got in the car, eyed me head to toe and blurted out, "You are fucking adorable!"

Oh hush... That topped the sushi guy. I batted my eyelashes; boy was I starved for attention. Camila was attractive with the exception of the aged look that former smokers can get. She was a hair shorter than me, and had an athletic to stocky build with moderate curves. I did not have a type in mind, but thought, *so far so good.*

It was a talkative fifteen minute ride to the theater. In that time, Camila asked if I had kids, if I was married, what I did for a living, and where I got my skirt.

"You know, Camila, I borrowed this car so I didn't have to pick you up in a mini-van. And now you're blowing my cover before I even get to enjoy pretending."

"Aww, mi Bonita—you did that for me? You didn't have to. It is fine you have niños. Thought I'd wait 'til I saw you to ask. I was engaged once, to a man. We were together eight years before I decided I prefer women and considered myself gay. So, I ended it." Camila brushed her hands together, as if wiping them clean.

"It's a relief that you understand the oscillation between dating men and women."

"Totally," says Camilla. She had the prettiest smile.

Camila and I watched the theater performance and enjoyed making sly comments here and there. We partook in the free coffee during intermission, and talked some more. When the play ended, I took her home, parking out front of her house. The tension of the moment was in the air... Were we going to have a first date kiss?

Camila undid her seat belt and asked, "Am I the first woman you have ever dated?"

"Why do you ask?" I said, unbuckling my seat belt with the car still running.

"Answering a question with a question, I see. My Spidey senses predict this might be true."

"Well señorita, I think it might be good to keep you guessing, especially since you seem to always get your answers," I teased.

"Oh, I do get my answers. Me no likey not know-y." Camila scooted her hips closer to mine and leaned a little towards me. Mmm, her perfume reminded me of a garden's morning dew.

Leaning over the console I whispered, "I think you can handle my taunting your instincts." I wrapped a lock of her hair around my finger. "Do you want to keep talking?" My eyes scanned her dark lashes and plush lips.

"Um, no – I do not." Camila closed the distance and pressed her lips against mine. Oh, they were so soft and full and responsive. My hand reached for more hair, pulling and supporting her head into a small rotation of kissing. We separated long enough to smile, then reconnected, this time with our arms wrapping into an embrace. Our lips parted slightly for a lingual caress. Women are so gentle. Their female regard is different, and wonderful. Yet, a woman did not quite fit the full equation for me. But I didn't want to be in my head space; I preferred enjoying the moment.

We rested our hands and created distance between us again. Camila asserted, "Okay Chica, perhaps you have dated women before. That was not a first-time kiss."

"Camila, I would like to see you again. I can't hang out very often... My situation is what it is, as I explained."

Camila perked up. "I would definitely like to get together again. You're cute, sane, and rather intriguing."

"I could say the same about you. I have not even asked what line of work you're in, or if you have kids."

"Ha! That's because you can tell I don't." She zeroed in for a final kiss goodbye and said while getting out, "You'll like what I do. I'm the shit." Off she sauntered beneath the moonlight. *Momacita.*

CAMILA and I met up at a bar a couple of times to shoot pool. Camila would start off giving me a chance to win, then pool shark me. After those casual dates, we began to meet at my apartment once or twice a week after I put the kids to bed. That only gave us an hour or so to hang out; being a mom came first. Camila's knack for interrogating was an actual skill: she was a head honcho for internal affairs; everyone reported to her. She did undercover work on sting operations, sometimes dressing up like a prostitute packing heat in a leg holster. Her team had caught on-line predators. Camila usually met the "perp" with a hidden team at a local fast food joint. The perp would think he was meeting up with a teenager then...*Bam!* Camila would break the humiliating news over a milkshake. I asked her, "What do most of these guys say when they realize they're busted?"

"Some deny it, of course. Then I repeat back the things they said online and inform them we already have a warrant to confiscate their computer. At that point, typically, they cry."

What did Camilla and I do to pass the time, besides making out on my second-hand sofa? Here's a fine example. Springing up from an epic kissing session, I announced, "Camilita, yo soy pensamiento!"

"Oooh, big Spanish word, Jesserita. How long you been working on that?"

"Two days. But I'm not just saying it — I do have a good idea."

Camila: "Glad to hear it. For the record, you don't have to try and impress me with your Spanglish. In fact don't, I'm afraid you might hurt yourself."

"Noted. My idea is..." I gave her my darkest, most intimidating stare. Camila bit her lip to refrain from laughing. "Let's arm wrestle."

Captain Camila immediately sat up, placing her knees against the coffee table. "You wanna throw, bitch? Let's go!"

I rounded over to the opposite side of the coffee table and

got into a high kneeling position. Camila stood up, proceeded to pull her arms across her body, then did some lunges.

"You're stretching?" I asked, half laughing.

"Don't want to pull a hammy," she said with seriousness.

Using my evil laugh, "Heh-heh, your head games will not help you." My right arm was in the ready position, elbow down, fingers outstretched.

"My mind manipulations are already at work," she remarked while cracking her knuckles.

I fought fire with fire. "At least when I walk into an Ann Taylor store, I'm not directed to the petite section." I cracked my neck, both sides.

"You leave Ann out of this!" Camila anchored her elbow on the table and grabbed my outstretched hand with a swift, firm grip. We locked wrists; we locked eyes. Camila slowed the cadence of her speech. "Better get some glue, cuz I'm 'bout to crush your soul. I will let you count."

Fast as spider legs, "One-two-three-go!" I blurted, and I pumped my right arm towards the table. Camila's forearm quickly yielded, but she locked out forty-five degrees off the table. Bulging veins appeared in her forehead. Her other hand grabbed onto the table.

"You can't use your other arm for leverage!" I grunted, seriously straining to keep her arm where it was.

"Yes, you can," Camila retorted through gritted teeth.

"No... you...can't! It's not *arms* wrestling...it's *arm* wrestling. It's all about leverage. Didn't they teach you physics in prostitute school?"

Camila relented and released her table grip. "Fine! Let me know when you start trying." She powered my forearm up, almost back to starting position.

Dangling a mental lure, "Hey Camzilla, guess what you and that sofa have in common?" I was desperately straining to get her hand back down. "I got you both on Craigslist – used. At least the sofa had good reviews."

"Grr, that's gonna cost you," and she muscled my wrist past midline until my forearm was leaning away from me. Combat mode: I rotated my wrist, angling it to gain some leverage; an old trick I used against Connor to maintain my alpha status. To no avail against her, this tactic only helped hold my forearm inches from the table. Camila delivered an accolade, "You are strong, I give you that little bird, but it's time to end this." Steadily, she took my forearm down...down...down...tap. My knuckles touched the tabletop.

In shock, I exclaimed, "That's sick! I move people in rehab all the time, plus my yoga workouts!"

Camila shook out her wrists. "Vinyasa all you want, yogi-bear, you were never going to beat me. I will have you know, back in high school, I held the record for highest bench press – one hundred and seventy pounds. I believe it is still the record to beat."

"Are you kidding me?"

Camila responded, "Nope. I am dead serious: one hundred and seventy pounds. Now get over here, little French fry arms. Yes, that is what I shall call you, mon petit wench fry." She indicated for me to come, patting a spot right next to her on my used sofa. I playfully obeyed.

WE HAD about a month of fun, though I offered very little towards the relationship. My feelings were not growing, and morally, I did not admire the choice—my choice—to dive into another relationship before my current one, my marriage, was handled. In addition, I was too strapped emotionally to throw another person into the mix. My kids were still young; they deserved a fully dedicated parent without having to ask for it, and I did not want to live a double relationship life. Having Camila pop into my life had been a nice boost, and a break from reality. She had expressed the desire for a serious, long term relationship so it was not fair to lead her further down a dead-end street. We mutually ended what we had started. I did not date again.

KIDS NO COME, SPOUSE NO GO

Fall leaves were dropping, the grass no longer needed mowing, and the kids were in the routine of sport schedules...all things autumnal seemed natural. Time to create a divorce-like parenting schedule with the kids. This meant having the kids sleepover, as if it were my turn. My younger two had already slept over a few times and had really enjoyed it. I wished to progress to all three kids sleeping over at my place, as well as establishing a turn for Josh to handle a day watching them. I picked Saturday for Josh because then I could work around the corner at a sub-acute rehab facility and be home in minutes if needed. This seemed like a good plan until Connor threw a monkey wrench into it. Connor refused to sleep over. He hated to leave his house. He wanted *his* bed, and *his* room, and he was giving me a very difficult time in front of his siblings.

We discussed the plan in my apartment. Connor expressed: "This is not my problem! It is your and dad's problem! I do not see why I can't stay in my own bed. It's right down the street."

"Connor, it's nice to be together. I have games here we can play; we can make blanket forts in the living room." I tried to be understanding, but not give him room to be the boss, a mistake frequently made with the first kid.

"I don't want to be here! All my stuff is at the other house." Connor was so agitated that the other two kids felt bad for him. They chimed in, making it worse.

"I would rather go home too," said Nicky.

"What?" I said. "Nicky, you said you liked it here."

"I do, but I want to go home too," he repeated.

. . .

SLEEPOVER NIGHTS BECAME A NIGHTMARE. Connor refused again and again, making it miserable for Nicky, Jolie, and me. I responded to these outbursts with a calm, cool explanation/validation approach, and I also tried the *suck it up, you don't have it so rough, kid* angle. No matter what I did or said, Connor had no off-switch. I was surrounded by misery and exhaustion, especially as his siblings followed suit, though Jolie not as much. In the end, Connor's attitude made it more difficult for me, and I didn't want a rift between the kids. I had bigger fish to fry—like getting my professional life in order. I put sleepovers at the apartment on hold.

Like a divorced couple might do, I gave Josh a solo parenting turn Friday night until Saturday dinner time. Perhaps Josh would step it up with the kids if I was not around to interrupt. The first two Saturdays in a row, Connor called me by 11:00 a.m., asking when I was coming home. Friday never became a special night. They all watched TV as usual, probably falling asleep on the sofa. Meanwhile, I listened to my friend Ashley complain about having three nights to herself, and to Natasha about having every other weekend without her boys – a weekend she spent with her boyfriend. The paradox blew my mind.

One night a week, I wanted to have the whole evening off to hang out at Barnes and Noble, surrounding myself with books. Nothing kicked Josh into gear to make this work. This was adding up to a lot of money. I had signed another six-month agreement, and I didn't know where things were going anymore. Josh still drank as always, yet remained fully functional. He went to work, paid the bills, rode his motorcycle...he even joined a men's hockey league. The kids were in a beautiful home, and I was working extra hours to live three blocks away. Was it worth it? I loved being at my apartment. I felt more worthy of my life without the belittlement to face. I had more freedom to think, and be creative. I enjoyed the space; it was so me. I did not know how bad it had become until I started experiencing the opposite: a space of reverence. This needed to be addressed with

Dr. Phoenix, whom I'd graduated to seeing every other week. Josh and I only went twice together, but it had been fruitful. I was able to tell him my version of what had happened that night. He had listened, and apologized. That had been his last visit. I was not his mother; I couldn't tell him what to do. I needed to accept what was and what was not a priority to him.

DR. PHOENIX LISTENED to my current situation of feeling stuck. She rephrased what she heard. "Let me get this straight. You can't kick Josh out and you can't kick Connor into staying at your apartment. And he makes it miserable for the other two children."

"Correct. And before I unleashed and projected all my anger at Josh out on Connor, I pulled the plug and honored how Connor felt. Connor and I were only going to get better at fighting; he would only learn to be a pawn. I was trying to work out the kinks of parenting time stuff before having to put it all into a custody agreement. I went to a county college workshop on learning about the divorce process. A couple of lawyers do it as a community service, mostly for women. They answered so many questions; it was very empowering. Hence, I was trying to get ahead of the game, and figure things out."

Phoenix: "Tell me, what do you think a divorce would look like for you two? What would be on paper? How would it play out?"

"Well, unlike most couples, I would want full custody, and as far as parenting time, I can be very flexible. Of course, I'd be the parent of primary residence. I think Josh would get that. I'd expect a fair financial splitting of things. There are objective numbers to crunch for those specific amounts. I don't fear a judge weighing in on the matters at hand, nor do I fear holding up my end."

Phoenix let out a teachable moment sigh and calmly replied,

"It is very rare that a judge will award one parent full custody. Custody is for big decision issues: something medical, for example. It is rare for one parent to lose those rights."

"I know, but in his current, parallel universe, Josh lets me do my thing with the kids. If he has joint custody, he might exercise his new power. If I could have a rational conversation with him, it would be different. Any medical issues the kids have had over the years were not pretty, and resulted in my handling everything alone anyway."

"I understand. However, I do not see how a judge would find him incompetent of having basic custody. I do not think that will go your way, which means, you have to get Josh to agree to give up custody of the kids."

"Is that all? For crying out loud, I am not getting divorced to have less power. No way! At least the way things are, I have the steering wheel to the ship. A divorce would give him a steering wheel that he doesn't even want. Josh would not give me custody —it would make him look bad. My point is that we can't ask Josh for anything! He can't handle the question. It's crazy! A judge will have to do it, and I am not going to fear a judge. I have to assume that a judge will be more rational than my husband."

Phoenix appeared to be enjoying my rage process. I guess she wanted me to grow a pair. Honestly, I didn't know what she wanted me to do. I sat back, crossed my legs and folded my arms tightly across my chest.

Phoenix placed her hands on her lap, palms facing up and asked, "Jessica, what are you going to do? What do you really *want* to do?" I pondered this. I had already asked myself this question repeatedly. In fact, I had already come up with my answer.

"I want to take a vacation, specifically, there is a yoga retreat coming up in Costa Rica." I unfold my tight limbs and open up my idea. "There is a new, sustainable, vegetarian friendly, modern, hippie-like resort that a major yoga studio from New York is going to open after Christmas. The rooms consist of outdoor cabanas. You take advanced yoga classes and, in the evenings, there are lessons taught by a Buddhist monk. There are white sand beaches and zip lines and wildlife. I used to travel on my own, before I got married. I traveled across the US twice in a two-door Pulsar. I stayed in youth hostels... We have them here. Who knew? Traveling was so empowering. You rely only on yourself, and you meet new people, and – oy, I could go on and on. I've suppressed this idea ever since I read about it."

Phoenix: "This is the first time I have ever seen you light up. I think you should go. If you can swing it, you should go!"

"I have not been on a vacation without children in seven years. Josh is probably the best or most stable he is ever going to be to handle me going away; it's a six-day trip. Of course, the kids would stay with friends part of the time, and my family can check on them."

Phoenix was most sincere in conveying, "Your apartment has been a saving grace, a sanctuary, as you call it. But I have not seen you find your light. If this trip can help with that, then I will personally shoot you if you don't go!" Her joke ended up revealing my main concern.

"I feel bad leaving the kids and—"

Phoenix cut me off to say, "Women always feel guilty. We are the nurturers. But with Josh, you are going to a tool store looking for a gallon of milk: it is not going to happen. And you are still so measured with everything you say and do around him. It would be nice to see you make decisions without being so measured all the time. It is okay to take care of yourself, and okay for you to take a break so that you can find your way. Josh only does what he has to, but he does it. For a week, with back-up, I'm sure the ship will continue to float."

Phoenix was right. What she was saying resonated with me, especially my behaving so "measured" around Josh. Wanting to grow, I asked her to show me; to tell me something else I could say, or show me another way to think, or another way to phrase things to Josh. Dr. Phoenix and I role-played conversations. We went back and forth, with her being me, and then being Josh. And even though I was only pretending to talk to Josh, I caved – I literally collapsed my overall being. It sickened me. I could not blame Josh when it seemed to be my spine that needed fixing.

BY THE END of the year, I was on a plane to Costa Rica. Our guest rooms only had three walls. The fourth wall was a curtain that opened to a rainforest. Every morning, I woke up to the call of Howler monkeys who made a back of the throat, swirling sound. First time I heard it, I thought someone was frothing milk with a cappuccino maker. The yoga offered there was challenging, and my trip mates were friendly. The homemade food was amazing and over-the-top healthy. My daughter made me a green and white sock puppet that I end up taking everywhere. I snapped photos of sock puppet lying on a towel by the infinity edge pool, zip-lining, getting the best massage ever, and even contemplative sock puppet next to a Buddha statue, meditating over Dharma teachings.

Sock puppet and I attended a number of Buddhist lectures. For five days straight, I observed and engaged in "normal" adult communication styles. My final morning in the Costa Rican sun brought me a level of clarity I could not have achieved before. I arrived home safe, refreshed, and ready to announce my revelation: Momma was moving back home!

Carpe diem 2009.

2010

A problem cannot be solved with the same consciousness that created it. -
Albert Einstein

My winter move back home slid in without a hitch.
Josh had nothing to say when I informed him. He
simply looked as if he had dropped a load in his
pants. Splitting myself up more and more was not helping, i.e.,
two homes, two different jobs, three kids, and two husbands: the
nighttime and the daytime version. I reintegrated into the house
by using our spacious third floor attic as my bedroom. My
clothes remained in the master bedroom, yet I retired to a lovely,
queen-sized bed upstairs, alone. If I believed Josh should not
have custody of the kids, then I needed to act that way. A court
wouldn't recognize this position if I resided somewhere else.

While I was in Costa Rica, the full week of parenting had led
Josh to his own revelation and made an appointment to see an
addiction specialist, and detoxed himself. Josh had kept the
horrible throws of detox from the kids. They thought he had
the flu.

"I'm tired of being this way," Josh said. "This doctor comes
highly recommended." He reluctantly told me the name of this

specialist, allowing me to verify his existence and confirm the appointment. Clearly, it was difficult to believe anything Josh said. Because Josh was making his best effort ever to address his issues, his health became *our* priority. Handling one thing at a time was fine by me. The apartment was mine for another six weeks—plenty of time for reselling items. I checked Josh's hiding spots and found no bottles.

Therapy and sobriety were very trying for Josh. He kept me in the loop about his first specialist appointment, which he had after work. Returning home, still wearing a crisp white shirt and navy-blue khakis Josh said, "This guy wants to see me three times a week!"

"Don't you think that is good news?" I asked him earnestly.

"I don't know. Why?"

"Because it means he thinks you have a serious problem and he is taking it seriously," I affirmed.

Josh plopped down in his reading chair, dropping his head back. "I told him I did not want to check into anyplace. I do not want to lose my job. Three days a week is what we agreed upon." Josh lifted his head, rubbed his chin and said, "He is a competent doc. Seems like a good guy." *Hmm, Dr. Good-guy. I like it.*

The following week or so was rough. Josh's mood varied from lost, to agitated, to despondent, as if he was a little kid and someone had stolen his lunch money. One time after a session, Josh came upstairs and flopped on my bed, a complete rag doll. "This is all really hard. Just tell me what to do. I will do anything you say." Josh didn't talk about his session. He remained a sad lump at the base of my bed, a pile of laundry with a face.

I reassured him that he should keep plugging away, do what the good doc asked. I told him I was proud of him.

Another time, Josh came to me, running his fingers through his hair, pacing in the hall, appearing as if he might cry. "I don't think I am going to get any better. There is no changing anything, and I feel anxious over things more than usual."

"Josh, you know what this is? This is depression: feeling a

lack of hope or that there's no way to solve anything; becoming more anxious and defeated... You probably have a depressive layer. Have faith that this is par for the course. Maybe there is a medication you should take."

"I do not want to take any meds. Maybe the alcohol was my way of self-medicating. But if I can control my drinking, then it is like doing the same thing with medication. I know I let my drinking get out of control. It was scaring me."

"Alcohol is a depressant, you know. Thinking you can control it is not a long-term solution."

Josh said, "I cry at almost every movie I watch. I cried over a commercial!" He leaned against the door frame to our Harry Potter closet under the staircase.

"Josh, I was waiting for the right moment to tell you something."

His arms dropped and hung from his body. "Please, no. No bad news. I can't handle it. Oh, never mind. What it is it?" lowering his head.

"I started going to Al-anon meetings. I also started listening to stories from alcoholics. Josh, this one guy, Brendan, was addicted to alcohol and painkillers. He never wanted to go to rehab and never thought it would work, but today, he is three years clean. He kept the wife, the kids, and the job, but more important, he said it was worth it. The way he feels now is way better than how he felt using alcohol. That is why people go to meetings. You are surrounded by individuals who really walked the walk, and their stories help create a link for you to climb out of your hole."

"What kind of name is Brendan? Sounds like a child's name." He frowned and shook his head.

"That's your take away from what I said?"

Josh turned and started to walk away. "I am sure the meetings are helpful. Everyone can complain about their deadbeat husbands." Following him, I maintained my composure and empathy.

"Ya know, I thought there would be complaining too, but there was none. I was totally surprised—zero complaining. People want to move beyond the effects of all the chaos and hold a sense of faith." Josh responded with an acknowledging grunt, a good sign coming from him. Continuing my nudge, "Brendan, a married, white collar professional with his shit together, is very willing to take you to a meeting whenever you might like to go," I said to the back of his head as he ascended the stairs.

"Thank you. I will keep it in mind," Josh yelled back, and he turned into the bedroom.

BEFORE IT GETS BETTER, IT GETS WORSE

The following week, Josh returned home from a session one night around 9 p.m. particularly distraught. He came over and slumped next to me on the sofa. I turned off the TV. The kids were upstairs, having some playtime before bed. We sat in silence near the soothing glow of his reading lamp. Josh gazed straight out in front of him and opened a conversation as if completing a homework assignment from Dr. Good-guy.

Josh began to share some personal information completely unknown to me. "The doc said it might be helpful for you to know...shame and ah, forms of humiliation are, I guess, *triggers* for me." Josh glanced at me. His eyes were red and sad, yet he seemed determined to keep on his assignment.

"Okay," sitting fully composed next to him.

Josh drew a deep breath and resumed. "There was a time, a time when my older brother was really sadistic. He would hold me down and choke me. He would put his hands around my neck and choke me until my last breath." Josh put his hands out like they were wrapping around a throat. While looking straight ahead, he said: "I couldn't get him off me; he was so much stronger than me. He would watch me struggle." Josh's breathing got heavier. "He could tell when he had me at the last possible moment before I would pass out."

"I am so sorry that no one was protecting you." He had hinted to me about his brother being rough with him before, but without any indication it was this serious. Josh was the middle son of three boys with a year and a half age difference between each of them.

"Yeah me too," Josh took another deep breath. "I am also supposed to tell you that sometimes when my brother finally let go of my neck, while I was gasping for air... he would... he would pour liquid in my mouth...sometimes it was dish soap. I would want him off me, but I couldn't get him off. And that is why I don't like turtlenecks and I stretch out my T-shirt collars. I don't like anything around my neck. Any sudden movements of someone's hands, and I think, *oh no, better look out!* So, you can't move your hands okay," Josh looks at me with a side glance, "You can't suddenly move your hands. Okay? It sends a chill up my spine."

"Okay, no sudden hand movements," telling my hands to freeze at that very moment.

"That is all." My husband stared off again.

"Has your brother apologized to you in any way, or does he realize that maybe this affects your life?"

"He apologized to me once before. I think he got some help, and from that he said he was 'sorry he treated me badly.' That was supposed to cover it all." Josh wiped his nose with the back of his hand and leaned into the sofa, turning his Nordic profile to me. "We were kids then. I stayed over at Henrik's house as much as I could. My mom must have known why I was always there; she was fine with it. I think my dad thought I was gay because I was always hanging out at Henrik's and reading books so much. My father made us play rugby. It's such a violent sport. I didn't want to get pushed around, so I was always aggressive when I had to be. And if anyone went after my younger brother, I would go after them. My older brother – believe it or not – watched out for both of us. No one wanted to mess with him!"

"I bet," bringing one leg up onto the sofa to turn comfortably towards him even more.

"Back then, I was a sensitive kid. They could see that, my dad and brother, and they didn't like it. They would say while hitting me, 'Stop crying faggot! I'll stop when you stop crying!'" Josh got up. "Anyway, this is enough or I will never get to sleep. I keep having nightmares that I am always trapped in some way. I'll be back. I'm going to the bathroom," and he shuffled away.

Take a deep breath. The emotions bubbling up in my chest were washed out by the shock waves I swallowed down. I considered it a blessing Dr. Good-guy let me in on the "humiliation trigger". Perhaps he had done that knowing I was a therapist. My understanding was that if Josh felt the slightest bit of embarrassment, he would go into high alert mode to defend against possible shame and indignation. He would fight back tooth and nail ten times harder. What Josh described in his past was horrific and devastating. When a child was not kept safe, that child's hopelessness, in my opinion, gave birth to depression and who knows what else. It also formulated a core of low self-esteem, as discussed in many psychology texts. This shed light on why Josh belittled people; it served to discredit anything they might say in order to maintain a safety zone of dignity.

The Road Less Traveled, by psychiatrist Scott Peck, makes a wonderful correlation between parenting styles and how God "thinks". Children form an association between the actions of their parents and the actions of a god. Many religious beliefs have been misinterpreted, allowing a handful of people to control the masses, or allowing one gender to be superior over another, or one belief system to trump another. Dr. Peck talks about the mental health breakdown under such conditions, and that perhaps clinicians should not view mental health and spirituality as two separate things. Dr. Peck advocates to include spirituality as it comes up. Twelve step programs suggest opening yourself up to something greater. The humbleness of that idea alone can help quell the ego, soften inner emotional scar tissue, and allow a starting-over to be possible.

Josh returned, and suggested we watch TV. "Sure," I said. "I am going to get a drink of seltzer water. Want some? We have three flavors."

Josh smiled. "Sure, anything but mandarin orange. I do not like that one." Sauntering out of sight to get our drinks, I compulsively stopped in the bathroom and did a search: toilet tank, behind the mirror...no bottles.

MEETINGS HELP

Brendan was a friend of a friend. He had taken it upon himself to offer up his phone number; I made the call. Brendan gave me hope that it was worth the fight to quit drinking. He missed it, but only sometimes. He preferred not living a lie. Brendan frequently used the word "alcoholic". Al-co-hol-ic, a word not found in the Josh and Jess dictionary, but Brendan owned it. He owned all of his behaviors. Brendan admitted that as soon as he had one drink, even a mere sip, it took over, and nothing else mattered. All the promises made or intentions set before that sip simply vanished.

Brendan remarked, "Once alcohol was pouring down my throat, whatever I said to my wife, my mom, or even my kids, didn't matter. From that moment, it was about what I wanted; screw everybody else out to control me. You want me to stop, hell − I'll drink more!" Brendan was fully open, offering, "My thinking was all bullshit. I thought I wanted to be away from my family, or my job, or my responsibilities. But honestly, I just wanted to get away from myself. It took over six months of sobriety before I could face things about my past without feeling a crushing judgment."

I could relate to Brendan's stories. For comparison, occasionally Josh would plan on a two- or three-hour motorcycle ride, but after stopping at a few biker bars, it would be five, six, or more hours before he came home, especially if he chose bars located two hours away. Brendan went on to admit that he had hidden back-up liquor bottles. He would unconsciously pick a fight with his wife, blame her for something – anything – as an excuse to storm off and drink from his stash. It reminded me of Ingrid and Caleb's storming off stories. Brendan said that at the time, it felt like his wife was trying to control him. "But, if you ask my wife, she'll say she was just trying to control all the loose ends coming undone. My wife really found some comfort, and probably some validation from Al-anon meetings. She and I both think you should go."

Their advice was one of the reasons I gave Al-anon a try. Another revolutionary reason, upon recognizing that alcoholics have a pattern of behavior, was my presumption there must also be a pattern of behavior for spouses, family members, co-workers, and friends of alcoholics. I wanted to know it, dissect it, and maybe even stop it. I began pointing the finger at myself as the only person I should "control".

Brendan also rocked my world by slipping the word "alcoholic" on both himself and Josh the way a shoe fits over a foot in a sock: it just does. Once I accepted that my husband was an alcoholic and I held that truth, all the issues attributed to alcoholism opened up, paving the way for me to admit, *Houston, we have a problem*. Josh's alcoholism existed whether there was a drink in his hand or not. Alcoholics lived from one drink to the next drink, and that next drink was always planned out. Someone might forget to stop and buy milk on the way home, but an alcoholic would never forget to stop at the liquor store.

Brendan expressed the importance of "hitting rock bottom". He had been addicted to both pain killers and alcohol. Brendan's rock bottom involved his wife's ultimatum combined with an awareness that he was going to lose his job. Brendan had given himself three days to wrap things up at work and to make sure his family's finances were in order, then he checked himself into an addiction rehabilitation facility. He completed a full, thirty-day inpatient treatment, followed with outpatient services. For additional support, he then joined a twelve-step recovery program. Three years later, Brendan was a seasoned, sober, AA member. When he talked about his past drinking behaviors, he had a solid, reflective disassociation from them. That was exactly what Josh could not fake: a spoken distance and reflective posture about his behaviors and his thought processes.

Josh considered a hellish, three-day, self-detox as the end-all and be-all to getting sober. He then gave himself the sage advice: *Next time, don't let the drinking get out control.* Alcoholism is a progressive disease that necessitates full-time support, and often specialized mental and physiological services. It was not a fight for Josh to take on alone.

CHANGES ARE A-BREWING

Josh had gone a month without drinking and seemed more at ease. Standing near my office door frame, he noticed me typing notes at the computer. He said, "I think the doc is going to hand my case over to one of his students."

"Excuse me? Why would he do that?"

"I think, maybe, he is not sure what to do with me. I have made a lot of progress."

"Yes, you have, but a therapeutic bond is essential. It doesn't make sense that he would put your progress in jeopardy. Did he actually say, 'I am transferring your case?'"

Josh remained very calm. "I got the feeling. I think he said something about insurance coverage and maybe that would be better. I don't know."

"Working in healthcare, you and I both know billing goes through the supervisor; it's not like the rate drops for the insurance company. Doesn't he want to see us together at some point? You did mention something about that a while ago."

"He has not mentioned anything recently," Josh turned and grabbed his sunglasses off the bookcase.

"Okay. Let the doc know I'm willing to come whenever he thinks it would benefit the cause."

Josh turned back around, spread his feet apart and lowered his chin. "What *cause* is that?"

Raising my chin, I said, "The cause to get you sober."

"I am sober. But thanks for saying I didn't cut it yet." The hall light reflected off his sunglasses. His boots scuffed the floor as he pivoted. "I'm going to work on the yard." The front door opened, and the front door slammed shut.

A melody from an old children's song floated into the house. The tune traveled down the hall, seeping into my frontal cortex. *There was an old woman who swallowed a fly. I don't know why, she swallowed a fly – I guess she'll die.*

My gut was talking. *Why?* Why was not the question. "Why" was the clue. *Why did she swallow a fly?* She had to swallow the fly in order to taste where it had been...in a pile of bull... Dr. Good-guy would not just back off and casually transfer Josh's case. I used a simple insight trick, probably the oldest one in the book: flip what was said to the complete opposite. Dr. Good-guy did not want to phase down the sessions...Josh did. Josh was prepping me. He was looking for an excuse, a way out of his therapy. Ugh, he gave me no credit.

What else? If Josh did not want to keep going for help, then he did not want to give up his best friend; my nemesis. *Where was the bottle?*

Double checking that Josh was busy outside, I looked through all the kitchen pantry cabinets. Nothing. I went downstairs and checked the ceiling rafters. Nothing. I wiggled each seemingly empty wine bottle on his homemade wine rack. There were at least twenty bottles; all of them empty. I checked the golf bag. Nothing. I went outside to his car...trunk, glove box, under seats – no alcohol. Okay, it couldn't be far, otherwise, it was too hard to get to it. I went back inside and checked his desk: nothing. I stared at his favorite resting spot which featured three things: a floor lamp, a guitar speaker that doubled as an end table, and his well-loved leather chair. Josh was very content to sit in his recliner and peruse a *New Yorker* magazine cover to cover. I peeked at them for the cartoons.

I sat in his chair and tried not to think. *Breathe. Use intuition. Breathe in... breathe out. Be Josh in his chair.* There was a pile of *New Yorker* magazines on top of the speaker, his 'to-read' pile. The back of the speaker almost touched the wall. *Almost.* There was a bit of space. I put out my hand and felt the back of the guitar amp, it was hollow. Reaching further, I explored inside the amp and pulled out a half-empty bottle of vodka.

There is an Eastern belief that our energy flows through pathways called meridians in our bodies. These meridians source out from seven chakras, up the center of the body, to the crown of the head. Two chakras are located in the pelvis: the root chakra, and the life-giving chakra. Upon seeing this bottle, both chakras in me surged a code red that ultimately landed an arc of decimating fear and sadness on my heart. For all the lip service, in my hand was the reality. This bottle was no longer Josh's best friend – it was his fucking mistress. He would always go back to her. *She* held all the cards.

At that moment, I realized that Josh was her pawn. He would not betray her, and he could not protect me. I needed to learn more about how to deal with addiction, but not through Josh, and not for Josh. If he wanted her, fine, he could have her; I did not want *her* ruling my life anymore, and living in my head like a compulsive parasite. My life was worth more than searching for bottles. I felt robbed of joy: joy in raising my children and having a fun marriage—that had been my plan. If I felt robbed, then I too, must be robbing my kids of my best parenting. That hit me with a despair akin to a malignancy. It made me feel weak. It all felt so complicated, and unending. I knew the simple fix...I would pour some vodka down the drain, but not enough for him to notice. That small act would symbolize my gaining some control over the insignificance he assigned to me. It would also symbolize my own ridiculousness. I still had much to learn about the chronic effects of addiction on the spouses of alcoholics and on codependency.

ADDICTION TIMES TWO

A few days passed. I kept my vodka discovery under wraps because Josh was still going to his sessions; it was the good doc's job to help him stop. Our evenings had been peaceful, I wanted to keep it that way. Quietly sauntering towards the TV room one evening, I happened to get within inches of the back of my husband in his reading chair. He was not reading a magazine. Instead, he was using his laptop. From behind him, I could see his computer screen. *Huh – shhh – don't move.*

My husband was scrolling through profile after profile on the screen. So many women... My husband was on a dating website. I felt a grinding in the pit of my stomach. As I stood there help-lessly watching, I felt sick. I wanted to throw up. Dating websites had recently become popular and less frowned upon. I knew of only two exclusive sites. He was not typing much, just peering. To avoid being heard, I trodden backwards very slowly, needing time to process. Plan A: point out the problem and we handle it together. Sure, and lead is the new helium. Plan B is the opposite: do not point anything out, and I handle it. Plan C: somewhere in between the rock and the hard place.

The next morning, I took the kids to school, returned home, and waited for the moment Josh turned on the shower. I dashed to the work bag, taking out his computer. His password was automatic. I brought up the internet and searched recent history. There it was—the dating website. Let's politely call it "Snatch.-com". Presto, clicking the link took me right to his profile. Guess he hadn't closed out his previous session. There was my husband, using a harmless professional photo: a very attractive picture of him with trimmed blonde hair, and a warm partial smile. He was wearing a white collared shirt and a dark blue suit jacket. This pleasant photo bothered me all the more because I did not get to feel an attraction for him since much of what he did was not attractive. Anyway, Josh put his relationship status as... Divorced! WTF! On his profile was a page of photos. Of course, there was his motorcycle, his car, and photos of...our kids! FWTF! It's like the kids were part of some package deal, and they didn't have a mom!

As a woman, I would never have put my kids' photos out there for strangers to see. No doubt Josh submitted those photos to seem safe, normal, and appealing. Unfortunately, I could not resist reading his profile backstory, or messages he had sent to other women. Yuck. I do not recommend anyone read a cheating spouse's profile page, or letters sent to pursue another. It sucks. There was a sliver of comforting news: Josh only recently opened the account, and none of the messaging indicated a relationship had started, or that he had met anyone. It appeared that my husband became a Snatch member before I moved back home, stopped his activity while he was getting help, then recently started back up.

WHERE'S ALL THE SANITY

There had been much to discuss in that week's therapy session. Dr. Rachel Phoenix, seated in her wingback chair, wore a rayon scarf dipped in hues straight from a Claude Monet lily pond. Her scarf fell over a black sweater that faded to matching pants. Beaming tastefully up from the floor were royal blue, velvet shoes.

I provided a complete spewing of my latest predicament. Dr. Phoenix remarked, "When most addicts drop one addiction, they typically pick up another. Some pick up gambling or smoking, others sex or overeating."

"Thanks for the Snapple cap fact. At least in your scenarios, someone gave up one addiction before taking on another one."

"I'm sure Joshua has had the coals raked over him in recent

weeks. We are seeing a lot of immature coping patterns," she said. "What age did he start drinking?"

"He told me at least thirteen. He remembers the feeling. Said he felt like 'he got it'."

"What does that mean exactly?" squinting her brows.

"I believe he meant understanding what it does for people: all the great wonders. Remember, his dad was an alcoholic. From my perception, I guess he related to why his dad, or anyone, escaped to it."

Dr. Phoenix imparted, "I have heard many alcoholics describe how it feels different to them. Not only that, they quickly gain a high tolerance. They drink their friends under the table." I nodded and took mindless note of her plants. It was hard to concentrate.

"So, what are you going to do?" she stated, bringing me back to focus.

"Good question. If we had a date to sign divorce papers, that would be one thing, but we're taking a courtesy break. Although, word on Snatch Street is that he already a divorcee." Dr. Phoenix pleasantly tilted her head side to side while I went on. "Our time living separately has ended; no doubt living apart was a grey area. I dabbled in the grey area of dating to revive myself, not to avoid reality, or have sex. Our priority is supposed to be his therapy. The only reason I am not totally freaking out is because I know he is not sleeping with anyone. He has not had the chance. I cannot imagine what women go through when their husbands are cheating on them."

Dr. Phoenix pursed her red lips. "Is not what Josh has been doing in the last year and a half of equal betrayal? I mean, take a look back from when you started coming here, until today. You saved him from going to jail, you moved out of your house, you took on more work, and you care for all three children as much as you ever did. You have never stopped supporting his well-being and you are still coming to therapy. Therapy that was supposed to be for you as well as your marriage. And he is still – Josh."

"Uh-huh. Yup," is all I could muster as the chakra at the third eye powered off. It's the chakra that balances the ability to formulate accurate gut feelings.

MY NEW REGIME involved checking Josh's computer first thing every morning. Within a week, my husband had arranged a date. He and a Snatch woman planned to meet for a motorcycle ride. They switched their communication to Facebook, which I could still follow. In fact, she posted out to her friends about her upcoming date. I had my short turn with dating only to learn that I did not want to take mental and emotional energy away from this family. I could empathize with Josh's need, or anyone's need for that matter, in this type of situation, which helped me keep a level, non-judgmental head.

On the morning of his date, I confronted him, saying I could tell that he was going on a date. Josh denied it. I covered my tracks, stating this information was leaked to me via a Facebook feed and that I double checked by visiting her feed. At this point, he hung his head and said next to nothing. I explained that I believed we should be following some basic rules of integrity, and having me babysit the kids so he could go out on a date while we lived together was a no-fly zone. Since he was the master of saying nothing, I left him to think about it, and get back to me.

Later that day, within an hour of date time, he had said nothing. This was his way of handling it. My way was slightly different.

"I'm going out. Find your own babysitter, and please, explain to the kids why you need one," closing the door loudly behind me. I camped out in my empty apartment which I had for a couple more weeks. Josh remained home and obviously had to cancel. I know because before going to my apartment, I parked in view of the house to make sure he did not leave the kids. The next day, Josh told me he would not try to see her again.

Things got better... No, actually worse. I started checking his phone – no pride there. Turned out that he had recently begun flirting with a professional peer and didn't need a Snatch catch. Through the history of their texts, it started out innocently enough. Actually, I knew who she was: a child advocate lawyer. She was very nice, pretty, had two kids, recently divorced and apparently under the impression that Josh and I were "almost finished" our divorce. He claimed he "tried his best". They were on the verge of boldly stepping out of their professional roles with one another into a private relationship.

On my end were interviews with lawyers to start the actual divorce process. Josh's crap behavior 'twas but a petty distraction. My eye was on the prize, but with no prize winners. None of the lawyers I interviewed thought it was possible to get the two things I wanted: first, I wanted the grounds for divorce to be "emotional abuse" versus "irreconcilable differences". "Nobody did that. It was 'too inflammatory,'" the lawyers said. *Well, he should have treated me better.* Second, I wanted full custody. "Full custody is rare, like 2%," they warned me. *Hey, those are my odds.* Eventually, a mediator met my expectations, and I received paperwork to look over.

My daily life included a healthy dose of looking over pre-divorce papers, reading the latest Snatch.com scenario, sneaking peeks at his phone regarding the lawyer woman, and checking his liquor stash behind the speaker. A line from the comedy film, *In Search of the Holy Grail* captured my attitude best. The valiant Black Knight is battling King Arthur and has just lost both arms to King Arthur's sword. The king thinks its' game over, but the Black Knight proclaims, "It's just a flesh wound."

Josh's text messages with the female lawyer progress to arranging a date – how sweet. This advanced intel allowed me to observe how Josh would proceed lying to me. Indeed, two days before the date, Josh told me he had a later appointment with Dr. Good-guy than was actually scheduled. I wasn't going to fret too much over a first dinner date. Josh would primarily enjoy the opportunity to talk about himself, and get a little positive attention. I therapeutically understood his need for this outlet; I too had needed a little shot of attention. On the morning of their date, Josh and the lawyer woman texted a confirmation. I hoped Dr. Good guy appreciated my distant support and patience.

THAT EVENING, when my husband arrived home from his "extended doctor's appointment," he came upstairs to the attic to say hi. The kids were already in bed; the house was extra clean. I had showered and styled my hair as if fresh off the beach, bringing out the shine of red and copper highlights. A coconut wash lingered on my skin, loose curls cascaded onto my freshly-washed, button-up Victoria Secret nightshirt. I had even given myself a mani-pedi with *Kiss Me Pink* nail polish. I was peacefully reading a book in my neatly made bed, completely at rest as my best self. Joshua emerged from the staircase wearing a tan wool blazer and a pressed white collared shirt, top button undone as usual. With his weathered, pretty-boy face and strong jawline, he looked dashing. I had to hand it to him... Some days, he could really knock it out of the park. Josh did a double take upon seeing me.

"Wow! You look pretty." He paused in his tracks before approaching the foot of the bed.

"Thank you," I said, returning to the book in my hands. Josh sat on a corner of the bed and began a pleasant conversation with me, I mean *at* me. He began to tell me about his day, news about a patient, etc. Closing the book with my finger as a place-holder, I smiled while offering my full attention. Not a single word passed across my fully moisturized lips. After his interesting monologue, he placed his hand on the duvet above my knee. Upon this very benign, thoughtful gesture I calmly uttered, "Do not touch me after coming home from a date. Do not spoon feed me pompous lies and do not think for one second that I deserve to be treated this way. Good night, Josh." And I went back to reading my book in my lovely space, undisturbed by my cheating, lying, drinking husband.

He was speechless. He did not get mad, yell, or even continue to lie. I gave him no platform to do so; no demands, no ultimatums, nothing. I kept the ball in *my court*. He could wait and wonder what I would do next. Josh descended the stairs in silence. Acting like a lady should have reminded him that I was one. *Boo-yah*.

THE NEXT MORNING, I sent my husband a brief, formal letter to his work email requesting the removal of his profile from Snatch.com. The letter expressed that, "as your wife, I find your dating activity to be very upsetting". To keep my intel source safe, I explained that news of his hurtful, deceptive hobby came to me from a single friend of mine who had come across his profile. Work emails had the high potential of being reviewed; the mere idea of that embarrassment should motivate Josh to respond and act properly.

Using his personal email, Josh formally responded in a letter that same afternoon. He apologized, indicating it was a mere "social experiment" that his co-workers encouraged him to do when I moved out. It was only a childish interest and he would "of course, shut it down."

This formal correspondence resulted in Josh taking a week long hiatus from his Snatch.com activity. He did not close the account; he merely added a profile block limiting those allowed to view him. I fully expected Dr. Josh would discuss all this hurtful behavior with Dr. Good-guy, and that those sessions would make us some headway. Josh's perseverance to continue therapy while these other "symptoms" surfaced was the only thing maintaining my empathy and buy-in. I knew he was still attending therapy, although I was not sure how often.

WE RECEIVED disappointing news about the good doctor. Josh told me: "He is transferring my case to a senior therapist. He feels this guy is better suited to me for the long term, and has a lot of experience in this field. I met him today. He seems very knowledgeable." Josh sounded genuine and volunteered the new doctor's name, saying I could look him up if I felt the need. "I have my first appointment with him this Thursday at six."

It was feasible to me that Dr. Good guy would find Josh out of his league and want a more experienced therapist to take over. "I'm glad you like the guy. I know you are at ease with the wise, elderly type – a familiar kinship to your grandfather."

Josh responded, "This is true."

I looked forward to finding out what his new doctor could accomplish.

COMMITMENT

Despite all the crap going on, every morning Josh still wore his wedding band. I took notice because somewhere in my mind, this was comforting; it symbolized a regard for our marriage, and our family, and his desire to hold onto that. On the Wednesday before his new therapist appointment, Josh had a naked finger when he came home from work. Confident the ring was not on the shelf next to his grandfather's watch that morning, I patiently made small talk while Josh put his work bag in the TV room.

Once Josh went upstairs to change out of his suit, I scurried to search that same ole work bag. Pulling the main zipper back, the polyvinyl sides opened out to reveal files, a clinical book, and a legal notepad. There was nothing on the bottom. Next, I checked the small outside Velcro pocket. Only coins there. Last spot to check was an outside, full-length zipper pocket. There was a wallet, eye drops, two pens, but nothing else. *Damn, I had been so sure. This didn't make sense. I had to believe myself – the first time.* I rechecked the side length pocket. This time, my wiggling fingers searched underneath the wallet. My fingertips began to fiddle and caress a hard metal circle. I pulled out his white and yellow gold wedding band. Unlike all the other days when he had remembered to fool me, he must have forgotten to put it back on his finger.

Different emotions raced to tag my heart; profound sadness reached it first. I was sad to be fooled, sad that our moral commitment had been discarded, and deeply saddened at the level of disregard for me and what we had co-created. Frustration rose in a fury that he would not be upfront, and set me free of this treatment when I was making a divorce very easy, and overtly fair. Other emotions continued fighting it out within me, as if opponents in a boxing ring. The announcer called:

It's a hard-square jab by betrayal. Oh! She takes a right hook from foolishness. Here it comes ladies and gentleman – Boom! – a sucker punch landed by stupid. Wait, here comes the combo: face punch, face punch, back hand! all delivered by the raw emotions of deception, annoyance, and a little she-devil we like to call silent rage. Ding! Ding! Match over. Can I have a woot-woot? No. How about a woot? Still no. Tough crowd. What do they want? Respect?

Before this moment, Josh had been riding on a clinical free pass due to the nature of his addiction, his haunting childhood past, and perhaps the struggle of dealing with a personality disorder. But this behavior marked the beginning of a new order. The decision to put on a wedding band when leaving the house, take it off at work to rouse his co-workers, thus gaining their support for dating, and then re-apply the band to make the wife think he cared, was absolutely a conscious choice of deceit. He did not have to wear the ring at all. He could have said, 'I am hurt and unsure', which was part of my statement when I got the apartment. I dated a little bit to exercise my full personality and get my shit together. I had already given Josh that same legroom. He was taking extra steps to convey a fake reality, yet I was not a fake wife, and we did not have fake kids. This mounting betrayal was not fake either.

THE NEXT MORNING, I searched the internet and obtained the phone number of Josh's new doctor, who was legit. However, Josh had probably not been expecting me to actually call and verify his appointment. Surprisingly, this doctor answered the phone himself. With the tone of a secretary, I stated that the purpose of my call was to confirm Dr. Josh's appointment for tonight at six o'clock. Perplexed, the doctor confirmed that he was indeed this exact doctor, however, he said that there was no appointment scheduled. When I explained the case transfer, he did not know what I was talking about; however, he did know Josh through his daughter. "Ah yes, Dr. Josh works with my daughter. Perhaps it is her that he is meeting." He tried putting pieces together for me, but I got the picture. I recognized who his daughter was, and Josh would never have dated her. This doctor was simply the unwitting alibi. I thanked him for his time.

Coincidently, making national headline news were the multiple, destructive affairs of a famous golf player. As the unfortunate, intimate tidbits of his cheating surfaced on TV, it seemed like the newscasters were talking to me in an attempt to clue me in. There was some comfort in hearing another wife's emotional reactions, such as smashing one's cheating husband's car with a golf club. *I feel ya, sister; I'm about to use my own nine iron.*

TIME TO END THIS

On the fly, Sara and another friend, Julie, agreed to help me. When they arrived, we got straight to work as soon as our kids had gone off to school.

"I brought a few boxes, like you asked," said Julie as she walked through the front door. "Oh, hi Sara! I see you brought your van."

Sara grinned. "Yup. I took out the back row; we have plenty of room."

"Great," I responded, slightly out of breath. "I already put all his clothes into trash bags. The bags are upstairs in the master bedroom. Julie, you can start by putting the bags outside by the van. We will pack them after the furniture goes in." Julie gave me the thumbs up and off she went.

"Sara, you and I will get his furniture from the study. There is a desk with a chair, a leather recliner and a floor lamp. Be careful with the lamp, it's his favorite. Oh, the amp speaker goes too, he needs somewhere to put his vodka," clapping my hands. "Let's go!"

It took only one trip with two cars and a van to haul all of Josh's basic daily belongings and typically used furniture over to my former apartment. With days to spare, there was still time to renew the lease. It took many trips up a long flight of stairs to complete the relocation process, also known as, *move your ass on out*.

"Welcome to your new home, Josh! Do whatever the hell you want with whoever you want!" I drop kicked the last bag of clothes into the completely empty bedroom. "Ladies, thank you for your service." Julie gave out hugs, and left first. Sara stayed to help with putting his things in order.

"It is pretty nice of you to set everything up for him: hanging his clothes, a set of dishware in the kitchen, a toothbrush, shampoo. I don't know if I would be that nice," Sara conveys while hanging up a bath towel.

"I am not being nice. I am handing Josh exactly what his immature, mutant brain wants. He doesn't really want a family and a wife, as I see it." I ranted while placing his watch, deodorant, and a few framed photographs of his grandparents in order. "We are always on a shelf, taken down for brief moments, and then put back up." I threw a pillow and a sleeping bag where there used to be a bed. "I just want him to stop, you know? Stop pissing in my boots and calling it rain."

Sara stood next to me and took my hands. "You have done enough here. You did not stoop to his level and take all of this to the dumpster, or leave it on the front lawn. You are showing him what he is missing: a classy lady who deserves better. When he walks into this place, you are showing him what treating someone with respect looks like. His stuff should be on the curb, but you hung up his clothes so he can pick up where he left off. He can pay his share of the bills and do whatever he wants. You deserve to run the family home in peace. Let's get out of here."

"Okay my friend." I glanced around the bedroom and grabbed the empty trash bags.

"Do you think Josh will be pissed off when you tell him?"

"Does a toddler enjoy his toy truck getting smashed? But, in time, I'm sure he'll be fine with it."

HAVE TO ADMIT—I underestimated that one. Josh was livid. This all played out over the phone. First, I called him out on the bogus therapist switcheroo; he said I was being invasive. Next, I mentioned I knew he was still actively dating; he denied it. Further into our conversation he ceased denying everything, but without admitting to anything. His final declaration before hanging up on me: "I am not leaving my house!" Click.

Huh. What do you mean you're not leaving? That was not supposed to be an option. Another woman in town with five kids had a husband who was repeatedly cheating on her. She had her dad and brother and her in-laws tell him to leave the family house. He didn't want to, but through this intervention of sorts, he saw what was best for everyone and got his own place. Why couldn't Josh own up, and leave? He wasn't welcome anymore. Didn't that matter?

I called Sara and asked if she could come over and be here as a buffer of sanity for when Josh got home. Honestly, I couldn't believe her husband, Liam, had let her. But Liam was very astute and willing to support a blow to Josh's arrogance. By the time Josh arrived home, Sara and I were playing with the kids out back. Josh briefly greeted us all with a palpable mood of agitation. He cleverly found clothes I forgot about in the hamper and changed out of his formal work clothes. Josh mentioned not a word to us and began to trim hedges in the yard while we played with the kids.

Sara and her son went home. Josh and I moved through the dinner and the usual night time routines without speaking. By bedtime, I mentioned he could go home to the apartment and I would finish up with the kids. Josh firmly stated he was not leaving and was adamant that if I did not return his things tomorrow, he would call the police to report I had stolen his stuff. He mentioned he even called a lawyer friend while at work.

This is not how I had imagined it all playing out. Suddenly, Josh was interested in being with the kids during story time. Fine. I gave Josh a book to take over reading to Nicky and Jolie. I went downstairs to call my dad in the hope that he would help persuade Josh to recognize the courteous thing to do here. I was barking up the wrong tree. My father had a more holistic view, and feared Josh would call the police, putting me in a legal situation. I told him I thought Josh was bluffing. My dad wanted to protect me from any negative strikes for an inevitable divorce, and strongly urged me to return Josh's things. *Dad, this is not why I called you!* My father agreed to come over in the morning to help work things out.

My brain pushed this unmanageable task aside. I climbed the

stairs to catch a final bedtime story – and halted. Half way up, I saw my six-year-old son, wearing red flannel Lego pajamas, come storming over to the top of the stairs. He folded his arms and screamed down at me, "You're trying to kick Daddy out of the house!"

"Wha-What?"

"You're trying to make Daddy leave! This is his house too!"

Marching up the stairs, I grabbed my son's hand and walked us into his little boy bedroom where Josh was laying on Nicky's bed, reading a book with my daughter. *Tea anyone? Cuz I'm about to boil.* Josh gave me a quick glance while swallowing a smirk, then shook his head like he was confused, barely hiding his amusement over Nicky's surprising reaction.

"Josh, what did you say? I was gone for ten minutes. Ten minutes is all you need to screw things up!" Jolie immediately got up to leave. "Jolie, what did your dad say?"

"Why do you want him to go? Why are you guys always fighting?" and she ran out. Meanwhile, Nicky crawled into bed with Josh, who cuddled him up. Josh pathetically mouthed to me, "I don't know," and continued reading. Triaging, I found Jolie, and brought her into the master bedroom for privacy. Speaking from my heart, I generated a calm, concerned tone. I sat on the edge of the bed, which allowed her to be taller than me.

"I don't want to talk to you!" Her blonde eyebrows pinched together and her arms crossed tightly.

"Jolie, something was said that is upsetting you and Nicky. If I do not have your help, I am completely in the dark and cannot do anything." Jolie clenched her mouth; her pink nightgown with dancing cats and shooting stars stretched down to the floor. Placing my hands together in prayer position I tried to persuade. "Jolie, no one is getting in trouble – not even your dad."

"I don't know who to trust! You say one thing; daddy says another!" She wiped a tear. "We're supposed to be the kids here, not you guys." Her hand dried another wet freckle.

"We are not acting maturely, you're right. I'm sorry. Let me explain something to you, okay?"

"Fine." She let me give her hand a squeeze. "Here, sit down." With Jolie at arm's length, I took a deep breath and went for it. "I am going to explain a clinical term to you called projective identification – big label, big concept – okay?"

"Fine. I'm not a little kid anymore."

"I know. You hit the double digits; bear with me. Let's say you are in your room playing with your dolls, Skipper and Belle. I come in and see the room's a mess. Immediately, I get mad because you didn't clean your room like we agreed. I bark, 'Clean this room now,' and leave."

Jolie flatly said, "And I start yelling at my dolls to clean their room and that's project whatever."

"Projective identification...and not exactly. You snap at Skipper doll who says to you, 'Hey Jolie, don't get mad at me. You made the mess'. Can you see that Skipper's feelings are not really thrown out there because of my outburst? In other words, Skipper has no bad feelings towards me."

"I get it, Mom. You are mad at me, and I am taking it out on Skipper, but Skipper is not mad at you."

"Correct; very smart. We are going to build on that. You probably feel embarrassed that you didn't clean your room like you promised. Maybe you feel super bad about it. Imagine pouring those feelings into a cup. Okay, you are holding a cup of shame." My hands came together like they were holding a wide cup.

Jolie, sitting up straight, imitated the cup and replied, "A mug of embarrassing tea."

"Jolie, I want you to slowly pour more of your reaction into your mug, because you are also upset that I am ruining your good time playing with your dolls. Everything was absolutely fine until I showed up. It's too much, so you tell Skipper that I am a 'c-r-a-z-y mom to come barging into your room, screaming at the top of my lungs.' You may even tell Skipper that I always say, 'I am disappointed in you as a daughter, and that you never do anything I tell you.' Remember Jolie, none of this example is true. You are awesome! But in this example, your exaggerated story is causing Skipper to feel bad for you. You get her attention and this makes you feel better because Skipper sees you as a poor, defenseless victim. Here's the home run moment, Jolie – Skipper gets mad at me! Skipper's like 'come at me, bro' mad. Your doll has embodied your twisted feelings that you cannot consciously manage in your cup. You become defensive and Skipper loses her insight because she has been manipulated by you and your exaggerations. This is hard on Skipper, because a little sense of herself gets crushed by this manipulation. Skipper is caught up in the sticky bubble gum of projective identification."

Jolie tilted her head and tried to grasp it all. "You never did anything to Skipper, but Skipper is mad at you. I can't handle feeling embarrassed, so I get mad at you for calling me out on my room being a mess. Then, I pour Skipper a cup of lies which gets Skipper mad at you, but you never did anything to her. Now my doll wants to mess you up. Mom, if I just cleaned my room in the first place, none of that would've happened."

"Pretty much, Jolie."

"What does this have to do with you and daddy?"

"Your dad's cup is spilling over because of things he has done. He is not handling his feelings and actions very well, so I suggested he could live at the apartment. He is telling you stories so that you guys think, *poor daddy*, and get mad at me. Meanwhile, he gets to pour his cup of embarrassment down the drain by believing his own story. You helped him, because he was feeling hurt. It's okay because you wanted to protect him, and stand up to me. But you lost thinking for yourself. You didn't question him, or seek me out to understand. You lost your individual processing ability because of the manipulations and his position of authority, or simply his being an adult over you. It's sticky, stinky stuff. It's not easy even for us adults to handle."

"Well, Daddy needs a bigger cup! He will throw things when

he's mad. He yells and curses. He gets really mad at Willie." A sparrow could have landed on my daughter's jutted bottom lip.

Holding her shoulders, "Jolie I am exhausted from dealing with small cups. It is making me bonkers sometimes; I am sorry for that. I am trying to get things straight. That is why I got the apartment, to get my head straight. Today, I think it is fair if your dad does the same, to get his head straight. That is what I suggested to him in my own way: to go stay at the apartment. Your dad does not like the idea. He is embarrassed and wants to stay here. You, my precious peanut, got caught in the middle. You probably feel split between daddy and I. You said you 'don't know who to trust.' That is why we are having this amazing, teachable conversation."

It took a minute, a hard minute, for my precocious ten-year-old to put these complicated pieces in place. She pulled away from me and burst into a tearful question: "Why would he do that?" Jolie hopped into my lap and melted into me.

"Oh my, good question honey," hugging her tightly, rocking side to side as mothers do. "Your dad doesn't mean to hurt you, or Nicky, or Connor. It is a defense mechanism. There are many defense mechanisms and we all use them. This one in particular kind of stinks. If you want to be a therapist one day and help people work on these kinds of things, go for it. Right now, I want you to know you can trust me. I am going to give you the scoop as best I can for your age, okay? Although, I totally went over your age just now cuz you're like a superstar and hung in there really good."

"Thanks Mom," wiping her face and standing on her feet again.

"Jolie this isn't the kind of stuff you mention to friends and townspeople. It is private, family stuff. You can talk to grandma or Pop-Pop or CJ, or just ask me about who you want to talk to. Understand?"

"Mom seriously," putting a hand on her hip and rolling her eyes, "I couldn't explain any of that if I tried. I'm going to clean up my room right now!" A whirl of golden hair brushed my face and a blur of ruffled night dress flourished out the bedroom door.

One down, two to go. I picked easier first. Thank goodness for this sight: Connor – having decided to visit me upstairs in the attic – had fallen asleep waiting for me. *I suck.* I gave him a gentle kiss and pulled the sheet up to his shoulders. Two down, one to go. In Nicky's room, Josh had already turned out the light. They were sleeping side by side.

I curtly whispered into my husband's ear, "Josh get up. I know you are not asleep." Josh did not move; his eyes stayed shut. Nicky's mouth had fallen slightly open. He was slumbering on the side of his dad's chest. My lips pursed inches away from Josh's ear to whisper, "If you don't get up, then I will grab Nicky, carry him upstairs, place him next to Connor and we will finish our conversation right here." My converse sneakers stepped away; my right foot started tapping.

Josh's chest rose higher and higher, then fell in a heavy huff. He kissed Nicky on top of his head and slid out from under Nicky's limp arm. On the way out, he glared at me while his jaw tensed and protruded forward. Josh went into the master bedroom, flopped belly down, facing away from me, and lay motionless.

Addressing the back of his head, my curtness continued. "I just spent the last fifteen minutes putting our daughter back together. She feels split and torn between us. Some of that is due to the crap you are saying to cover up your behavior. You are cheating on me, or rather, trying really hard to do so. You stopped seeing a therapist, you're swapping bogus session times for date slots, you started drinking again—big surprise, I can tell —and now you're using the kids as pawns. Own it, and stop it! Or take the grand prize: keep doing all those things, and go live somewhere else! I made it real comfortable for you to move out; no one did that for me. You never checked on me to see I was safe, didn't help me move, and never once asked if I was okay. In fact, someone told me you said, I moved out 'because I was gay!' 'Poor Josh, that must be why their marriage is on the rocks, his wife is gay.' Brilliant story; now you have a reason to drink."

"Enough already!" Josh blurted out.

"How much am I supposed to take, Josh?"

Josh lifted his head, facing the mattress in a pushed-up position. He gave a big sigh. "I am not moving out. I am not leaving my family or this house that I take care of and pay for and then not live here. I can't do that. That's what I am fighting for don't you get it?" he demanded in a high-pitched voice.

I softened my demeanor. "You're in over your head, Josh. It was easier to be by your side when you were getting help. It was like you finally admitted needing a life preserver. But now, you pretend you're not drowning." Kneeling by the bed. "You know what a drowning man does? He pulls the closest people down too, the ones trying to help. I thought I was swimming, Josh, but I'm not. I'm drowning too. You need professional help, so that you don't pull everybody under."

"That doctor was going to put me away."

"Josh, no one is putting you away. Worst case scenario, rehab is not jail."

"Rehab is too jail! It would feel like that to me."

"Rehab is to keep the world from harming you while you heal. It's not the other way around."

Josh acknowledged this truth with a "hmm" sound. That was as good as it was going to get. I hung up my animosity and left to check on the kids one more time. They were all asleep. Jolie's room looked wonderful. I curled up in bed with my daughter; she would probably dream that I was a big cat beside her.

THE NEXT MORNING, my dad came over, just before the kids needed to get up for school. He would bear witness, and perhaps set Josh straight. Upon hearing my father's concerns, I reluctantly conceded this might come back to haunt me. I went into the master bedroom where Josh had fallen asleep.

"Josh, wake up. My dad is here so we can decide what to do about the apartment. Please come downstairs where we can all talk privately." Josh opened an eye, lifted his head, but the lips did not move. I smiled at him, and rejoined my dad.

After ten minutes of waiting, Josh did not come downstairs. Excusing myself, I went back up to find he had crawled into bed with Nicky. After re-hinging my fallen jaw, I lifted Nicky out of his warm bed, handed him his clothes, and told him to get dressed in the bathroom. Without saying a word, I left to get the other two kiddos up, telling them to grab some cereal for breakfast. I announced, "You must put at least one fruit in your cereal bowls."

Back downstairs with my dad, I explained the situation. This freaked my dad out a bit. He could not believe this was the action of a grown man. As the kids came downstairs, we went up. "Cereal is on the table, kids." *Oh boy, am I looking forward to my dad defending his daughter – in your face!*

I opened Nicky's bedroom door. Josh, still lying under a quilt with zoo animals, immediately rolled towards the wall. *Are you kidding me?* I walked to the bed; my dad stayed in the doorframe, maintaining his distance. *Uh, okay Dad.* I began by saying to Josh: "I will compromise, which means I do not like the solution either, but I have to agree it is fair. Together we got into this mess, so together, we will both move your things back to the house. If you are going to live here, then you are going to stop dating other women and get off a dating website while you are my husband, otherwise, leave." I glanced at my dad, he added nothing. I glanced back at the lump, aka my husband. He said nothing. "Eh-hem, Josh, does that sound fair? Or do we need to literally stand here all day?"

Facing the wall, Josh clearly stated, "That sounds fair."

"Wunderbar!" I briskly walked past my silent dad, feeling like

I had just had one of the most pathetic moments in my entire life.

Once we're downstairs, I said to my dad, "I thought you might say something to him."

"I did not want to agitate him."

"Clearly, you did not."

"Honey, you were handling it very well. I was only your back up. You kept your cool, stated a fair plan and got his buy in – his verbal agreement, anyway. That was the goal."

But Dad, I wanted you to make him stop! Snap him out of it! Tell him your daughter does not deserve this. Tell him to either hand over a divorce, or grow up. My whirling head resigned that my father did not own a magic wand.

My dad, aka pop-pop, offered to take his grandkids to school. Right before they all headed out the door, Josh came downstairs. His hair was sticking up like Rod Stewart. He said a brief hello, and meandered into the kitchen to make his coffee, only to yell in dismay, "You took my coffee maker too?" My dad covered his mouth to dampen a heaving laugh.

"I wanted you to be comfortable!" I yelled back.

My father put his hand on my shoulder, a gleam in his eye. "I'm proud of you, honey. Call me later, as soon as you guys are done. I want to know how everything went."

"Okay, I will," I said before hugging and kissing my munchkins good-bye.

CLEANING UP THE MESS

Josh and I gathered up his things from the apartment—my fourth time moving stuff in and out of this place. It was Josh's first time in the apartment, ever. At one point he started to cry, which took me by surprise.

Josh gave me a hug saying, "I never knew what it was like for you. I never thought about what you gave up. I know, I drove you away. All my mistakes… I know, I know." He wiped his nose and sniffed.

"You know, it took me six months before I could shower somewhere my kids did not; it was not a home without them," I said standing under him.

He gave me another hug and whispered in my ear, "I'm sorry. I'm really sorry." Politely thanking him, I suggested we get through the day, which we did, like two adults for a change – a united humbling. I officially turned in the keys, and stopped paying for that price tag on my mental break.

It took some doing for Josh to completely end his dating endeavors, which was code for I actually handled it. I visited the lawyer woman at her office; we had met years before at an autism clinic. We had a five-minute meeting of complete under-standing as I explained she was a little fish in a big pond. She disclosed that she had divorced her husband for his infidelities; she wanted no part of a repeat. She said, "I won't mention you were here. Josh and I have a client together and that is all our communications will be." Worked for me. Felt good to trust someone.

Next battle: Snatch.com. I called an unknown woman from Josh's phone record and explained exactly who I was: the wife. She had a hard time believing me at first, but then confessed that she did not want any part of this mess and had another guy of interest. She asked if it was true that Josh and I were getting divorced because I was gay, adding that it was okay if I was. "Being with my husband may make women seem more appeal-ing, but no, I am not gay."

Tactically moving into enemy lines, I covertly logged on to his Snatch.com account and enhanced his profile. I began by changing Josh's dating age preferences to be between 65 and 85 years old. Next, body type: nothing less than two hundred pounds. Under hobbies, I typed: "Ever since I was released, I enjoy collecting blunt axes, machetes and shanks, as well as eating refried beans straight from the can." The final embellishment went to the self-description section where I erased and replaced his current bio twenty times over with... "Married man. Married man. I am a married man.". I pressed submit, and a pop-up bubble appeared stating that all changes would go under review. I was counting on it.

The relief from knowing all these avenues were closed was tremendous. The angst of mistrust when someone has an affair is crippling. Plus, I had been acting like an obsessed, crazy person reading messages, checking phones, looking for bottles, and trying to outsmart his devious behavior with my justifiable devious behavior. I didn't want to behave this way. Alas, I had but one nail left for Josh's behavior coffin. His peers were still under a spell of lies.

COMING SOON WAS our fourteenth wedding anniversary. From a remote place inside my heart, I pondered the tiniest of questions, "What would I do if we were celebrating fourteen years of love and happiness? What if he was my ideal love partner?" Oh, the mere idea of this lifted my spirits with a swell of energy. I would yell from a mountain top, "Happy anniversary, darling!" For a moment, I held the feeling as true; it morphed into a high road idea.

On the spring day of our anniversary, I used Sara's social media account to post onto Josh's Facebook page. After introducing myself as Josh's wife, I authored, "Happy Anniversary to my darling husband of 14 years! I know we've had our ups and downs, but after all the effort we are both pouring into our marriage, I am hopeful we will share many more. Love, your wife, Jessica."

The post was released during his drive to work so there would be at least an hour before he would see it. The anniversary party boat did not stop there. I messaged and asked a dozen mutual friends to wish Josh and I happy anniversary on his social feed because their support would be nice as we got through some rough patches. Everyone was happy to help, which meant that all day long, at random times, his social feed blew up with happy anniversary messages. Certainly, these message-grenades would obliterate any lingering loose ends in my husband's dating world.

Did it work? Hell, ya. On his feed, his friends were all dazed and confused. Another female he was courting told him privately, *hasta la vista*. In addition, the lawyer woman I had met privately posted to Josh: 'Do the right thing. The world needs more decent men, and you certainly should be one of them.'—a traveling pants of sisterhood moment. Josh could not erase the incoming anniversary messages fast enough.

Josh arrived home earlier than usual on this special anniversary day and sat in his black leather chair, appearing quite beside himself. I turned off the TV, having just watched The Oprah Winfrey Show. Josh could not ignore me because I was lovingly staring at him, which also meant he could not reach behind the speaker to commiserate with his vodka. He appeared at a loss for words. I decided to wait until he found something to say. *One potato. Two potato. Three potato, four.*

Josh mumbled, "You...you - humph."

Five potato, six potato, seven potato more. Volunteering emotional support, I offered a complete sentence. "I was compelled to shout 'happy anniversary' to my husband." Josh squirmed. He began to state that he knew why I had all our friends post him messages, but then stopped before his dominos of guilty-as-charged started to fall. Observing the collision between his world of lies and a comet of reality was a bizarre sight. Moving forward, unless my husband wanted a smear campaign, he'd best fly straight.

A TRUCE HAPPENS

Finally, we had peace in the house. Josh emitted more healthy energy and sanity from not living a double life as a cheater, and I had more time and emotional energy back on my plate. Josh and I attended one mediator session, then he was no longer interested in going. He was an anchor in the mud and I was at the end of my rope. Therefore, I officially took a break from filing a divorce. There was not enough of me left for an uphill battle. At this juncture of cultivated peace, I only wanted to be a mom and an occupational therapist. Further soul searching: I had not been much of a friend to anyone, or a daughter, or a sister, or an aunt. I had not gone out socially, or read a book. I needed to start living as myself again.

Josh was still drinking, but leaving *it* alone seemed to help Josh maintain his balancing act. My living back home had provided a natural lid on the libations. We agreed to not argue over wine and beer. Josh had stopped any and all professional help for his issue; it was dead in the water. For daily functioning, I limited my nighttime engagements with Josh, and made fewer parental demands on him – the wave of our future.

AS SPRING BLOSSOMED INTO SUMMER, my job switched to summer school programs which meant fewer work hours. My caseload included a couple of handicapped preschool groups which were a lot of fun, and treating about ten individual students, all with severe developmental delays and/or autism spectrum disorders.

Some of the balls juggling in the air were the efforts to manage our beautiful home and property. It took both of us to float the house financially; Josh did the lion's share. I knew I'd be very comfortable in a smaller house. Around the block from our colonial mini-estate, a perfect downsized house was up for sale.

It was so cute, with half the house and property of our current home. Downsizing could solve many problems. I arranged a private showing ASAP.

The agent, a nice, older gentleman, provided the tour. The craftsman style house was 2,800 square feet with half an acre of property. It had a modern layout with an open concept and plenty of windows. No more boxed in colonial rooms. Financially, if we downsized, we could pay off both mortgages with money left over for college funds. Our second $100,000 mortgage was for a bad business deal Josh made on a town deli that bombed. I had co-signed that deal and that was on me. Now, we were part owners of a commercial building nobody wanted. Anyway, real savings would come from lower bills in not running a big house, and the decreased stress. In my mind, I could handle this marriage longer with the scale tipping in so many other positive directions for the family. This only had true value to me if the kids liked it too.

The agent was very amenable to arranging a second showing for my kids. Much to my relief, the kids liked the house. The basement was set up like a games room which they found exciting, and although Jolie expressed that she would greatly miss her view of our backyard gardens, she could envision herself doing artwork on the porch. Surely, Josh would see the wisdom of this swap. He was the one who complained the most.

A major reason we were able to purchase our large house was because I had read three books on selling FSBO – For Sale By Owner – and sold our Hawaiian home within three weeks at full asking price. When I mentioned my current downsizing idea to Josh, he downplayed his history of complaints and asked if I liked our house.

"Yes, of course," I said, "but I am trying to be realistic." Desire held power. Letting go of desires allowed other options to become clear. Releasing our life in a grand house with numbers to paper, revealed a valid option. Josh opened up to my point of view. After hearing the kids talk about the other house in a positive manner, he agreed to see it.

Two days later, the kids and I ambled over to meet the agent. Josh would meet us once he washed up from working in the yard. We greeted the agent on the charming porch. He welcomed us inside; the kids immediately began running around. It was a turn-key house. Fifteen minutes of small talk went by. I began calling Josh to see what was the delay. No answer. Another awkward ten minutes went by before it hit me: Josh had blown us off without the decency to say he had changed his mind so that this agent was not stuck waiting around.

Disheartened, we all wandered back to find Josh drinking a can of beer, surveying our vast yard. I sat in a chair next to him as he continued to gaze out yonder, and then spoke as if I were an audience member who paid to hear him. "This is a dream house I can leave to the kids. I put so much work into this home. That should stand for something. I cannot let that go." Converting the lecture into a conversation, I mentioned the lack of courtesy he demonstrated, and in fairness, giving my idea a moment of honest consideration required little effort on his part. This notion appeared intriguing to him. He nodded.

My quick acceptance of the situation didn't mean I was giving up. My brother, Greg, was in the mortgage loan business; he could test the validity and options of my idea. Greg and I discussed at length whether or not I alone, could buy the house, and break free of my dependency. A recovered friend of mine casually mentioned the term *codependency* to me. I wondered if this was what she meant?

Greg's answer regarding my ability to purchase the house: "No way; no chance. Not even close, sis."

My brother spelled out the figures and a tutorial on how to assess purchasing a property and getting loan approval. How did women with fewer resources in worse situations ever get out? It was fair to want something stable and functional and beautiful. Women needed a plan when they left a relationship: determination only got you so far. My kids were not old enough to be left alone very long, and Nicky couldn't leave school without an adult picking him up. It was back to the drawing board.

I began with heart space thinking. What would be my ideal life for raising a family? I remembered: back in Hawaii, Connor had gone to a Waldorf preschool. It had rocked our world.

CHILD EDUCATION

Waldorf schools use a developmental approach to teach children. Waldorf's core beliefs are in line with a certain cluster of parenting values that has made this private school system renowned. There are over 1,150 independent schools all over the world. Rudolf Steiner, an Austrian philosopher, architect, and leader of social change founded the first school in Germany in 1919 to avoid heavy government influence over education. Next, Waldorf came to England in 1925 and the first US school was in New York City in 1928. A child's natural intellectual, creative, and artistic development, as well as a focus on practical skills forms the central, holistic approach for fostering a child's natural curiosity to learn. Tools and toys made of natural materials are used in order to keep the younger child in tune with nature, for example, cloth dolls, wooden toys, and woolen hand-felted creatures. Students are protected from social marketing and media influences, i.e., video games and excessive television watching. A healthy diet is also stressed. Many parents, myself included, considered a Waldorf school to be a sort of co-parent. This was exactly the co-parent I wanted for my children, and in some form, for all children.

I had tried pursuing a Waldorf education option for our kids when we moved here, but the closest school was a fifty-minute commute, too far for a kindergartner. I decided to call that same school again; they had openings in the grades my kids were entering that fall. Dream first, reality later.

I knew that Connor would probably not want to leave his

friends, which would be a cost advantage. Connor often found his siblings annoying. At times he could be harsh to them. Even when he play-wrestled with Nicky, Connor was often too rough, poorly grading his strength, and inadvertently hurting Nicky, or causing Nicky to be sad from being overpowered. Hence, if Connor was not on board – though I'd like him to be – my teenager would have to sit in the world of his consequences and acquired entitlement. Right then, I wanted to keep the dream alive; cost and logistics were not on the table yet.

ALL THREE KIDS reviewed the school online, but only Jolie and Nicky were interested. The art studios alone wowed Jolie. The number of subjects and material Waldorf can cover because the kids are curious and engaged is beyond a typical American education. The kids go outside every day, rain, snow, or shine. In fact, they will puddle jump or go sledding for recess, then come back inside alert, pleased to be warm, and ready to give their attention to the next subject. The same teacher remains with her class from first grade until eighth grade. This not only nurtures the natural bond developed from a young age, but the teacher, having an incredible mastery of many subjects, enhances their fullest comprehension versus teaching to the test. We visited the Waldorf school and once again, it was an incredibly robust, multicultural, multi-sensory environment.

After a thorough interview process to make sure we were a match, the kids were accepted. Okay, next hurdle: the long commute. The cost to pay a driver was... ah... about the cost of renting a small apartment. I looked up small apartments and found a newly renovated place near the school. We could live there Sunday night through Friday afternoons, and if we came home every Wednesday for dinner, then I would be with Connor four out of seven days a week. Plus, the Waldorf school calendar has about thirty fewer school days than Connor's.

If my mom or dad saw Connor on one or two of those other

three days, it could work. Josh could step up his bond with Connor without my "controlling interference". All of Connor's practices and games were handled by the junior high school. Connor had received my priority mothering dedication for twelve years; I owed the younger two children the same. Jolie would be entering fifth grade, and Nicholas first grade. I felt that I had some making up to do with them, especially the middle child. My dad had broached the middle child syndrome with me about Jolie. Pop-pop thought she was not getting enough parental attention. If true, then I was not going to throw my hands up about it. At ten, she was still young enough for me to try and make-up for any shortcomings. Jolie was a vessel of creativity: very bright, caring, and creatively self-directed. If Josh would not help provide the right environment, then I would. The fact that we were **not** divorced made it easier.

The cost of private school took me by surprise. I had been squirreling money away, and that acorn would cover the initial payment. Once again, I needed to make mo' money, mo' money. The fields of Occupational and Physical Therapy have so many rewarding options, I began searching for a better job. Becoming an OT had been one of the best decisions of my life. *Thanks to my mom for supporting that endeavor.*

CALL IT GOOD FORTUNE, but my job research honed in on the specialized area of Early Intervention (E.I.) for the population aged 0-3 years. Because this period of development is so critical, national laws support related educational services before school age for special needs children. I have often treated a preschooler wishing I could have worked with that child sooner. E.I. is a coveted specialty.

During my interview, the program director explained the children were seen either in their homes, or daycare centers. She said, "This agency serves some wealthy areas; but mostly, we serve one of the poorest cities, with one of the highest homicide rates in the country. We offer security for the worst areas. It's a tough caseload. When you carry above ten cases, the pay rate goes up in significant increments until a max of 30 hours."

The director was impressed with my natural, floor time play approach and my former NDT (neurodevelopmental training) certification. She offered me the job by the end of the interview. It was a deep, professional leap. I said yes with mixed emotions of worry and excitement about providing quality therapy. I had faith that I could make a difference as a therapist, especially after nine years of parenting. With the new income, Waldorf was a go!

No court, no judge— I simply told Josh that this was what we were doing. I explained to Connor how this would affect him, and that self-reliance was a tough skill to learn; that is why middle school was hard, but I knew he could do it. Connor was aware that some days I would be next to him, other days not too far behind, letting him grow. Connor held fond memories of his Waldorf preschool experience, i.e., the puppet shows, making homemade bread, and the teacher flooding part of the school yard to sail homemade paper boats. He agreed it was a good school and opportunity for his siblings.

PRIORITY CHILDHOOD

Jolie and Nicky are the sun, and I, Mother Earth, revolving around all their childhood needs. The kids help set up the apartment and it was adorable. We even had a fairyland area made of cedar tree stumps, crystal stones and silk scarves used to create imaginary landscapes of hills and water. The kids made hand-felted woodland creatures from hand spun wool and fairy sized hammocks. Our apartment had tons of books, no TV, and no video games. A string instrument was required for Jolie. She took up the cello, which stood in the corner of the living room.

When traveling between homes, all the VIP stuffed animals

commuted with us: teddy bears, a sock monkey, a polka-dotted elephant, a lion, and a beanie hamster. They loved the adventures too. My kids had the opportunity to meet other children of all colors and races at the new school, as well as in the elevator of our new apartment. We shopped at the local, organic, earthy crunchy store and we made new friends. My kids were learning they could change their environment and be okay. Connor even gave them credit for taking on such change, admitting he might not have fared so well.

When I picked up the kids after school, they immediately started talking about all the stuff they had learned. They went on and on with enthusiasm every single day. They had NEVER done that before. A symbiotic relationship between child development and school philosophy fosters children to blossom in the most natural, loving manner. This is one of the ways to make the world a better place.

CAREER WOMAN

My early intervention job cases constituted the next ten kids on the county's waitlist. The majority of the cases were children with severe medical needs. One of my infant clients had a capped-off trach-tube opening in his throat, a feeding tube and no ears, just nubs without cartilage. Another client, a toddler, could barely use his hands and needed the support of pillows to sit. It was difficult for him to acquire grasping skills when sitting upright took so much effort. Other kids had developmental delays and thirty second attention spans. All that said, I procrastinated in scheduling one particular little boy. I had never encountered anything like what I read on his case sheet.

The specifics of Trey's disabilities had become a blocked-out blur in my memory. I tried to recall them as I parked in front of his family's duplex, a chain link fence surrounding the compact yard. Trey was almost three years old. It was odd to receive a child that old because he would age out in a few months; hence,

I was not sure if he had had any therapy services up until that point. Sometimes delays in services happen.

I put my canvas bag of magic toys down on the concrete stoop of Trey's home and reviewed his case sheet. Trey was unable to walk, talk, or crawl. He was not toilet-trained, nor did he perform any dressing skills. He could not feed himself, but was able to briefly hold a sippy cup. To me, this was all challenging, yet familiar. Trey's data continued in handwriting smushed to the edge of the paper. Trey was deaf, unable to use both hands together, and unable to play with toys due to poor manipulation skills. His limited attention span ranged from two to three seconds, and he exhibited severe and profound deficits with vestibular, tactile, and proprioceptive systems. Profound was written in all caps. Fortunately, Trey was able to swallow.

Indeed. Well, all things considered, I hesitated to knock on the door. *Pep-talk to self 101: Every time you dread a client because a case is complicated, weird, or profound, you stand to make the biggest gains. This is a job for an occupational therapist! Knock on that door. You're specially trained with neuro disorders – get in there and do your best. You'll be out in an hour.*

I could do this; proprioception was my jam. It was probably why I loved to teach yoga. Proprioception is the awareness within muscles of where the body is in space; it's position. A simple test is to ask a patient to close his or her eyes, reposition one arm, and see, if he or she can imitate that exact position with the opposite arm. It's like playing visual Simon Says *do this* with mirroring body parts. If there is a deficit, the client cannot tell if a therapist has positioned his arm up or down, bent or straight. Vision is the compensation. Kinesthesia is slightly different; it is the awareness of movement verses position. Therapists can use "normal-movement" treatment strategies to retrain the brain to interpret information about the location of body parts and joint positions. Other starter treatment approaches involve weight-bearing activities, multi-sensory activities and closed chain movement patterns. This was where weaving in my Neurodevelopmental Training brought out significant outcomes. I knocked with determination.

"Hi, I'm Jessica, Trey's new OT."

"Come on in. I'm his mom, Donna. The physical therapist was here yesterday; they worked in the living room. Trey's in there." She pointed to the only large room in the home. A kitchen was also in view. I figured that the bedrooms must be down the hall.

"I look forward to meeting him."

"If you don't mind, I'll be in the other room doing laundry. Holler if you need anything."

"Sure. It's fine." She walked out of sight into another room. I understood. Quite often, parents were burned out. Even in the smallest of homes, they disappeared just to get a break, get caught up, or have a nap. I didn't judge; I let them clock out of responsibility for a while. There would be time to connect with them later. Besides, I preferred a one-to-one interaction with a child; it helped me get "in the zone".

As I entered, Trey was rolling around on the floor. He paused, sat up for a moment, and then went back to his rapid turn overs. His arms and legs did not react with full extension; he stayed ball-like, ready to roll, even when he stopped. Trey didn't notice me. I looked around the sparse room and saw a light box. Someone else might have thought it was a homemade footstool, but I knew if you pressed the bar, it turned on a bright light. Trey proceeded to roll up to the sofa and stop. He came up to a kneeling position, wavered his head, and then like a transformer, went back to rocking and rolling from wall to wall again. It would appear that my office forgot one small detail: Trey was also blind.

He's blind too! Up to that point in my life, I had never said or thought the following words: *uh, fuck me.*

. . .

TREY'S OT sessions always began with him sitting in my lap. My limbs became an attached shadow to his. The goals were to normalize his movement patterns, build on them, and create forced skill development. In other words, get Trey to use his hands for his own occupation, that of being a child, who needs to play and feed himself for starters. We changed position every minute or so from crossed-leg sitting, to side-sitting while leaning on one arm, to weight-bearing on all fours, then up to kneeling, then back down to all fours... repeating as able. My body provided stability while he became accustomed to holding these positions for longer periods of time. Over the course of my visits, we started to crawl together—me on top of him, my knees pushing his legs forward. This strengthened his muscles and – double action – increased his attention span. When I tried to have him stand, he buckled over at the waist like a dramatic, wilting flower.

After our gross motor neurological warm-ups, it was natural to progress to acquiring some hand control. My arms and hands were figuratively Velcro over his. We played with pop-up toys, and cause-effect toys, as well as we filled/emptied and poured/dumped items into various containers which demanded the use of two hands, all while he sat in my lap. At times, I held his pinky and ring finger down so he had to use a pinch and tripod grasp. His palm arches were flat because he only used a primitive raking grasp. Holding various cups with weight helped to develop his palmar arches and intrinsic hand strength.

Trey started using his finger tips to grab a marble out of a cup. He progressed to holding items with a pincer grasp for three seconds. Once he mastered a five second hold, it was a quick dash to the kitchen with a bundle of boy in my arms. Trey would get plopped into his high chair to work on self-feeding. Bulging from either side of his rib cage were rolled-up dish towels. I used them as lateral supports to keep his trunk upright

.

Sir Trey would not initiate picking up any food and had no

history of feeding himself. He could not see the food nor was accustomed to searching for food with his hands on his plastic landscape. To entice Trey to feed himself, my fingers helped his fingers hold a raisin long enough to reach his mouth, then I let go. His hand naturally came back down without my touch: thank you, gravity. Next, I guided his wrist only halfway up to his mouth and Trey brought it the rest of the way to his lips, but then he had difficulty isolating his fingers to push the raisin all the way into his mouth. This we practiced, and he improved.

We advanced to searching for the food on his tray. If I tickled his index finger with a raisin, his fingers searched for that raisin and pinched it. He began holding the raisin long enough for the tentative journey to reach his mouth. Then, Trey's fingertips heaved the raisin over his lip with slow-motion speed: one, two, three self-fed raisins in a row! I yelled to Donna. She came into the kitchen. Donna watched while bringing a hand to her mouth, then darted away. She was quick to return with a cell phone in her hand.

"Do it again, Trey baby. Come on, baby!"

I tickled Trey's lip with a raisin, then after touching his finger, put the raisin down on the highchair tray. Donna recorded her son's hand as it searched and found a raisin on the tray. Trey used a flat palm to pat the dried fruit, but then remembered he could isolate his finger movements. His index dragged toward his thumb, making a circle to pincer grasp the raisin on the second try. Trey managed to hold that raisin for the tenuous ride up to his mouth. He rested the raisin on his lower lip, and stopped.

"Come on, baby! You can do it." Donna, still recording, looked up to watch her son compete in his own version of the Special Olympics.

"Don't help," I whispered. I held my breath and clenched my hands because I saw the drool; I wanted to push that wrinkly, dried grape into his mouth... He had such trouble with this part. *Come on, man! Get it off your lip before your arm gets tired.* Trey lowered his head a tad, popped the raisin into his mouth, and began to chew.

"My little king!" Donna shouted. She began kissing Trey's head, and hands as well. Phew, that's one way to break a sweat.

As THE FALL months rolled on, navigating the new adjustments became easier and my family made it to a long, relaxing, winter break. My caseload remained challenging; however, I found a therapeutic groove, and a shorter commute to the bridge. Connor was balancing things on his end. For Josh, a private clinic opportunity had come along. Feasibly, he planned to work at the clinic from 5:00 to 7:00 p.m. a few days during the week and a half day on Saturdays. Josh seemed pretty gung-ho about this opportunity. He got my passive "thumbs up" as that was what we did for each other. We seemed to be living out our dreams, but driving in separate lanes.

As a family, we had made a lot of progress by the end of 2010. If this was the worst it got, I thought, we would be more than okay. Life felt predictable, like the tides. Sure, the swells were surprising and sand castles got swept away, but the ocean had become calmer and safer. Maybe I had seen the sign, "Warning: Riptide", but it's not until your legs are swept out from underneath that one can truly realize how powerless you are against the current. Tossing and churning like seaweed in the tide, you become disoriented, and lose sight of the surface. At that moment in time, I felt that the kids and I were safely back on shore. I had done not only what was needed to survive, but also to thrive.

Sweet dreams 2010.

Some people are like clouds. When they disappear, it is a brighter day. - Not So Lao Tzu.

Winter seemed to put Josh in touch with his Icelandic heritage. He bought the family one of the best gifts over the holiday: a freestanding fire pit. Josh was good at telling stories, the perfect talent to show off when gathering around an evening fire. Snowstorms were plentiful that season, which helped Josh develop a talent for snow sculpting with the lawn tools. He carved some amazing life-size sculptures of the following cartoon characters: Sponge-Bob, Patrick the starfish, and the miserable Mr. Crabs. Expanding his creativity, Josh sculpted a hockey player in a cross-check position with a carved snow stick and a Canadiens logo on the jersey. The next morning, all in good fun, a playful neighbor had draped an American flag around his sculpture.

Behind our property in the woods was a small pond, wishfully referred to as a lake. Somehow, Josh maneuvered the John Deere tractor along a quarter mile of trail with the plow attachment and scraped it smooth for ice skating. Other families in town joined us for pick-up hockey games. Our border collie, Willie, made for an energetic mascot, scooting around effortlessly on the ice. His preferred activity was to kangaroo prance through snow drifts, leaving a trail of magical, crystalizing puffs in the air. Indoors, I organized my own version of winter sports.

"COME ON KIDS, let's go dog sledding!" I grabbed Willie's thick and hardly used dog bed and set it atop the staircase – wood banister on one side and plaster wall on the other – creating the perfect luge.

"Mom, no way! Can I go first?" asked Nicky, scrambling up the stairs ahead of his siblings and a barking dog.

"No, I'm the test pilot." Upon sitting on the dog bed, I immediately realized, "Kids, we need more padding at the landing site." Connor loaded the bottom of the stairs with sofa cushions and throw pillows. "All set, Mom!" Connor's face was a beacon of anticipation.

Smiling back at Jolie, Nicky, and a pacing dog, I said, "Count with me – one, two, three!" Whoosh! It's a rapid, bumpy run to the bottom with a flop of a stop.

"I'm next!" Connor yanked the sled out from under me. The commotion had Willie, who rarely made noise, barking and whining. This roused Josh from the TV room.

"What is Willie so upset about?" Joshua took note of the cushion pile, then focused on Willie.

"Watch, Dad!" Jolie yelled. "We're sledding on the stairs!"

"All clear. Go ahead, Connor!" I proclaimed. No sooner said, and Connor sprang off the landing, bobbing down each step with a decent amount of speed. Connor did a dramatic flip, landing into the cushions at the bottom for stuntman effect. Willie chased after Connor and sniffed his face at basecamp.

"Jessica, they are going to break the bannister, or break their skulls," Josh said while Connor scrambled past his feet.

What a buzz-kill. I yelled to the kids, "Don't grab the rails, and don't break your head."

Nicky asked from up top of Stair Mountain: "Connor, can I use your karate helmet?"

"Yea. It's in my—"

"I know where it is!" Nicky disappeared. Jolie did too, into her room.

I started rubbing Willie's ears. "Poor Willie, so worried. He never gets this agitated."

"He's a herd dog. It's in his nature," Josh said, stepping left then right like he did when he was not sure what to do. "They are trained to herd animals. Willie probably thinks one of the kids is escaping."

Gingerly scratching our dog's neck, "Oh Willie, you're such a good flock herder. Hey Connor! Call Willie and hold him while your little brother and sister take a turn."

"If this bannister breaks," said Josh, "you know I'll be the one who has to fix it." Josh's bushy eyebrows looked so cool when they came together as one.

"I'm ready!" shouted Nicky, who was posing with a padded helmet and fists on hips, a real pint-sized Captain America ready for an episodic seizure. Our padded superhero readied himself on the sled.

I turned and said to Josh, "You might want to step away from the blood-bath zone," waving my arms around to depict an enormous amount of predicted carnage.

"Open the front door, Mommy. I'm going to the neighbor's house!"

"Just go, you little scrum-num," Connor said. He gave his brother a push while holding Willie steady. Adhering to Newton's law of physics, Captain Half-Pint's mass did not provide the acceleration he was expecting; he stalled in the middle of the luge.

"Hop on your butt!" Connor yelled. Nicky re-gripped the front corners of the sled, and pulled back, as if using riding reins.

He contracted his body, jolting up and scooting down the next few steps until the momentum gave him a sliding finish into the landing cushions. Josh walked away without saying a word.

Nicky angrily kicked the dog-bed back at the staircase. "That was so lame! How come Connor went down so fast?"

"Because you have a chicken butt," Connor said as he came down the stairs to get the bed sled.

Jolie finally reappeared. She was almost as wide as the staircase. She had tied a pillow to her bottom with a scarf. Serving as a chest protector were two stuffed animals attached with a belt. Jolie had also donned a kerchief and tied it neatly under her chin. If we weren't dog-bed sledding, I would have thought that she was running away, hoping to be adopted by a nice Russian family somewhere in Kazakhstan, probably without brothers. Jolie and Connor took turns sharing a ride with their lightweight brother, doubling the mass so Nicky could get in a good run. Willie was soothed with doggie-biscuits; all was well.

GOODBYE OLD FRIEND

As the snow melted for the last time, we received sad news. A Vietnam veteran friend of Josh's had passed away. Antonio was a motorcycle rider Josh had befriended at a biker bar about a year before. We had all been to Antonio's house a couple of times; he loved to make homemade Italian sauce and let our kids try his paintball guns. Antonio had been so pleased to finally meet me. Privately, he told me: "Josh said you were the devil. I knew he was lying."

I recalled another conversation I had with Antonio.

"I know a lot of guys who drink," Antonio said. "When we get drunk, we blame our wives for everything. Me and the ex-wife haven't talked in years. I came back from Vietnam all messed up. I'm still messed up. I was a heavy drinker then. My new gal, she knows not to try and change me, but I'm upfront about it. I leave my bottle out in the open and I don't get effed

up and drive. Holly trusts me. I want to keep it that way."
Antonio said this to me under the influence of the bourbon
sitting on the counter.

I responded, "I'm glad you and Holly worked something out.
At least you own who you are and you're not breaking promises.
Josh isn't upfront with me. We can't problem-solve anything,
because Josh will not allow a problem to exist. If I get one to
exist, he spins it into a web of something else. It drives me
crazy."

Antonio often talked out the side of his mouth. He said, "I
can spot bullshit and bullshitters. I try tellin' Josh, but he won't
listen. I can see he's gonna to end up like me. Ya know, I don't
see my daughter – haven't seen her in years. I got grandkids I
don't know. It tears me up. Your husband don't listen to me."

"It's nice to hear someone sticking up for me. Thanks,
Antonio."

"To hear doc Josh talk about you, I thought you had horns.
Now that I met you, I get it. He didn't want me to know you're
an angel."

"Well, I don't know about that."

"I ain't shittin' ya, Josh is a big drinker. He drinks more
than most guys at the bar. He's out with me for hours. I'm the
one saying we should get home. It's like he forgets he has a
family. I get you Jess and I get Josh, but I can smell bullshit. I
used to say nasty things about my first wife, but really, I was
the nasty one. Never been right after coming back from
Vietnam."

His wife, Holly, a petite lady at least a decade younger than
Antonio, confided in me a few details that her husband left out,
like that one time he almost choked her to death, and that she
had left him for a while. After the choking incident, Antonio
had started seeing a therapist and got re-involved with VFW
activities. Holly had come back under compromised conditions.
Holly said Antonio was honest about the bare minimum he
needed to drink and that was their compromise: half of that

amount they imbibed together. Holly liked her wine and the occasional lemon cello shot.

Holly also confirmed the poor relationship between Antonio and his daughter; they had been estranged for years. Holly had mentioned that I was the same age as Antonio's daughter, and that might be a part of the gentle liking he had taken to the kids and I. We probably helped fill a familial hole. If time with our family was a small reward for the service Antonio did for his country, it was an honor. The last time we had seen Antonio had been to eat his homemade lasagna.

Josh's visits with Antonio gradually faded away. He said Antonio was getting into fights at bars. I questioned this because who would mess with an old guy wearing a Vietnam cap? Then Josh clarified they were not fights, but rather moments of Antonio's high agitation with everyone. This eventually led Josh to feeling uncomfortable hanging out with him.

Sad news soon followed. Josh said he found out from other riders that Antonio had died of brain cancer. He was not sure when the funeral had been because the riders were only acquaintances; no one had called him. Our kids were very sad and tearful to hear about Antonio's passing. I felt somehow that Josh should have been at his funeral. Maybe we all should have been there.

ADRENALINE RISING

The yard showed signs of spring with crocuses and the tips of hyacinthine poking through the mulch. On a daily basis, Josh was coming home a little earlier from work which meant he started his habitual drinking routine earlier in the day. It was still too cold to ride a motorcycle, hence Josh only had his introverted hobbies, such as reading, playing his guitars, or watching late TV to keep him occupied. Boredom has been documented as a key factor with addictions. There was no reversing the effects of alcoholism under these conditions. The monkey on his back was growing into an ape.

Usually, it was hard to tell if Josh drank a lot because his baseline demeanor stayed relatively unchanged. These days it was more obvious in the evening as he appeared either *punch drunk*, or clearly not in the present moment. His tall tales were taller, his temper snappier, and his behavior could range from childish to elitist. It was all easy enough to ignore until his behaviors seeped into my parenting territory. He was crossing the line when I tried to get the kids to bed.

We had one TV, so at night, the kids often watched with their dad. When I would come into the room announcing it was time for bed, Josh would continue watching as if I wasn't there. I'd give it a while, but still, he did not turn off the TV or even mute it. "You don't have to listen to Mom," he would say. Then I would get snappy, and the kids would come.

In private discussions, I pointed out that he was making me the bad cop and himself the good cop, which in turn, made my job harder. I suggested alternative phrases he could say such as, "Kids, we need a good night's sleep." or "Staying up late doesn't help us wake-up for school." But his replacement phrase in real time was, "You better do it, or Mom will get mad."

Josh said I was asking him to fix problems that I had created; I should have listened to his advice in the first place. At times, Josh did suggest good advice from theorists' books he had read. Other times, he said that giving kids rules amounted to trying to control them. According to him, if our kids respected me in the first place, they would listen, and I would not have any problems.

I suggested, or rather confronted Josh with the possibility that he was unable to handle setting boundaries. He replied with angst, "It would ruin my relationships with the kids." Clearly, this part of parenting was above his pay grade. I asked him if having a child look both ways before crossing the street or expecting he brush his teeth, were signs of a controlling parent, or a caring parent?

"I see where you are going with this," Josh had said. "There are things that keep a child safe and healthy and probably prevent them from becoming a societal mess, which would happily put me out of a job. I'd be thrilled for all kids to grow up loved and cared about."

"That's the goal, Josh. I'm not at my best all frustrated in a game of us playing against one another."

"I know, I know, you really are great with the kids. You are amazing with them. You keep track of so many things. If I tried to jump in and start making rules, I would be like some ogre," Josh confided.

Despite our somewhat fruitful parenting conversations, it happened again. One particular evening, as the screen faded to black, Josh wrapped his arms tighter around Jolie and Nicky. The kids responded by blowing me off, and hugging their dad back; a real loving, screw-you-Mom moment. An empty wine glass rested on the table.

Turning my frustration into an adrenaline rush, I went behind the full-length couch, grabbed the bottom frame, and flipped the entire sofa containing my family up on its front end. The kids and Josh were dumped onto the floor, spilling over each other in a heap of shocked faces. I eased the empty sofa back down to the carpet. The kids belly laughed while getting to their feet. Josh could not help but smile. At that moment, it was a breeze to pleasantly usher my bumpkins up to bed, instead of turning into a raging witch. Meanwhile, their dad remained in a stupor, devoid of any alpha energy to lead our pack. He had nothing to say. Addiction ate his personality like a cancer. He had resources and a wife, but as sure as this disease left him no choice, he had obviously made one.

GET HERE SCHOOL FINISH LINE

The spring semester at Waldorf went smoothly for Jolie, Nicky, and myself. Contrary to our positive experiences, Connor complained about being alone so often. His junior high friend-ships were shifting, he was no longer invited to the same homes, and a best friend had changed schools. Connor had fewer places for escape, and was finally missing us. His grades began to slip, particularly in math. Connor swore that his math teacher was awful at teaching. I asked to see his textbook so we could check his homework and read over his lessons. I explained, "It may take a few reads to fully comprehend the subject matter. You might need to look over your book every night."

"Mom, we don't use textbooks. Everything is on a smart-board," my son was quick to add. "And don't talk to my teacher! You'll make it worse!"

Naturally, I talked to his teacher on the down-low. There's more than one side to every story. I like to assume teachers care and that they are willing to do their part. Also, I believe parents have to help solve the problem, not just advocate on behalf of their children while blaming the school. After speaking with Connor's math teacher, I learned specifics regarding where Connor was not keeping up with the rest of the class, and where he needed to make extra effort, i.e., completing homework assignments. I informed Connor that I had spoken with his teacher, and that we both cared about him doing well. We concluded there was at least something each one of us could do. Connor, with hesitancy, said he appreciated the efforts.

His teacher gave us an old textbook, which proved useful once I taught Connor how to use it as a resource. Math and English teachers were available in after-school study halls to assist students with their homework, plus a late bus ride home was available. Despite his protests, I had Connor attend those classes twice a week. Perhaps he feared asking for help, or more plainly, he preferred to go home and play video games. What-ever the reason, too bad. I privately requested that his math teacher reach out to meet Connor half way because he was too shy, and he did not want her taking time away from the class to explain something to him. She was very agreeable to this plan and to fostering a more comfortable communication between them.

In a couple of weeks, Connor was understanding the math, and keeping up with the class. Josh was not privy to any of this which was the norm. But since missing homework was a contributing factor, I asked Josh to make sure Connor was doing his homework – his math in particular – on the few days I was not at home. Josh was very agreeable, and mentioned that he had helped Connor with his math in the past. I knew this to be true because Connor mentioned that his dad's help had been confusing and quite frankly, had contributed to many incorrect homework answers.

I MAINTAINED my mental health as a priority and continued therapy sessions once a month. Every so often, I also attended a Twelve Step meeting and read Al-Anon literature, learning a little too late that the things I did to stop my husband from drinking—fun times involving emptying bottles down the sink, adding water to his bottles, or smackdown confrontations—were never going to succeed. One time, I had pretended to chug half a bottle of vodka right in front of Josh. Secretly, I had already switched the contents to water. He protectively screamed at me to not drink it and harm myself. Those actions only forced another promise to quit; a promise that would and did fail since there was no support system in place.

My boundaries were gradually getting firmer. I was not intimate with Josh and had not been for a long time. Dr. Rachel informed me that engaging in sexual relations would send mixed signals, and worse, be "misleading". She had probably wanted me to start somewhere with setting boundaries. Sex would be seen as an act of giving myself away. As with any man, I turned away advances in a non-harmful, polite manner. Not sure if this was the best way to handle sexual advances, but it was not a skill someone taught me how to do any better.

Unfortunately, Josh's behavior escalated one weekend over Connor's math grade. Josh happened to see the kids' report cards on my desk. He had never asked about them in the past, and I was not hiding them. Anyway, my husband saw Connor's report card on my desk and came at me, completely red-faced, asking why Connor had received a "D" in math, and if I had known about it.

Calmly, I confirmed my knowledge of his grade and added "not to worry" – it was already being handled by the teacher. Josh started hurling insults about the math teacher, whom he had never met, and then insulted me. He went on and on in a quick rant, ending with the question, "What are *we* going to do about this?"

Claiming my territory, I first informed Josh that we had recently obtained a textbook from his teacher and that I had taught Connor how to utilize it. Next, while Josh hard stared at me, I mentioned that whenever Connor found math confusing, he was expected to go to an after-school study hall with a math teacher for assistance. Finally, I explained how his teacher was initiating more communication with Connor, both to put him at ease about seeking help, and to make sure he felt cared about as a student. The "D" had already been in place when these measures were rolled out.

The logic train had come and gone. My man could have boarded that train, but instead he opted to take the loco-moco ride. No doubt in my mind, Connor's "D" made Joshua look bad to an imaginary audience of millions. Josh's thick blonde hair became prominent against angry skin as he blurted: "I have seen "their math" helping Connor with his homework – it's ridiculous! Who teaches math like that?" His irate eyebrows became two albino caterpillars head-butting one another. "Either this teacher is stupid, or our son is stupid. Which one is it?"

Only my lips moved. "The answer, Josh, is that neither one is stupid. I have seen the homework papers you helped with, and they were incorrect. It contributed to confusing Connor. You usually help him after you've been drinking which – doesn't – really – work."

"Are you trying to tell me this is my fault?"

"I am telling you that Connor is not a stupid child. Algebra is a struggle; we have solutions in place. Connor got an 88 on his last test, not that it crosses your mind to ask. Your disinterest and intoxication do not help his math. But rest assured, Connor's grade is improving, if that's what you actually care about." I returned to my magazine, and began to ignore him.

Josh stormed out of the living room and into the adjourning TV room, slamming the slender French doors. My magazine sentences blurred into crinkles created by my hands fisting the page. My chest started to pound. I sipped some mint iced tea. *When the stone skips the pond, let the ripples go.* Josh returned, crossing the room towards me in an instant. He grabbed two fists full of my sweatshirt and stood me up from my chair. Then he swung me over and up against a wall. The cup was still in my hand.

"You like messing with me. You know I can't physically hurt you, but I can financially hurt you."

"Let go, Josh."

"Do you know how fucked up you are? Do you? How does that feel to know how fucked up you are?"

"It makes me feel like splashing this drink in your face," which was inches from mine.

"You splash that drink on me, and I am punching you in the face."

Neither of us moved a muscle. Our poker hands were on the table.

From behind his clenched jaw came out: "You are so beneath me. You are like a slug between my toes." He released my shirt and walked away, storming out the front door and down the street. I could see him through the window, receding out of view.

My thoughts were racing. *Do not ignore this. Do not ignore this. Do something. I cannot ignore this.*

This was all I repeated over and over and over until something that made sense punched through my head. I dashed upstairs...*need a plan...need a plan...*and peeked in on each child sleeping soundly. *Make a plan...make a plan...* I washed my face and hands... *Do not do nothing...do not do nothing.*

Going into Jolie's room, I sat on the floor at the foot of her bed, settled into a lotus pose, and took in her magical, innocent world. Her dress-up dolls were in baskets. Her Rainbow Ponies were lined up by a castle. Her favorite Beanie puppy and kitten were clothed in dresses and bonnets. Everything she owned was meticulously cared for sending me a reflective message to care about myself, my family, and to assess if Josh was a danger to us.

Immersing my mind into a meditative state, I became grounded, letting emotions run their course. I gave no attention to them—only observed the emotions like rising bubbles that eventually popped at the surface, clearing my mind of thoughts so new ones could emerge. Staying in the present moment meant latching on to the freshest idea that moved me forward onto the next thing. This took effort, but I did it. When I felt centered, I stepped outside of Jolie's room.

Jolie's door was at the end of a short hall and faced the entire second floor. Closing her bedroom door behind me, I sat right down like a little yogi. On my right side was a full view of both Nicky's door, and next to it, Connor's. In front of me, but off to my left side was the top of the stairs, and to the left of that, the master bedroom. Here I sat in the dark, waiting and observing.

It wasn't long before I heard Josh come home and move about downstairs. I did not hear the usual pouring of wine in a glass, nor bottles tapping back down on the counter. Perhaps he was looking for me. I heard him walk up the steps, more slowly than usual. Reaching the top, he did not see me, and he turned into the master bedroom. The light went on, there was a pause, and the light went off. Josh came back out into the hall and passed me as he headed towards the attic. Then, he stopped in his tracks, and turned his moccasin slippers in my direction. His slippers headed toward me, the knees of his jeans bent down, and I heard a harmless sigh. Josh squatted to my level and said, "Hey kiddo, what are you doing?"

"I'm contemplating."

"Contemplating, hmm." He sat on the floorboards, crossing his legs like mine. "That is actually a good idea. I think I did some of that walking around outside. I needed to get outside. I felt pent-up inside. I feel trapped when I feel pent-up."

"Uh-huh."

Josh appeared to take a moment to assess me further and then said, "I'm sorry I was rough with you. I overreacted. I way overreacted. You were handling things well with Connor. More than that, you were doing all the right things and I glossed over it and got upset. I am sorry. I know you may not believe me, but I am."

His parroting psychology statements merely beaded off my psyche. My next step would not involve Josh; I did not need his permission. I did not want this situation to blow up in my face, nor for Josh to think I was taking him down and lose the ability to function. My husband could only keep his own ducks in a row.

"Obviously, I want some distance from you right now. I only want everyone to be okay: you okay, me okay, the kids okay."

Josh put up two open hands. "That's all I want too, I swear. I want everyone okay." His hands moved to resting on his knees.

"Then we're good. Let's call it a night. I will sleep with one of the kids."

Josh breathed a relieved sigh. "Okay. I'm tired. How about I make French toast in the morning? The kids seem to like that. And I can make homemade bread for supper tomorrow."

"I want tomorrow to come too, Josh. French toast sounds good. How about you make the dinner that goes with the bread?"

This made him smile, as intended. "Okay, I will make dinner

as well. Happy to." He stood up, waved goodnight, and went into the master bedroom. I heard him flop on the bed. I went into the middle room and kissed Nicky's hair about ten times. Then, I lay next to him and waited. For about an hour, I lay in wait before hearing Josh snore. I exited the house. To avoid any chance of being heard or noticed, I rode my bike at one o'clock in the morning to the police station.

ONCE THERE, outside the entrance was a special phone to call the dispatcher, who sent an on-duty policeman to meet me at the station. The older, broadly built officer who arrived asked me to give a brief rundown of what happened. In short detail, I explained Josh's threat to punch me in the face, and that he had physically grabbed me. The officer asked if I wanted a restraining order. I responded with a request. "Please explain exactly each step, if I do that."

The officer explained that first I would need to write a statement; next he would call a judge, right then, in the middle of the night. The judge would talk to me and determine if the situation was threatening enough to issue a temporary restraining order. If yes, the police would immediately go visit my husband and provide him the following choice: either leave voluntarily, or be removed from the house. My husband would not be allowed to return until after a decision was made at a hearing, which would be scheduled within a week's timeframe. The hearing was where a temporary restraining order had the opportunity to become a permanent restraining order.

Was I ready for all that? Starting today? Wanting to explore all options I asked, "What about making a record of this event? Something indicating this behavior is going on in my home?"

"Ma'am, there really is no record. If you think he is going to harm you or your family tonight, then you can request a restraining order. The judge will talk to you over the phone." The officer was in a firm state of neutrality and he certainly was not offering a therapy session. "What is your husband doing right now?"

"I believe he is sleeping."

"Do you feel like you can go back home? Your kids are there, right?"

"Yes, I feel like I can go back home. I need to make some progress here. Is there some way to record there was an incident, that I felt I needed to come here?" A momentary hesitation came and went.

"You could make a statement."

"I can make a statement of what happened, and it would be on record, here in the department?"

"Yes. It would be an incident report, kept on file."

Uh-huh. Good thing I persisted. "Then I would like to make a statement, please." *Sorry to make you do paperwork. I need to show I am not crazy.*

We went inside; I wrote out my statement with a shaky hand. It was not until the officer read my statement and got to the very bottom where I ended with Josh calling me a *slug between his toes* that he softened in his demeanor, just enough, that I felt he considered me a victim – someone who was perhaps in over her head, and might need protection. He said that all the reports were reviewed the next day. "The team will be aware."

"Thank you, officer. Have good night."

I rode my bike home and finished the night sleeping next to Connor, up on his top bunk bed. The next day, we all had French toast as promised for breakfast, and a delicious Mediterranean supper of curried chicken with roasted chick peas and tomato, homemade Naan bread, and cucumber-feta salad with fresh basil from the garden.

What we think, we become - Buddha

DUCKS IN A ROW

Forget the lawyers. Forget the mediators. My black leather clogs swanked across the courthouse threshold where Josh's case had been heard two years previous. "Second floor Miss," said the security guard. Past many conference rooms was a small office that contained the holy grail. The clerk was a middle-aged, black woman.

"Hi. My name is Jessica. I believe this is where is can get divorce papers to copy...papers that I fill out, and file myself."

"You sure can. It's the white ring binder over there on the desk behind you. The photocopy machine is down the hall – ten cents a copy. Feel free to look it over here in the office, but if you take it down the hall, I need you to leave your driver's license." She talked as commonly as if listing the side dishes at a drive-thru.

Stunned by the simplicity, I turned around and approached the desk. Sure enough, there was a beat-up, dirty white binder with the title: "Motion for Divorce". Opening the well perused binder, I found seventeen pages individually placed in plastic sleeves. The first few pages were instructions on how to file. This was what everyone feared... All the angst and fighting and thousands of dollars for this? Most of the motion involved filling in the blanks. How I pitied our society.

"Excuse me, do people frequently come here to photocopy – or uh – to file themselves, without a lawyer?"

She answered while looking over the rim of her glasses. "They sure do."

I was still reeling in shock. "It's a thin book. There are instructions that spell out how to file the motion. It's not written in some kind of legal mumbo-jumbo."

She moved her glasses to the end of her nose. "Once you turn this into the first-floor clerk, it starts the clock ticking. In that same binder is the timetable and all the instructions to follow as well. Those deadlines are important. You might want a separate calendar."

"About how many people come by a day to do this?"

"It varies. In a week, I would say sometimes fifteen to twenty people."

"Wow! Can I ask you something else?"

"As long as you ain't asking legal advice."

"Oh, no. On the papers where it asks for the reason for the divorce: do people ever put 'Emotional Abuse'? I had a lawyer swear she doesn't know anyone who uses that."

Without hesitation she said, "Folks put that reason down all – the – time."

BACK HOME, I scrutinized the forms, highlighting the timetable of submittals and mailing specifications, usually it was by certified mail. The most difficult aspect was the case information sheet, the CIS. It was a compilation of everything financial, and the value of every piece of crap you both owned. Every dollar spent must be accounted for and placed in some category. Alas, I realized we did not have a strong handle on the monies a comin' and a goin'. First order of business: make a copy of everything we owned including the car, the motorcycle, and the retirement accounts. I could not count on my husband ever filling out this sheet. Fortunately, we were both organized; Josh more so. Our receipts, bills, statements, etc. were all kept in appropriate files.

Diving into those files, I photocopied everything from paycheck stubs to credit card summaries. The credit card summaries listed how often and how much Josh spent on alcohol; it wasn't pretty. Any receipts that substantiated his drinking went into a unique personal file...nothing less than full custody. I fully believed that after a private conversation with Josh regarding my rationale for custody, he would sign off on that particular dotted line. Besides, he realized I did right by the kids and he was best behind the scenes—a self-description he had coined. All divorce files were kept either in my car or my dad's house.

———

JOSH GOT one paycheck from his second job and spontaneously came home with a brand new 2011 Toyota FJ jeep cruiser with four doors and built to haul. It was all white and huge...as if an Eskimo had squatted an igloo on our driveway. Josh had traded in his paid-off, old Jeep Cherokee and signed up for five years of car payments. He already had a Harley motorcycle – his second trade up – and a treasured old, TR-6 convertible which somehow managed to pass inspection; he was very into vehicles and enjoyed tinkering with them. Guess my husband was going to get himself whatever he wanted before the divorce. More equity for his side. Thankfully my mom raised me to be independent; hence, Josh and I had separate credit cards. If we hadn't, I would have cancelled them. We also had separate bank accounts. It was nice that we were not up each other's butt about spending habits; we valued our autonomy.

MILLION DOLLAR DATE

Never ever had I met a millionaire. This particular millionaire had so many *buckaroos*, he loaned money to banks. Yeah...I know. Buck had many successful real estate deals that led to more wealth-earning investments. Buck enjoyed collecting, among other things, handmade glass art sculptures by a local artist. My dear friend, Mike, collaborated with Buck to create an elaborate photo book about the collection, and the artistic labor process behind it. This was an incredible client to have on board. Mike, Kate, and I chatted about him on occasion because it was all very interesting.

Buck made rare visits to John's backyard photography studio

to discuss pending photographs of the detailed, hand-blown glass orbs. One day, while Buck was visiting, my kids happened to be there playing. Mike invited me over to meet Buck for nothing more than my lame, star-struck curiosity. Briefly, Jolie, Nicky and I made small talk with the millionaire in Mike's studio. My kids politely shook his hand, made eye contact and thoroughly answered his get-to-know-you better questions. My chat with Buck included a laugh or two before I left, never expecting to see him again. Buck was nice enough; however, he was not overly attractive to me, and I had heard Mike describe him as difficult to work with. But hey, I guess some arrogance comes with climbing the corporate ladder and then buying said ladder.

A couple of weeks later, Mike passed on a message from Mr. Buckaroos. "He thinks you're hot and he asked if you were single. I explained you recently separated from your husband and that I believed it was dissolving into a divorce. Anyway, he is going to a charity event and wants to know if you would be his guest."

He was asking me out? "Whoa! I have never been asked out by a millionaire before."

My friend laughed. "Yeah, that doesn't happen every day. This event is $400 a plate. It's next week. He probably expects an answer soon."

"Shut the barn door! Four hundred dollars! On me? One date. That's crazy!"

"He's paying for me, too. I don't know how I feel about you two going on a date, not that it matters. It's really up to you, Jessica. I don't have any advice for you."

"Let me sit with it for a while. I'll call you back tonight."

"Okay, Jess. Talk to you later."

It is amazing how you can instantaneously picture your life going in a totally different direction. I was already on a yacht, sailing the ocean, with my kids running around the deck asking who could take the next turn on the water skis. Imaginary trades-offs flashed in my mind: the sacrifices of a one-way, romantic chemistry, and being of servitude to this rumored-to-be demanding man in exchange for a totally upgraded lifestyle: travels, college education for the kids... Would I even continue working? It already felt like a sell out to my future self, not to mention giving the gift of inauthenticity to my new suitor. I did not want a business deal as a personal relationship, even though trades and negotiations were par for the course.

On the other hand, was I really giving this polite, decent looking man a chance? He had made a generous offer for us to get to know one another at a colorful event, and we would have the ice breaking companionship of Mike. Was Buck not worth one date to get to know him better? Buck thought I was worth it. Dramatic thoughts aside, I assumed we would enjoy our evening – me being "the hot woman" on his arm, a phrase I cannot say with a straight face, though I appreciated the compliment.

It was one evening, yet, I was still married, still somebody's wife, and a role-modeling parent. I was these roles and these roles were me. I remember thinking, *I cannot be a savior if I am looking to be saved. Am I not more than a woman looking to be saved? Can I not see that I am more than my situation?*

My evening call to Mike was straight to the point. "Please thanks him for the generous invitation and tell him I am very flattered; however, I must decline. In all fairness, I am not in a position to invest in dating, and I think it will be a while before I am." My friend seemed relieved at my decision.

If I wanted a million dollars, then I would have to make my own.

RESTRAINING ORDER

The kids were on spring break, bringing us all together in the same house for the week. It was a welcome hiatus from commuting back and forth to the Waldorf school. Only seven weeks to go and private school would be done. Connor was due to finish junior high a couple of weeks after Waldorf. Connor's grades were up and his spirits were too. He was definitely appreciating his siblings more. This was good, because he seemed to have too much power in terms of making or breaking the mood for the rest of us. Over the school break, Connor arranged a sleepover at a new friend's house in a different town: a nice kid— I had already met his mom. Thus, Connor would keep his track record for not being home during another unexpected incident, one in which Josh played Jolie against me.

AS USUAL JOLIE, Nicky, and Josh were watching TV in the family room after a late dinner. Jolie was asked to put the dinner dishes from the sink into the dishwasher. As I walked around doing household chores, I noticed she had not done this task prior to watching the TV. I ventured to the sofa to discuss this with her. Jolie half looked at me and half looked at the tube. We came to an agreement: when the show ended in ten minutes, she would finish the clean-up task, then get ready for bed. Josh ignored me. Nicky pulled a blanket up to his chest. It was not worth turning up the heat to demand Jolie respond that exact moment; I understood she was easily lured into watching television with her family.

Jolie's allotted ten minutes passed. She remained in the TV room, waiting for the next show. I approached the sofa. Josh held out the remote, actively channel surfing. Jolie looked at me, made an *Oh no* expression, and turned to bury her face into more of a snuggle with her dad. As usual, Josh acted like I was not there. He continued to change the channels, and with mild jovialness whispered to Jolie: "You do not have to listen to Mom."

Moving my stance to where it blocked the remote signal, I looked directly at Josh, then locked my Irish eyes with Jolie's Nordic eyes. I held up one finger. Waited. Held up two fingers.

Waited...not blinking. The final finger went up as did my reluctant, quasi-obedient daughter. We had a One-Two-Three Rule in the house that was used for rare necessities, such as when I needed the kids to get out of a pool, or leave a birthday party. While other parents screamed at their children, I held up fingers. It worked because the consequence of failing to respond was cleaning out a trash can; a gross task that was over quickly and turned everyone's emotions around to focus on a job well done, and then move us onward without judgements, shame, or ridiculous impulsive punishments. Conner washed out a kitchen trash can once, then hated getting to two fingers. Jolie ended up cleaning every inside trash can and one outside trash can the day she tested that rule, but then it had worked every time since. Nicky only needed to watch his older siblings to be on board.

"Nicolas, get your pajamas on," I sternly laid out to my son.

"Yes, Mom!" Nicholas was gone. I walked out in silence and met Jolie in the kitchen.

"Let me tell you Jolie, the little game of acting like Mom's not there when I am standing right in front of you is NOT gonna fly. And just because your dad's behavior sinks to that level, does not mean yours should. I expect you to know better."

"Yes, Mom."

"And why, Jolie? Over dirty dishes in the sink from a meal I made for you? Is that worth it?"

"No, Mom."

"You can clean out the kitchen trash can to remember that it's not worth lowering your behavior just because the person next to you goes low." I knelt down and said with sincere softness: "You're a good kid, sweetie, and I'm a good mom."

Jolie wrapped her arms around my neck. "I'm sorry, Momma. I'm really sorry. Daddy says I don't have to listen to you."

"I know he does. But is that what your life needs? Not to listen to anything I say?"

Jolie grins. "No-o-o."

"Good," returning the hug. "Off ya go." Jolie tended to her duties.

Storming back into the TV room, I crouched down to where Josh's head leaned against the armrest. Whispering through clenched teeth I said, "Perhaps you'll be even more satisfied to know that Jolie gets to clean out a trash can because I expect her to behave better than you. I know you think that glass of wine on the table isn't hurting anyone; same for the vodka you're tapping behind the speaker—the bottle you think I don't know about. It all has consequences that everyone else pays for, even when you think it doesn't. Our little girl is paying for it right now." I exited the room. This facade that none of his behavior affected anyone else in the family pissed me off!

I fully expected Josh to mentally ferment about what had I said, and then go back to the TV. I did not want an argument; I did want to jam down his throat how his behavior affected us... and swallow. I was going nuts trying to understand and empathize with his nuts. In fact, my latest hobby was reading clinical books about alcoholism, narcissism, dissociative identity disorder, depression, anxiety disorder, and the effects of child abuse on the developing personality. Any one of those was challenging... A dual diagnosis was not a good time, not that I was trained to formally make one.

Occupational therapists are trained to combine physical, mental, social, developmental and behavioral theories with therapeutic strategies to improve functional daily living skills. Active addicts seem to have limited awareness that they are tied to a train wreck about to happen. That is why only a complete surrender will do. Zero usage. Nada. A well-intended, half-ass surrender earns next to nothing, as told to me by recovered addicts who completely stopped "using". They know the urges will come, so they are proactive about temptation, and attend meetings. Soul-soothing to me was listening to those, who had crossed over into recovery, talk about the positive trajectory their lives had taken. A recovered person sounded whole, sometimes more whole than those of us who never became addicted in the first place.

Jolie was in the kitchen, ungrudgingly cleaning a trash can. I had gone upstairs to check that Nicky was brushing his teeth. Upon visual confirmation of Nicky's stellar oral hygiene, I returned downstairs, fully anticipating giving Jolie a hug for a job well done; however, she was not in the kitchen. *Huh.* She was no where in the room.

Jolie suddenly appeared from the back door panic stricken. "Mom! Mom! Dad is freaking out!" Her eyes were wet; she grabbed my arm. "Dad came in here and grabbed the trash can out of my hand. He threw it outside. He's out there, kicking the trash can all over the yard. He's cursing and yelling and saying the F-word!"

"Okay, Jolie, okay. I'm sorry he scared you," giving her a hug. "Where is he now?"

Jolie's sky-blue eyes were wide and damp. "He's still out there, calling you names." Nicky came in wearing Batman pajamas.

"Jolie, what's wrong?" Nicholas reached out both arms to console his sister.

"Dad is attacking the trash can! He is really mad!" They held each other.

The backdoor opened, then slammed shut. Josh stormed in, seething mad. "Ahh!" Jolie screamed. I placed her and Nicky behind me.

"Why is our daughter cleaning a trash can! Are you sick?" Josh panted from a few feet away. His red and yellow eyes were held in sockets dry as gourds. Nicky started to cry.

"Josh, you're scaring the kids."

He took a step towards me. "I don't care," his jaw barely moving.

"They care, and they don't like it. We can talk outside." I kept still. My voice was steady, almost monotone.

"I don't care. They're going to see this."

I turned to the kids, who were still hugging one another. "Please go to another room. I will be right there."

Jolie rushed with Nicky down the hall, and out of sight. Josh stood there, seething. "Why is she cleaning a trash can?"

"It's part of the consequence system from THE 1-2-3 MAGIC book. A parent makes up a consequence that can be carried out effectively and suits the age of the child. It helps make expectations clear. It's the book you recommended to me and you recommend to your clients, but obviously never read. Too bad—it's quite helpful. I highly recommend it."

"You like to bring up my drinking every chance you get! You just love to embarrass me!"

"I don't try to bring it up. It's always there." Josh took a step towards me and I stepped back.

"You just love," clenching his hands, "to control me!" He kept walking towards me, forcing me to back away and put the kitchen table between us. The table was good, but it sat in a nook. I had just boxed myself into a corner.

"I want to raise our children—Jolie, Connor, and Nicky—in a safe home. Right now, you are scaring them." Mentioning the names of our children might de-escalate him.

Across the black lacquer table, Josh was pacing from side to side. "Do you know how bad I want to punch you in the face, and then leave? Just walk out of here?"

"That's nice. Anything else?" Because that's all I needed: a serious threat of harm.

"Do you know how crazy you are! You can't cook; you can't clean. You're fake! Everything about you is fake."

"I'm leaving now." I started to leave. He stepped left; I reassessed, and went right. He stepped right as well.

"I am leaving now, Josh. Are you going to let me?" I asked him this because he had a choice, his own life choice. *What's it all worth, Josh?* My husband said nothing; his behavior did not escalate. My only defense was that he knows I will absolutely tell; I will not keep quiet. I am not like his mother.

I strode forward. He did not move. I had to turn sideways to squeeze by him, leaving an inch between us. He did not flinch. Keeping my still attached head up, I grabbed both purse and keys from my office alcove and continued down the hall to the base of the stairs, calling for the kids. Josh followed like a shadow.

"Where do you think you're going?" he asked from behind me.

"I do not feel comfortable staying here." I searched for the kids while ignoring him. "Jolie! Nicholas!" I yelled. No answer. I avoided eye contact with Josh, and calmly addressed his concerns. I could feel that the kids were near, so I didn't go upstairs quite yet. I rechecked the living room, noticing one end of the sofa was pulled out. *Aha.* Trying to hide, Jolie and Nicky were lying longways between the furniture and the wall. I quickly pushed the sofa out and bent down. "Come on, guys. We're leaving." They looked at me, but they did not move.

"Now! We are leaving now!" The kids stood up. I heard Josh ask, "Where are you going?"

"I am either going to my dad's, or a friend's house. Neither is far away." The kids were up and I had an arm around each of them.

"You are not taking the kids!"

"You do not get to make decisions when you scare them." I headed towards the front door. Josh quickened his steps.

"Mom, we don't want to go!" they pleaded from a huddled standstill at the base of the steps, three feet from the door. I stopped two feet from the door. Josh planted himself in front of the door and barked: "You are not taking them."

Is someone friggin' kidding me right now? I'm jackknifed by scared-to-death kids on one side, and a psycho-ass spouse on the other, and they're all on the same team! I downed that shit like a shot of Don Julio tequila, barely noticing the worm.

There was an ace in my hand and I was laying it down: I bet everything on Josh not wanting to physically harm me. The prospect of jail time had already been too real. I extended an arm to reach for the door handle. Josh stepped out of the way, clearly avoiding an act of "blocking or touching me". Opening the door with my back turned against him, I locked my feet into position, and kept hold of the door handle. Laser focused on Jolie's confused eyes, I stated: "Get - in - the - car." My other arm reached out towards her creating a guard rail between Josh and the passage to leave. Jolie hesitated, then shuffled out into the night. Neither Josh, nor Nicky moved.

Wiggling my fingers—I couldn't quite reach him, "Nicky, it's okay. Please get in the car."

"I don't want to go." He was incredibly sad.

"Nicky, it is not safe here. Get in the car."

"I don't want to leave." His superhero pajamas were the only thing holding him up.

The more fucking sad he got, the more fucking stoic I became, so that we could all get the fuck out of there in one fucking piece. "Boo, you can either walk out this door, or I will carry you out." My one hand was gripping the door as if it was a poltergeist exit. My other hand strained within inches of reaching my son.

Nicky's head sunk down as his shoulders and torso pulled into gravity. Molten legs carried my little Batman past me of his own accord. Joshua grabbed the top of the door, preventing me from closing it as I followed Nicky's back. As I navigated the front steps, I clicked the remote, unlocking the car doors. Jolie got into the back seat. I corralled Nicky with my body until he was also inside, next to Jolie. I closed the door, and remote locked the doors. Josh's hovering footsteps were near. "You are not taking the kids!"

I faked going around the trunk towards the driver's side. As he whipped past in an effort to block me, I backtracked from the trunk area to the back-passenger door where Nicky had gotten in. Grabbing the door handle, I clicked the remote to unlock the doors, pulled the handle, and immediately clicked and re-locked the doors before entering the car. Josh tried to open the driver's side door, but he was too late. I snaked inside the back of the car, closed the door behind me, and vaulted over the console into the driver's seat. Like a crack of thunder, Josh pounded his fist on the driver's side window. The kids screamed; my hand trembled while making multiple attempts to line up the key into the ignition. Josh pounded more windows. *Bam!* He smacked at the back window. The key turned over starting the engine.

"Daddy's on the roof! He's on the car," they yelled. Turning to the back seat I saw the kids clutching each other. Jolie cried out, "Mom! He's up there! What are you going to do?"

With a slight nod: "I am going to drive my car."

Calm down. Headlights on: check. R is for reverse: check. Pedal under right foot: check. Push pedal, make go: check.

I backed the Nissan Pathfinder out of the driveway nice and slow. *Bam! Bam! Bam! Bam-bam-bam! Fists pounding on the roof, scaring me: check.*

Gently, I backed the car onto the street. The road was all clear at that time of night.

"Mom! You can't keep driving!"

"Mom! He's on the roof!"

"Mom-m-m, Dad's still on the roof!"

Kids screaming: check. D is for drive: check. I started driving down the street at five miles an hour. My grounding focus was going from streetlight to streetlight. Josh stopped pounding on the roof, perhaps to grab hold of the roof racks, which would explain how he was able to kick away at the passenger side mirror. The police station was eight blocks further down the street, though may as well have been eighty at our ridiculously slow speed. Josh kept trying to punt the passenger side mirror until it finally gave way, dangling limply like a flag without wind.

My side mirror was hit next. Shoe-to-mirror, shoe-to-mirror... I swerved the car. The shoe stopped for a moment. Then, the shoe forcefully returned, stomping relentlessly at the driver's side mirror which somehow didn't give way. Grabbing my cell phone, I dialed 9-1-1.

"Kids, it is going to be fine. Please stop screaming. I have to talk to the police. I will keep going slow, so I don't hurt him."

"Why is he doing this?" the kids yelled. A fist pounded on the roof above our heads, *Bam! Bam! Bam!*

On the phone, I confirmed with the dispatcher: "Yes, I need the police." The police station was approaching, five blocks to go. It was likely no one would be there, but even the sight of police cars should help.

Josh dangled his feet over and onto the windshield, reached down, grabbed a wiper blade, and violently started shaking the wiper from side to side, trying to rip it off. *What an A-hole.* The kids freaked out and escalated. I could not understand what the dispatcher was saying. An idea surged into my imagination to spray the entire windshield with washer fluid while Josh ferociously grappled with a wiper refusing to break. The idea of blasting him up there on his perch was so incredibly tempting. Alas, I could not pull the trigger and risk pissing him off even more.

The second dispatcher, the one for the police asked, "What's your emergency?"

Is this a trick question? Where do I begin? Fumbling my words, I tried to explain a request for police back up. I was not able to say much before the kids screamed: "He wants to get off! He wants to get off!"

How he indicated that to the kids, I did not know, but I stopped the car. Josh jumped off and headed toward the sidewalk. I told the dispatcher, "He's off the car. Got-ta go. I'll call you back." Foot to pedal, Momma sped off, catching a glimpse of Josh in the rearview mirror as he stomped away.

Holy crap! Holy crap. Holy crap-crap. Focus. Crap! Focus. No police cars at the station and no visible lights inside. My friend, Natasha, lived nearby – yes...somewhere safe. I called her. All my calmness rapidly dissolved when I heard her familiar voice.

"Hi, Jess."

"Tasha! Are you home?"

"Yes. Why? Everything okay?"

"I'm coming over."

"Jess, what's wrong? What is it?"

"I can't talk. I'll be right there!"

"Jess what is it? Tell me!"

"For crying out loud Natasha I can't! I'll be right there!"

"Jess tell —"

I hung up on her. Ugh, of all the people I decided to call, Natasha was the one who immediately went "to the dark side" as she put it. One time, within seconds of feeling a pimple on the back of her neck, Natasha assumed it was a mosquito bite, then feared it was Lyme disease. No, she decided, to big—it was a lump...in seconds, she had a cancerous tumor on her neck. Putting Natasha's dark-side aside, she was a fiercely loyal friend, and a dedicated mother of two boys. Her oldest son, Lucas, was a best friend of Connor's.

Moments from hanging up on Natasha's overwhelming concern, I pulled up to her house as she ran out the door. I got out of the car; she grabbed my arms and asked in utter panic if this was about her son. "Did something happen to Lucas? Jess, tell me!"

Stunned, I answered: "What? No. No! Why, I wouldn't —"

Natasha folded over in relief, then hugged me tightly saying, "Honey I'm sorry! You know how I get."

"I'm trying not to freak out, okay? I cannot handle somebody else freaking out right now. You cannot freak out!"

"What do you need, honey?"

"We need to stay here tonight. Josh went off the rails. I will explain later, okay? I want to get the kids inside." They had already climbed out of the car, and were clinging to my bewildered friend.

The kids quickly calmed down inside her house. Natasha was one hundred percent attentive and nurturing to them. My phone rang. Per caller ID, it seemed to be the police. At that moment I could not answer their questions. Ignoring their call. I dialed my father. With rambled speech I explained the nut and the nutshell of what was going on then handed him the relay baton.

"Dad, feel free to go over there." *Defend your daughter and her honor!*

"Has he been drinking?" my father asked.

Well, duh. "Yes Dad. No more than usual."

"I don't know if talking to him while he's been drinking is going to do anything."

Say what? You told me to call you! You got upset before when I didn't call you. Well, now I'm calling! "Okay Dad... You don't have to. I thought you could make sure Josh was still home so I could inform the police."

My dad requested that we stay at his house for the night instead of Natasha's. Quite frankly, I needed someone to takeover being a mom for me, which my dad was not adept to do. I reassured him that staying here was best. My dad offered to drive by our house: no way he could just sit at home if I was not coming over.

As I hung up with my father, another call came in from the police dispatcher. I answered. The dispatcher immediately put me through to an officer who calmly asked me to explain my current situation. Despite a deep well of swallowed fear and nerves, I reported that the kids and I were safe, adding that I wished to make a formal statement. The policeman offered to come pick me up and take me to the station.

"I can see the station from my friend's house. I prefer to walk." It was a subconscious need to briefly be alone, and to protect the kids from seeing me talk to an officer about their dad. Natasha was more than willing to hold the fort while I went to the station. "I don't know how long I will be," I warned.

"Don't worry about the kids. I can sleep with them 'til you get here, then I can take the sofa."

"Thank you," hugging her goodbye. "I am trying to handle

one thing in front of me at a time." I kept the sentiments short; I could not afford to come undone. After using her bathroom, I was ready. No sooner did I begin walking to the station when my dad called. He informed me that he saw Josh outside our home, and they had talked.

My dad recounted the conversation. "Josh was in the front yard when I got there. We spoke out on the lawn. I said to Josh right off the bat that I did not need to know all the details to understand the situation. I told him the stuff between you two has got to stop. Josh mumbled a bunch of stuff, and then it was like a switch went off or on, I'm not sure which."

"What are you talking about, Dad?"

"His whole demeanor changed. Suddenly, he thanked me for coming over and expressing my concerns. Then he shook my hand." My dad sounded dumbfounded, and still in shock.

"He shook your hand! Are you joking?"

My dad calmly responded, "It was the weirdest thing."

"Weird? Dad he was playing you. The words 'I'm sorry' are what you should have heard." By this time, I had reached the police station. An officer approached me, but before I let my dad go, I needed to find out something. "Did you question Josh, or did he say anything about what he did?"

"Honey, I figured if he was drunk – and I could smell it on him – talking was a waste of time."

"Uh-huh. A policeman is here: I need to go." My dad's answer left me beside myself. I had not called my father so that he could shake Josh's hand. Although I bit my tongue to avoid making my dad feel bad, somewhere in my head, I knew that my father sounded reasonable.

"Jessie—you and I are having breakfast at 7:30 tomorrow morning, sharp."

"I'll be there, Dad. Thanks. I love you."

"I love you too, peanut."

Embers of acceptance ignited within me; I could not handle

this myself. There were laws to protect me, and I was going to use them because I was in that kind of situation.

The officer asked, "Do you want a restraining order?"

"Yes – I – do."

HERE COME THE JUDGE

As previously learned, a restraining order can only come from a judge. It was almost midnight when the officer called the judge, explained what he knew, and then passed the phone to me. The judge requested that I explain the incident. He then asked some standard questions about my safety. It was difficult, but eye-opening to admit that I did not feel safe in the house with Josh. The judge had no hesitation in issuing a temporary restraining order. We would receive a court date via mail within the week. At that court appearance, a more permanent order would be assessed. Go me – so educated had I become on the matter of restraining orders.

Time waits for no man. The officer left to hand-deliver the restraining order and essentially kick my husband out. Technically, at that point, I could have gone home, but I chose to stay at Natasha's for the night. I still did not feel safe.

IN THE MORNING, I went back to the station for a copy of any paperwork filed the previous night for my special "just-in-case" divorce file. The same cop was about to finish his shift, so I asked how it had gone with Josh. The cop shook his head, a wave of agitation washing over his expression.

"Ma'am, I'll tell ya, I was so close to locking him up. I was thinking, 'Is he really gonna start something with me?' He was yelling this and cursing that."

"Let me guess: he thought *I* should be the one to leave the house."

"Oh, he said this was all part of some big conspiracy you have going. I told him that I had seen the car damage he caused, and I could smell the alcohol on him." The officer shook his head again. He paused, as if trying not to say too much.

"He did leave though, right?"

"Oh, there was no option. Once I made it absolutely clear I was not kidding around, he got some things together, and he left. I watched him drive away. I circled back around the house throughout the evening, but he never came back."

Thinking ahead I said, "He will probably need work clothes. Can I have an officer come to the house while he does that, at your convenience?"

"Yes, we can do a one-time thing. He needs to get clothes for a least a week, until the court date."

"Great. Thank you. I do not want to talk to him. I need to protect myself from anything he might say."

"Good luck with everything," said the officer who escorted my husband out of his home. Wait, it was my home too.

I kept my promise to meet my dad for oatmeal. Over break-fast, Josh texted me, asking what he should do about clothes for work. I told him: "Already thought of that. Go to the police station and arrange an escort. Remember to get at least a week's worth of stuff. You have till 10:00." I asked him who he had stayed with last night. Josh texted back that he had slept in his car. Boy, I got that wrong. I had imagined Josh explaining *mea culpa* to whomever he had to ask for a sofa for the night. Doc Josh did not seem to check his actions or thoughts with anyone.

WHEN CONNOR WAS INFORMED the next day of what had happened, he became visibly upset. I thought he was sad or empathetic for his dad who was kicked out of the house, but that was not the case. "Mom, I'm sad for Nicky and Jolie. That must have been really scary for them." This gave me hope I was not losing my teenage son.

Josh's absence provided me some breathing room, albeit using the same constricted lungs. With my raging, stubborn, alcoholic husband out of the house, I had what I could not get before: a refreshing balance of power. He had ignored multiple opportunities to leave in an honorable way. I told myself I did not need to feel bad for him nor battle him. I simply wanted a life based on respect and a reverence for child raising.

According to Tao, rough waters can carve out organic beauty among the rocks.

COURT

Sitting on wooden pews in the open court room, I observed case after case going before the judge. Josh and I sat, without lawyers, on opposite sides, waiting our turn. I welcomed the chance to speak for myself. The various cases before us ranged from five to ten minutes long. In each situation, the judge gave his full attention, which happily surprised me. It appeared as if he had already familiarized himself with each case. I had always thought that a judge knew nothing until he or she opened the file, right there in the courtroom.

Josh was wearing an older gentleman's button-up cardigan I had never seen before. He also had a fresh haircut. He was staying with Mary, his secretary; the sweater probably belonged to her retired husband. In my peripheral vision, I could see Josh looking warmly over at me, but I completely ignored him. Once we got to our podium spots in front of the judge, the incident itself was not discussed. Instead, the judge asked if I wished to drop the restraining order. That must have been Josh's prior request, or maybe this was how it always started.

Straight-faced, I responded: "No, Your Honor, I do not wish to drop it."

Josh was asked if he would like to come back with a lawyer, and he responded: "Yes – unless she would like to dismiss the order," glancing my way. I looked at Josh, looked back at the judge, and shook my head, *no*. Gavel strike. We were postponed for another week and that ended that. Walking away from our podiums towards the center aisle, I declined Josh's attempt to exit together. I sped up, heading out the door, and did not look back. The most significant development was not having to converse with Josh; I was alone with my thoughts. I did not have a lawyer nor was I seeing Dr. Phoenix any more; therapy can end as quickly as it began. Not having professional advice was a double-edged sword.

Since Josh was getting lawyered up, my family was coming at me hard to retain a lawyer as well. The restraining order situation was not a complicated process; I was not in favor of paying a lawyer to stand next to me and answer for me. Eventually, I caved at the idea of having someone in my corner, and spent $1700 to obtain counsel. A week later, my lawyer spoke for two to three minutes. Sparing the details, my lawyer was not impressive and was borderline rude to me from the get go. Admittedly, more time was spent on the handwritten agreement that was added to the restraining order on the morning of our court appearance. Our agreement stated that Josh could return home so that I could finish out the last month of school with the kids, and see my apartment lease through to the end. Josh was to pay for the damages to my car, and give me support checks during that month so that there would be no negative financial consequences. After a month, it was expected that divorce proceedings would take over, and it did not look likely that Josh could stay in the house. Combined, Josh and I had spent almost $4,000 to go back to the way things were. I was done with lawyers.

When Josh and I first spoke again, he said he thought something was "wrong with him" and he was trying to cut down on drinking again. *You do you, and I'll do me.*

THE LAST MONTH of school flew by without complications. I briefly reached out to Josh's older brother, who politely declined hearing any details, but understood that Josh needed to pull his act together. His brother thought I had not been working a career job for years, and that I was making Josh pay for private school – something he didn't want. Josh also gave his family the impression I had left the kids when I got the apartment. The smoke screen placed in front of his family was too big for me to address. The call to Josh's brother ended up being of no help at all.

Ready to move forward, I was locked, loaded, and prepared to file divorce papers. Every line item was filled out and everything on the checklist had been crossed off. Triple copies were made, and the certified mailings were ready to go. I requested full custody and full parenting-time. The section that asked about any legal domestic incidents had my attachments. A calendar had been filled in with all the dates and timeframes needed for the next several weeks. The day I sauntered back into the courthouse complex and turned in my divorce motion, the clock started ticking. Josh did not even have a hint it was coming. He would find out when he got served.

SUMMER OF COEXISTENCE

Once Nicky, Jolie, and I were back home, we took it one day at a time. I was not working as much, so I could be home with the kids for a chunk of the day. The paycheck stubs I turned into court would be from these weeks. Josh was working more at the new practice, equaling another month of bills paid and credit card debt lessened. Next on the divorce calendar to do list was submitting my case information sheet (CIS) which got turned in after filing the motion.

Compiling this data had been the most tedious part of the whole divorce packet. I can only imagine the nightmare other couples go through if they are not organized about their receipts, or worse, if one partner takes all the files, as happened to my friend. My "ahead of the game" position helped to avoid the latter situation. I had no agenda to take Josh down, as was the case in many other divorces. His retirement monies, his motorcycle, etc.— were his to keep.

Josh was agreeable to getting his own apartment; however, he seemed to lack the time, and perhaps the motivation, to hunt for a place. Having lots of motivation, I searched for him. Josh did manage to find enough energy to buy a trailer to carry his motor-cycle and his stuff. He said he wanted to protect his motorcycle, fearing any apartment complex would not adequately do so. I was definitely mad when he bought a trailer at the cost of $2400 instead of renting one. Best I could do besides complain was to copy the receipt and put it under his list of assets.

While Josh was on his restraining order hiatus, I moved back into the master bedroom, hence Josh slept in the attic bedroom. We did our own thing day and night, meeting in the middle like associates for home/family related tasks: a functional peace. With that routine, it took me a while to notice: one summer morning, I spied Josh taking a swig of vodka straight from the bottle before going to work at nine o'clock in the morning. He had never done that before. Concerned, I gently approached him right there on the spot, bypassing any opportunity for denial.

Josh was forthright and explained that he was having symp-toms he could not control. He was unable to sleep through the night without getting up for a drink. If he didn't take a sip before going to work, he got the shakes. Beer or wine was not enough— drinking vodka was easier. He admitted to being scared. When I tried to take those facts and parlay that into addressing the situ-ation, he shut down, said he would be fine, and left for work.

I called my AA comrade, Brendan, who said, "Having the shakes all the time is a definite sign your husband is really bad. He will not be able to stop without rehab. In fact, trying to stop cold turkey could lead to seizures, or worse." Brendan added with more seriousness: "Do not get in the car with him under any circumstances! Do not let the kids get in the car with him! He needs professional help to stop. He needs rehab." Brendan was the only one to give me point-blank advice. He was applying his role as a recovered addict to help someone else, through his own experiences and story. *One day, I'll write a book and do the same.*

Josh's biggest concern about rehab was that he would lose his job, or it would affect his professional reputation, especially if someone there knew him. With Josh drinking throughout the day and night to avoid the shakes, it would only be a matter of time before he was fired. His last excuse was barely holding water, in fact, the vase was leaking.

Continuing to afford our house and lifestyle meant that Josh had to keep doing what he was doing, and it was destroying him. He could not make a rational decision about this imbalance, and I was no longer buying into the status quo. Josh held power over me with the mission to keep the house. If I could let go of that desire, I would release the power it had over me. In the search for salvation, letting go of the house was key. My husband no longer had a seat at the decision-making table.

It was a solo trip to the local hardware store. The summer sun reflected brightly off the red and white "For Sale by Owner" sign stuck in the freshly mowed grass. Publicly, I spread the word we were selling our house." Privately I thought: *for the redemption of our sanity, we are selling the house.*

I had sold our Hawaiian house FSBO; I could do it again. Josh was informed that we could split the earnings 60/40, me/him, since I needed a house to fit four people. Josh said very little. He did not engage in any conversation beyond the mundane. Accepting was the opposite of arguing, hence, this must be Josh in an acceptance mode. The following month our kids would be back in school; that was when Josh would need to be out of the house and in an apartment – that was our agreement. The restraining order was outdated, but it was easy to see he had futile negotiating power. With each passing month, I appreciated another round of bills and debt getting paid. Once the kids were back in school, I'd be freed up to earn more income. My goal: make it to the end of summer.

ODD BEHAVIOR

Josh began carrying his pewter grey backpack with him everywhere he went; it was next to his bed when he slept. I knew he kept a vodka bottle in it, but this seemed excessive. Josh did not think to take it with him when he showered. One day, the second I heard the shower faucet, I was inside that backpack like a bee to a hive. There was a seltzer water bottle filled with vodka, as expected. Hmm, he also had his passports in there. Who carries around their passports all the time? Uh-huh. *Okay Josh, let's see if you can pass for an eleven-year-old girl or a seven-year-old boy.*

The following morning, when he took a shower, I switched out his two passports for the kids' passports. The booklets were the exact same navy-blue color. Unless Josh opened them, he would never know. His passports went to a lockbox with other papers I had at the bank. My dad had the only other key.

I also found a few opportunities to use Josh's debit card and make a monetary withdrawal. No pride in this, but I felt the need for a financial security net. I also perused Josh's personal calendar organizer. He had meetings scheduled out for a couple months which was a relief. On the side of his calendar page was his "to do list". Oddly, he had listed: 'cancel the cable and the electricity'. *Don't try to control anything. Stay one step ahead.*

Apartment hunting on Josh's behalf had been grueling, but successful. I found a suitable place, and gave him the information so he could check it out himself. If he didn't like it, he could search on his own.

Josh increased his packing efforts. Files, tools, and other things were all going into the trailer as I searched while he was at work. I was operating on high alert, but not really sure why. In the trailer, I found a folder marked "documents". Apparently he had packed the original birth certificates of our kids, and our marriage certificate. Maybe some kind of memento? Straight up, I took them back. Those records were needed for all sorts of reasons; I did not want the headache of replacing them all. I took the certificates to my dad's and hid them alongside my court documents. Admittedly, this was mutually screwed up cloak and dagger shenanigans. In that shady spirit, I removed a blank check halfway into Josh's checkbook in case, for some reason, I needed to write one last check. Yes, I would have to, let's say "reproduce" his signature, but in my mind, it was proactive defensiveness. Certainly, the sale of our house should give us both enough financial security to avoid being petty or scared about the future.

IT WAS LESS than two weeks before school started, and the calendar was counting down. One morning, there was a hard knock at the door. The kids were still sleeping; Josh and I were both mulling around, getting ready to leave for work. Josh answered. It was a total gift he got the door while I was down the hall to bear witness. As Josh signed for the courier, it hit me; time slowed down. *I know what this is.* Josh had thought this would never happen. He had been trying to avoid it with every ounce of his being, yet he had just been served. I slid back to where I could still peek at the front door. As my husband pulled documents out of a large manila envelope, the earth's rotation paused for the quiet realization... *Your wife of fifteen years is divorcing you.*

I remember the particular reaction my dad had soon after my parents divorced. My dad was unaware that when they got divorced, my mom had also filed to revert back to her maiden name. She did not think it needed to be discussed with him, nor did she need his permission. However, the court automatically notified all affected parties. Her name change bothered me a little because it was also my name, but I got over it. My dad was extremely hurt by my mother's decision. He got super mad when he received the documents in the mail, and began yelling at her over the phone. "What you're saying is all those years my name was good enough, and now it's not!" Neither of my parents were typically yellers.

My mom, too stunned to say much of anything, was courteous enough to let him vent over the phone. Well, not thirty minutes later, he came by the house. The front door cracked open, an arm threw a big manila envelope inside, documents flew all over the floor, and the door slammed shut. I felt bad for my father, even though I knew he was being childish. He was crushed, and there was nothing to do but allow him to be hurt. Watching my husband get a manila envelope resurfaced that same empathy.

Josh exhibited no anger. He appeared numb as he spoke. "I guess you know what this is."

"Yes."

His eyes seemed empty, and his head went down with an about-face turn. Soon, Josh was outside, pulling the trash cans up the driveway. I finished washing up the dirty dishes, and put them away.

HANGING ON

After that day, we did not speak of the divorce at all, though we got along fine. Josh exhibited a limited range of emotions. At times he admitted to being scared about how much he drank, stating that he was trying to hold onto another day for the sake of me and the kids; other times, he was aloof. Work was demanding for him, and I got the sense he was having a hard time keeping it together there. I revisited the idea of rehab, explaining that it was only while he had a job that his stay would be covered... Why blow that? Finally, he let me show him a highly respected rehab place online. We read reviews that the food was good and the grounds were nice. Breakthrough: rehab was not jail; after all, it was supposed to be a caring place. We read success stories of people who never thought they could stop. Folks addicted to both narcotics and alcohol had managed to make it back to a recovered life they valued.

When I pushed the envelope about actually going and emphasizing this was about his life, Josh became indignant and refused to attend rehab, or a single AA meeting. He was quick to list fear after fear until finally, I had to inform him that his fears were not that special—particularly that of being a white-collar worker having to mix with "the others". There were always plenty of highly educated folks to fill those rooms. Addiction did not discriminate.

I expressed to Josh: "Who do you think you're working for anyway? You work for the bottle. You're da bitch. You are not better than anyone else at rock bottom. Don't you think that is where you are, rock bottom?"

"That's the problem with me. I hit rock bottom and start digging." Josh admitted that my points made sense. Consideration was progress.

THOSE AMONG US

Two new friends, or perhaps angels, had recently come into my life. Ellen and Michael were the parents of Nicky's newest best friend. They became privy to my current situation and frustrations. Turns out that the universe, as it does, handed me the support I needed. Unbeknownst to me, Ellen and Michael were living a life in recovery, and were immediately willing to be vulnerable about their past behaviors and their helplessness around getting well. They admired the compassion I had for Josh, and the way I was trying to handle the divorce. They also threw out words like 'codependency' and 'enabling'. I thought in my head, *You mean me?* They offered that alcoholics need multiple chances to get sober. It takes time, someone has to want it, and there are going to be failures along the way. Michael admitted that after finishing his first rehab stay, he went straight to a bar. They admired my ability, at times, to separate Josh, the individual, from the pain Josh had caused me: a difficult aspect, but so tied into the disease. We talked a lot about rehab, and how it led to their love story – that's where they had met. Of all the couples I knew, they laughed the most.

Talking with them gave me a renewed source of energy. Knowing that my husband's job was already at risk, the divorce was happening, the infidelities had ceased, and that Josh no longer denied he had a drinking issue, I gained the motivation to help Josh get into rehab. I called a couple of intervention specialists and listened to their strategies as well as their price. An intervention specialist costed around $5000, whether Josh agreed to go to rehab or not. Even with their success rates, Josh was a tough sell. I considered doing an intervention without a hired specialist. Mike and Ellen attested that families often did interventions themselves, sometimes utilizing the help of recovered alcoholics.

FINDING the right people for an intervention with Josh presented a challenge. The only family around were my small unit, and Josh's only friends—ones who were not heavy drinkers — were four core people he had worked with over the years. Three were therapists, the other was Mary, the office secretary Josh had stayed with during our restraining order period. I ended up calling George, the only male therapist of the group, and the one I had previously spoken with the most.

George was not only supportive, but also in favor of the idea. Turned out, he had helped a former girlfriend realize she needed treatment. George admitted he was not surprised about Josh due to what he had witnessed at work. He revealed that the CEO had recently been asking questions. There had been times that it was hard to find Josh at work, and the CEO sensed there was a drinking problem. As alarming as that was, no one had offered to get Josh help. No one called me as a reliable source of information, nor checked to see if I might be drowning too. The balance between minding one's own business, and reaching out to someone is always a delicate line.

George offered to speak to the other two therapists and confirm whether they were on board with attending an intervention Labor Day weekend. I spoke with Mary and asked if she and her husband would come; she agreed. That was all good news, but the amount of influence felt too small. Josh's deceased friend, Antonio, came to mind. If I was Antonio's wife, I would have kept my recently deceased husband's cell phone around as a lingering connection, just in case someone called whom he had cared about. In my secret file was a phone list of Josh's contacts. I decided to call Antonio's cell phone in hopes that his widow, Holly, would pick up. I thought if she came to the intervention, she might provide a meaningful presence. I dialed, and the phone rang...a good sign.

"Yeah hello," a familiar, brisk, male voice answered. *Huh – not female.* I was expecting... Umm, hold up. I was not expecting—

"Uh, hi there An-ton-io?" I sputtered.

"Yeah, I know my name. Who's this?"

"An-too-nio, it's me – Jessica... Josh's wife." *Calling from the other side.*

"Oh, sorry kid. I didn't know the number. I don't need any deadbeat bill collectors callin', ya get what I'm saying?" Antonio laughed to himself.

"Ye-ah, Antonio, I get really tired of crap too." This was unbelievable. I quickly whirled my head in the law of psychological opposites. If Josh had said that Antonio was getting out of hand and he could not deal with it anymore, that really meant Josh had been getting out of hand, and Vietnam vet Antonio just did not take anyone's crap.

Antonio asked, "So, why ya calling? You okay? That husband of yours okay?"

"Well, I've been better. We're selling the house. Nothing is stable anymore. It's sad, it's such a beautiful home. The kids love it here."

"Sometimes you have to give up things, Jessica. You can always get another home, but you can't replace people. I'm sure the kids will be fine. Pissed off for a while, but they'll be fine."

"Yes. So, I am calling because Josh is not fine. Perhaps you noticed he has—a drinking problem. I mean, a severe drinking problem."

"No shit Sherlock. He drinks everyone under the table. But I haven't talked to Josh in months. Did he tell you what happened?"

"Well, here's the thing. Josh told me—I hope you're sitting down—Josh said you were dead. Guess he gets to avoid telling me what happened, if you're no longer around."

"Are you shittin' me? I'm dead? He told you I'm dead! I'm talkin' to you and I'm dead!" Antonio went right into a marauder sort of laugh. "How did I die? Did I shoot myself in the head cause I'm crazy?"

"No... Brain cancer."

"Brain cancer! So now I have brain cancer and I'm dead," spewing even more evil laughter.

"I don't mean to be personal, but do you even have cancer?" I wanted to be polite.

"No, I don't have fucking cancer! I have a hemorrhoid, and its name is Josh! Mother of all! Let me ask you somethin'... How come, if you thought I was dead, you're callin' me?"

"Good question. I thought Holly might not have been ready to turn off your cell phone yet. If I lost someone I loved, I'd still want to call them; hear their voice message. I'd wait a bit. Anyway, I was calling to speak to your widowed wife."

Antonio did not seem to care much about my answer, instead he went off again and again about how dead he was not. Eventually I had to cut him off. "I get you, Antonio. Listen, Josh is making my life very difficult and I'm handling it. I just served him divorce papers."

"You just served him divorce papers... I knew it! Josh lied. He said *he* was divorcing you months ago, and it was almost done. I knew he wasn't divorced. Jessica, are you still living with him?"

"Well, yes, and I have been. But I was living in an apartment a few days a week with the younger kids so they could attend another school. Honestly, I didn't want to keep raising them with Josh, and I couldn't put the brakes on his drinking."

"Ha! He told me you moved out to go live with a black woman."

"What? Why would she have to be black?"

"You're getting divorced because you're gay, right Jessica? You're gay? It's okay if you are."

"I am not gay, Antonio. Women are beautiful, but I'm not gay."

"Ha! You're gay and I'm dead! Together, we're two happy ghosts! You're calling a dead guy!"

"Oh my gosh, I thought your poor, mourning wife would still be carrying around your phone."

Antonio cut me off. "Hey, this way I have an excuse of why I'm late for dinner. I'm out back gardening, six feet under!" Antonio was perhaps what some may call a "dry drunk", that is, unless he was drunk right then. I couldn't tell: it was the only way I'd ever heard him talk.

"You're obviously enjoying this, but I was calling to see if your wife would come to an intervention for Josh to go to rehab. He is still a father to three kids and contributes to society. I'd like him to have some tools in a sobriety tool belt to get better, and avoid any worse case scenarios."

"You're a good mother, Jessica. I could tell the day I met you. You don't deserve how he's been treating you. I'm going to be straight with you because you deserve to know. Josh said the divorce was almost final and that you were crazy, controlling, and

living a gay life. I didn't know any different at the time. So, Josh
starts dating one of my lady friends. He's kissing her and telling
her she means the world to him and all this crap. But I start
figuring out that he doesn't seem divorced, something ain't right.
I saw messages on Facebook about your anniversary. I told him
off, and my lady friend dumped him."

Okay, enough callous details. "Antonio, I am aware he was
trying to date other people. That's all been squashed. And Josh is
on a path to lose his job, or hit someone with his car, or die in
my house with a TV remote in one hand and an empty bottle in
the other. I'm taking responsibility to try and prevent any of
those things from happening."

"I tried telling him that he's gonna end up like me. He didn't
want to listen, so I told him off."

"Josh can't stop drinking long enough to think straight.
Rehab will give him a tool belt and lessons on how to use them.
My goal is to hook a link between faith and rehab, and I am
going to hold steady whether he is lying, cheating, belittling,
narcissistic, or a Dr. Jekyll and Mr. Hyde. I am strong enough
now to do that while kicking his ass out of the house. And, I'm
taking full custody of the kids while I'm at it. So, don't feel sorry
for me, Antonio. I'm good."

"You're fucking frontline, Jessica."

"Thank you, sir."

"I can't be at the intervention, Jessica. I would not help the
cause. I don't believe rehab can work. I know drinking works for
me, but I already lost everything. Now I got a peaceful life and a
woman who loves me, broken as I am. I learned to respect her.
Keep in touch with me, okay? Let me know if you need
anything."

THE INTERVENTION PIECES were coming together. The rehab
place Josh and I looked at was on board to admit him, if he was
willing to go. They took his insurance, although final insurance

approval would occur at the time of admittance, and he could very well be denied at the door. They had a bed available, but that too could change. The most difficult aspect was that they needed to speak to Josh directly to make an intake appointment; I wasn't able to just drop him off and go. They were open until 8:00 pm every night, and would keep his basic information on hand.

George said that he and his two co-therapists agreed this was the best option for Josh. George took over the burden of further contacting Mary with the updated specifics. We coordinated the intervention for the evening before Labor Day. Out in the front yard, *House for Sale* information sheets were going like hotcakes. I had already given one house tour to a prospective buyer. I felt as though things were coming together.

PLANS UNHINGED

The kids and I were outside playing by the pool when I received an explosive phone call from Josh. "You switched my passports, Jessica!" *O-o-o kids, Momma Bear gonna walk away for dis.*

"I did what exactly, Josh?" innocently spoken.

"You switched my passports! That is a federal offense! You went through my stuff. You cannot take my passports, Jess-i-ca."

"Did you look in the file cabinet? Maybe you grabbed the wrong ones."

"You think this is funny? I'll have you locked up! You can't take someone's passport – it's international property! It's an official government document! Identity theft is a federal offense!"

My voice deepened to a brisk growl. My lips pressed against the phone as I spoke. "I'll tell you what's a federal offense: pulling a loaded gun on someone is a federal offense. So don't tell me that you're sending me to jail. I'm the reason you're *not* in jail. You want your passports? How 'bout fessing up as to why your passports are stuck to you like toilet paper?"

Josh stopped yelling. "Because I didn't want you taking my passports."

"That does not answer the question."

"Are you going to give them back or what?"

"I'm not even saying I have them. I will help you look for them. By the way, we have a few details to sort out...you know, the next phase of the divorce. We need to come to an agreement on some major issues. How about you have that conversation with me, and I'll try really hard to find your passports?"

"Fine."

"Tonight. I will have someone here with me, and you are going to talk to me like a human, or we are not talking at all."

He hung up.

After explaining the passport situation to my mom, she arrived, ready to be in my corner while Josh and I discussed the terms of our divorce. My parents had cultivated a genuine friendship over the years. They leaned on each other in times of stress, especially with regard to their daughter not living the safest or happiest life they might have envisioned. My mom informed me of my dad's biggest most paralyzing concern: Josh was going to either hurt me or himself. My dad's longtime partner, CJ, sadly and tragically lost her son to suicide by hanging. The first person she called was my dad, who not only saw her son hanging from a tree, but also brought his lifeless body down from the branch in order to calm CJ's understandable hysterics. Living in Hawaii at the time, I was very removed from it all and did not know the details, nor understood the impact it had on my father until my mom said, "Your dad never, ever wants to have those feelings about one of his own children, and he can't help but go to that memory. That's why he sometimes feels at a loss."

"Wow. I didn't know. Sometimes I transfer situational feelings onto Dad—it just kind of happens."

"We both love you so much, and we both had alcoholism in our families growing up. We admire the strength it has taken you to handle everything with integrity." She put her hands on my shoulders. "I heard it takes most people four times in rehab before they get clean, but then, they are living a much fuller life. Josh deserves that chance, if he's not too stupid to take it," she said in a humorous, frustrated yell while shaking my shoulders.

"I know Ma – if he doesn't drive us crazy first."

WHEN JOSH CAME HOME, the three of us met outside on a brick patio edged with colorfully raised flower beds and miniature round boxwoods. Our back property line blended with the view of conservation woodlands. Against the skyline, treetops gently swayed with the breeze. Josh sat down in a wicker chair, holding a mug of coffee and the inner tension of a sailor's knot. His arm robotically rose from a stiffened spine to bring the coffee mug to his taut lips. He and my mom said nothing more than a hello. Once again, the presence of my family lent restraint to Josh's expression, but zero sign of remorse.

Josh asked about the passports. I reminded him first things first: I wanted a fair divorce and in return, he got to do what he wanted, when he wanted, without going behind my back to do it. I reminded him that I had already given up staying in the house, and lived the apartment life. I was not a hypocrite to expect he did the same.

"You forget, Jessica—you are kicking me out of my own house."

"Our house. I'm losing too, Josh, and so are the kids."

"I work my ass off for this house, and you want to kick me out and have me give you money for the rest of my life?"

"Did I ever say that? You know what, I am not going to remind you of the path that got us here. And I am not going to play the game, *Who is more entitled?*. First on the agenda is the house: a 60/40 me/you split so I can get a house that fits four. You'll have enough money to buy all the things you want, and live a comfortable lifestyle. I am not trying to sacrifice your lifestyle for mine. We both should stay afloat."

"Fine."

"Next, one parent's home has to be what the court labels the "primary residence" for the kids. It is the place they live most of the time. Since I take them to school every day and manage their lives, I think it makes sense that I—"

"Yes, yes. I don't deny you look after the kids." He was looking straight down at a spot next to my feet.

My mom chimed in, "Thank you for recognizing Jess is an attentive mother to your children, Josh. I believe that is what you were saying." Her tone shot across to Josh like a banked billiard ball, causing Josh to acknowledge his audience.

Josh replied maintaining a conversational gaze, "Yes, she does." I did not bring up the full custody issue, I had decided a judge could handle that with fairness.

Next, I brought up money. Men and their money... "At times we have more going out than coming in. Overall, we are not on top of things."

"You know I have that new job I started with the practice; that is taking off. And I can work Saturdays."

This response seemed absurd because it lacked both admittance and analysis of our financial situation. In addition, it implied that the solution was for Josh to work more. I was trying to balance financial security for us both while coping with a male ego that identified success with wealth and status. I could not expect Josh to feel generous and helpful if he already felt sucked dry of money and appreciation for his hard work. He had dedicated his life to acquiring a professional career through his talents and skills.

I explained to him, "You've always been able to focus on your career and make advancements because I raised the kids. I chose a career, always intending to contribute financially, yet back away to raise a family. I am still doing that. My point is that there has been a balance of contribution and effort from both of us, but mine is not measured in dollars, and you don't see that. Your view is very one-sided; hence, you see everything as unfair to you. I am trying to be objective."

Josh was still actively listening.

"Here, I wrote down all the numbers. You will pay overall much less than what you output now because I am basing it on the cost of a smaller, yet typical home in this town. We both love this town for the kids. I think we are in agreement to remain here." Josh glanced at the paper for a moment, then folded it in half.

"I wanted this yard for them," said Josh, hand outstretched. "All this for them..."

"Honestly, the kids are becoming a bit entitled and maybe we are too. They do not contribute at all to taking care of this place. The family across the street are all out there doing yard work together: shoveling snow together; inside chores together —you hate that. You have never requested our children do a single thing. Without expectations, I am constantly asking the kids to do basic things over and over. This house is above my skill grade. It's above us both, since we aren't working together."

"I wish I shared your view, Jessica, but I don't. I can't." His shoulders relaxed; his coffee mug dropped to rest on his leg.

"Let's get past the money part of the divorce, Josh. We're on the home stretch. Your contribution is less than half of what you make, and I contribute everything I make working part-time. There doesn't even have to be alimony."

Alimony represented taxed income for me. Without consulting a professional, I decided that keeping Josh's payments strictly as child support had an advantage, plus the situation would be less inflammatory for Josh.

"Fine."

"That exact amount is fine?"

"Yes, Jessica," his jaw tightened. "I will give you money." No matter how I presented it, money was still a hot button. Next.

"Visitations are all one big hassle. Let's see if we can keep it as free flowing as possible. I hope to have family dinners...probably more so than we have now."

"Yes, that's fine." Unlike some dads, Josh did not seem concerned with who saw the kids more.

"And I prefer we do not use lawyers – as long as we can communicate effectively?" I said this with a sincere inquisitiveness.

"Yes," he said with exacerbation. "I can't stand using lawyers."

I sat back and waited. I was waiting for Josh to realize he did not have to be in the back seat, and never did. It took about forty-five seconds before he asked, "Can I have my passports back, please?"

The air was cool with not a single cloud in a clear blue sky. My mom had not budged. She was emoting a forced neutrality like no one's business. Tapping my fingers on my crossed arms I inquired: "Let me ask you something, Josh. Why are you carrying your passports around? You look like a man who's about to bolt."

Josh looked down to the ground, and moved his head to the side.

"Can you look at me, Josh? This family needs to be taken care of."

Josh lifted his head. "I was thinking I wanted to visit my family. I haven't seen them in a while. I didn't think I could trust you with the passports. I feel like an outsider here in this town, in this country – no offense. I want to feel like I'm home. My dad said I could visit him for a week or so. He is hosting a family reunion soon. He's coordinating with my brothers to fly in for it."

Straightening up, "I don't mind that. But you're not talking about this visit like you normally would."

"It just came up. I wasn't thinking anything through. I'm not even sure if I'll go," Josh solemnly added.

Planning or rather needing to visit his family resonated as

honest. Guess I had gotten what I came for. "I'll get the passports. Wait here." I had already retrieved them from the bank lockbox; hid them in the house. Once inside, I noticed that Josh had already put the kids' passports on the kitchen counter.

Back outside, I thrusted out the passports still clenched in my hand and was suddenly overwhelmed with emotion. My chest tightened. Swallowing a huge ache in my throat, "You promise to meet our agreement? I just want to be okay in this."

His wrinkles softened, the tight sailor knot showing signs of frayed edges. "Yes."

Again, without thinking, the words kept coming out. "You promise?"

"Yes, I promise." He made no motion towards me, and only took the passports when I placed them in his hand.

"Come on, Ma. Let's check on the kids." She and I went inside the house. I had done it, right there on the patio, let go of all my rights to control anyone, much the same way a bird releases its droppings. From now on, I had no say on how or where Josh would land.

A REUNITED FRONT

After a couple of days, things lightened up. Josh came home early and joined us in the pool. First, he dove in and got right out of the water as usual, but the kids asked their daddy to watch them as they showed off their dives. Soon enough, a competition arose, and Josh and I were the judges calling out whacky styles to be attempted off the diving board. After the competition, Josh joined the kids and performed a wide arm swan dive, curling into a ball at the last second, creating an enormous, unexpected splash, much to the kids' delight. Our family laughed and Josh grilled a delicious dinner. We feasted poolside.

As the stars took claim of a midnight sky, I had the rare treat of reading to all three my children in one blanket wrapped bed. After tucking them in, I retired for the evening. During all this,

Josh watched television. However, in an unusual fashion, before I fell asleep, my husband came upstairs and plopped down beside me. A palpable air of melancholy surrounded him.

"I realized I was downstairs all by myself, and my family was up here, right upstairs."

"Welcome to my world Josh," turning to face him.

"Hmm, yeah," he sniffed. "That's my fault. I'm not being smart, I know. I'm really scared. I feel like I am hanging on by my fingernails." Wiping his eyes and nose, he grabbed a pillow and put it under his head.

"Josh, I hate sounding like a broken record, but you need rehab. You know the fable of the emperor who wore no clothes, right? This highly distinguished emperor continues to walk around town, completely unaware, he's going commando. Nobody wants to upset this emperor or feel his wrath, so everybody tells him what a fine robe he is wearing."

"Yes, I know the story," Josh said with interest.

"Everyone knows he's buck naked, including his wife, but she is the only one with enough courage to say, 'Yo, put some pants on, your ass is hanging out!' Is it fair she's cast as the villain for pointing this out? Bravely, I think she was using humor to address a rather embarrassing issue because she really cared." Josh smiled and wiped his face in the pillow.

"Hmmm," he said, "you're much stronger than me. That's why I picked you. I didn't think it was fair to pick someone who wasn't strong enough, and you were so different. You were the least narcissistic person I'd ever met. I guess I get so hard on you because I'm hard on myself. People often say I'm like a robot: I just keep going – like at work. I am always doing more cases than everyone else."

"I remember when we met, your supervisors would tell you to slow down, but at the same time, they gave you all the hard patients they didn't want." We talked as mirror images facing one another except I was under the sheets, and he was resting on top.

"I know! They kept giving me mixed messages. What was I supposed to do?"

"Take the feedback. You needed to learn to pace yourself."

"Everyone has demands on me. I can't stop going," he said. "I don't know how long I can hold on for you and the kids. I am – trying. Every day I am trying to get through another day." His breathing rate increased and he squeezed his pillow corner. "I am tired of being the bad guy. I'm tired that people don't get me. This doesn't seem like my life."

"That's a lot to handle."

"Yes, it is!" he lifted his head, put it back down, and then closed his eyes. We engaged in comfortable silence before he stated, "I need to get a drink of wine. I can feel the shakes coming on. Do you mind?"

"No, go ahead. I know you can't stop on your own."

"I'll be right back," and he planted a sweet kiss on top of my head. I uttered a quiet "uh-huh" to myself, a release of unproductive sarcasm. He could only be real for so long, yet I waited for him. He did not return.

I WOKE up with a countdown in my head. Today was Thursday. Our family Labor Day barbecue was all set for Saturday afternoon, and the intervention was scheduled for Sunday evening. Feeling that I often dismissed my family, I wanted to host a barbecue for them before everything else took over. When I informed Josh of the party, his face went blank. It was kind of weird, but when wasn't he weird? Before we went to work, I left a few checks filled out for the monthly bills on his desk to be signed. Usually, I organized the bills and wrote out the checks; he signed them and stuck them in the mailbox. Other bills I paid directly from my account. This split in duties had worked for us since we have separate checking accounts. When Josh came downstairs, I hovered around to observe him sign every check, which he did. As normal, he placed all the envelopes into the mailbox. I had also left apartment information on his desk for his move out. The pile appeared as though he had glanced it over.

After he left for work, I decided to check our mailbox. Inside there should have been four envelopes; there were three. The mortgage check was missing. My lower chakras started spinning. Josh must have put it in his backpack. He unceasingly continued to take that thing everywhere. The inside pouch maintained a bottle shape even without one being there. *Don't panic...you have a safety net...one blank check.* That evening I would look for the missing envelope. Intervention Sunday was only two days away. *Hang on!*

Communications with George continued to be very supportive. He and I agreed telling Josh about the intervention at the last possible moment was best. It would quell Josh's option to not participate, yet avoid coming off as an ambush. Josh's buy-in for the intervention was a key step towards accepting what we would recommend. Surprisingly, Mary had little to say when I called to reconfirm everything was a go. Mary simply stated that she and her husband would be there.

BABE RUTH AT THE PLATE

On Friday Josh came home early, and packed up more tools and items from the basement. I found the mortgage check in his bag while he was loading the trailer, and immediately mailed it at the post office. The errand was a good reason to take the kids for a bike ride. We had dinner separately from Josh, who was writing reports all evening.

Saturday morning arrived; the family barbecue was planned for later that afternoon since Josh and I both needed to work a half day. Before leaving, I headed up to the attic to wake Josh so he wouldn't be late to the clinic. His grey backpack was right there, leaning against the bed frame. *Resist the urge to crawl on the floor and sneak another look, or take his passports again.* I was tired of choosing that life. Besides, he would probably hear me and wake up. I gave Josh a slight nudge; he popped up.

"What?" he said startled.

"You need to get up for work soon."

"Oh, thank you," returning his head to the pillow.

"Remember, my family is coming over today. Today is the party."

Josh opened his eyes and stared straight at the ceiling. "Okay," he said.

"I'll see you later."

The kids were asleep, even so, I liked to peek at them. I let the dog outside, gave him some quick attention with a ball toss, then got in my SUV which was parked beside Josh's Jeep. I backed out of the driveway, past the trailer in the street. My thoughts drifted to making sure I had everything for tonight's family barbecue. My mom, sister-n-law and CJ were all bringing side dishes. My dad would bring the whipped cream—his standard contribution. The refrigerator was stocked with hotdogs, hamburgers, bottles of iced tea, and water...beverages that satisfied my family just fine.

Naturally, I was preoccupied with concern over whether the intervention would work or not. Just because someone wanted to drown, did not mean you shouldn't offer a life preserver. If the preserver was there, at least he or she had a choice. Without a preserver, what choice was there?

––––––––

THE LONG-TERM CARE center had given me an extra patient to treat, but by 12:45 p.m., I was cruising down my tree-lined street, almost home. Enough foliage had changed to a golden hue creating a natural backdrop for the early leaves turning red. The wide, clear street in front of our house came into view, along with the sycamore trees and a row of boxwoods lining our empty driveway. The driveway was empty—as it should have been, but it was vastly empty. Wait...the trailer was missing...and Josh's Jeep was gone. The Jeep...with the trailer...was gone.

He's gone? He couldn't be gone.

He left.

He left us?

Without stopping, I drove past the house in case I had just missed him and he was on the road ahead of me. *No...no... No! Son of a bitch, you did not just abandon your kids.*

My frantic fingers called his cell phone. *You just left a 7-year-old boy, an 11-year-old girl, and a 13-year-old kid, but you made sure to take the motorcycle!* Calling his cell phone two, three, four times.... He did not pick up. I drove until the road turned into endless highway. I pulled over. My clutched hands let go of the steering wheel. My head dropped, my heart hit the floor. I was chasing the phantom of a man. I was now the crazy one.

THINKING that this could happen was totally different than it actually happening. I compared it to what it must have been like watching Babe Ruth step up to the plate, and point an outstretched finger to a place beyond the stands...

The crowd would sense that Babe might smack one out of the stadium. They would watch from the edge of their seats as the pitcher lifted a leg, wound up and relinquished all throwing speed toward the mound. Babe Ruth would swing his bat, crack the ball dead center, and launch stitched leather over the infield while the fans would jump from their seats, yelling: "Going, going..." but not until the actual moment when ball crossed wall would everyone know, including the wife... It's gone.

CLEARLY, this man had planned to leave his family for quite some time. I decided to phone his close friend and drinking buddy, Roger. If my husband was the alibi for when Roger was with his mistress, perhaps Roger was in the know about Josh leaving me. But then again, Josh never admitted his real thoughts or actions to anyone. If he had, they might have pointed out that he was—

"Hello."

"Roger, it's Jessica. Is Josh with you?"

"No. Is he supposed to be?" Roger had recently gone camping with Josh and had seen him go through withdrawal symptoms. Roger had realized then why I had wanted a divorce.

"Roger, Josh left. I mean, he packed his stuff, took his passports, and left."

Roger cleared his throat and softened his tone. "Look, Jessica, I don't know nothing about what he is or was planning, but to be honest, it doesn't surprise me. You know how many times I just wanted to up and leave my wife and kids? The whole thing... Just leave it? A bunch."

"But you didn't."

"Because I don't have the balls. But Josh, he looked like a man on the edge. I'm sure he is doing *a walkabout*. Every guy wants to... Has a need to get away – be a man, grow up a little, clear your head, and then, he'll be back."

"You know he has a drinking problem?"

Roger paused. "Yes. I didn't know, but I can see it now."

"Well, however bad you think his drinking is, it's ten times worse. He's not running from a problem; he is running with a problem. I'm holding the bag here, Roger. I'm not the one causing the problems. I just get the luxury of pointing them out."

"There is always a 'he said, she said' and I'm not here to get into that with you."

"Did HE tell you that he has to wake up in the middle of the night to drink, otherwise he gets the shakes? And that he drinks vodka first thing in the morning, same reason? It's hidden in his car, behind the speakers. Do you think taking *a walkabout* and leaving your kids is braver then facing your actual problem?"

"I don't, Jessica. I'm sorry. He doesn't tell me everything. If he calls me, I'll tell him you want to talk to him. But I'm not calling him. Obviously, whether it is right or wrong, he needed to get away."

That was the most he could offer. Roger was not the one I needed to yell at.

AMONG THE ASHES

Back home, I ran into the house and investigated whether the kids sensed anything. Nicholas was seated on the sofa watching cartoons, two chewed apple cores by his side. I asked him if he knew where Daddy was.

"I think he's upstairs."

"No, he's not upstairs. Did you see him today?"

"Wait... Yeah, I did." His attention remained captive by the characters on the screen.

"Nicky, look at me and not the TV!" I said, leaning by his side from behind the sofa.

"Sorry, Mom. Daddy went to work. He gave me a hug and a kiss, and he gave me this Lego guy." Nicholas grabbed a Lego figurine off the coffee table to show me. "He said this guy is really rare. He gave it to me for my birthday."

"Your birthday is over a month away."

"I don't know. That's what he said," and my son went back to his world, clueless. He probably won't even remember this day. I dashed upstairs to his sister's room. Jolie was there, painting away on her quilted bed. Doll clothes and books scattered around the floor.

"Hi Momma!" She was the cutest, dearest, most creative little girl.

"Hi Jolie-cub," I said, leaning against the doorframe for support.

"You okay, Mom? You seem out of breath."

Hanging onto her door knob, "Yeah," I said with that happy mom smile. "I like what you're making. Are you almost done?"

"Yes, but I might change the color. It's too bright," she said dipping her paint brush into a cup of darkly clouded water.

"Hmm. Hey—did your dad come in here this morning?"

"Yes. He was leaving for work. He came in to say goodbye."

I tried to imagine him feeling a heavy sense of sorrow. "Did your dad seem, ah, any different?"

"He seemed strange; like he was sad or something. Gave me a big hug before he left."

"And that was it?" *Just keep smiling.*

"Yeah." Jolie shrugged her shoulders and went back to her paints. She'd always loved painting. Jolie could already crochet and needlepoint, and that year, she had learned how to knit. Jolie was and is so many things, so full of life. At that time, she loved dressing up her stuffed animals; she loved to wear crushed velvet dresses in July.

Jolie and I had painted white and lavender clouds on her pale-blue ceiling. Some of the clouds had interesting designs. Floating up there was a rabbit cloud, a crescent moon, and a cumulus cat chasing a ball of yarn. At the tender of age of eleven, Jolie was sweet and smart and harmed no one. Her Dad should be there to defend her, uplift her, teach her to fix her own car, and to never settle. Those tasks were now my responsibility. Next, I headed to Connor's room.

Upon opening the door, I found Connor lying on his top bunk, playing a handheld video device. His room was tidy except for some Nerf guns on the floor. Opposite his bunk bed was a wall with a hand-painted mural, my first. It had a Hawaiian mountain scene inspired from a children's book about the Hawaiian goddess Pele. The lush, green Pali Mountains mural began on the right side by the doorframe, stretched across a third of the wall, then sharply dropped off to ocean water. The majority and focus of the mural was an underwater scene that included Bikini Bottom, hometown to Sponge Bob Square Pants.

All the main characters and their homes were there, including the pineapple house, Patrick's rock house, and the Crab Shack. SpongeBob was holding a jellyfish net in one hand while racing to catch a bright pink jellyfish. Intricate corals and ocean plants anchored the far left side. The mural captured glimpses of the boy I was losing to the inevitable teenage years.

My eldest son's face lit up when he saw me. "You back from work, Mom?"

"Yes. Had hoped to be home sooner." I walked over and placed my hands on the wooden bunk rails, peeking up at him.

"That's okay. I had a bowl of cereal. Is today when everyone comes over?" asking about the only thing he had to remember for the day.

"Yup. Your aunt, uncle, cousins and grandparents are all coming. Wow...soon." Rising up on my tiptoes I asked, "Did your dad pop in here?"

"Yes. He was leaving for work."

"Uh-huh. Did he seem unusual at all to you?"

"No."

"Do you remember what he was wearing? I wonder if he has to change before the party."

"He was dressed for work. I think he had a suit on. Maybe not."

"Did he give you a hug?"

"Yeah, he climbed up here with me. Are we having hamburgers on the grill today?"

"Burgers are the plan, Connor. That's the plan." I climbed up the wooden ladder just as his dad had, and gave my son a hug. "I love you so much. You are such a good kid. No matter how tall you get, you're still my pumpkin." He let me bestow kisses on his cheeks when we weren't in public.

"I love you too, Mom."

Once back downstairs, I called Josh's office to see if he was there. He was not, and they were wondering where he was too. He had not even called out sick, which meant patients had shown up and sat in the waiting room. Covering for him, I threw out that Josh hadn't been feeling well and perhaps he'd gone to see a doctor. I could only handle my own reaction in the moment, not anyone else's.

Call Josh again. Josh did not answer. I did not leave a message. I would not give him the satisfaction of hearing that I was distraught or needy or freaking out. He appeared so gutless to me at that moment; rage began coursing through my veins. My initial shock and panic provided no fuel. Rage, on the other hand, was pure octane. *Focus. Validate your ground.* I walked around the house only to find more of Josh's personal belongings missing. His grandfather's watch, and even his wedding band were both gone.

———

MY MOM AND HER HUSBAND, Mark, arrived first. They knocked and came in as expected. Seeing my mother's cheerful face tugged at the laces holding me together. Why? Because my mom always lights up when she sees me. Both of them were happy to see me and the kids. They made such a basic family experience so simple. Josh made it so complicated.

Hugging my mom, my face right next to hers, I revealed, "Ma, the trailer's gone. He took the trailer. Josh is gone. No doubt in my mind he went to Canada."

"Son of a bitch! He left?" jaw dropping, her hands already in a fist. My voice box shriveled up; I went speechless. My mom filled Mark in on what she had already figured out. With mild disbelief, Mark asked all the appropriate questions regarding other possibilities. I shut those all down, shaking my head *no*.

Mom asked whispering, "Do the kids know?"

Bouncing back, I responded, "No, they think Daddy went to work. He hugged them all goodbye; gave Nicky a Lego figure for his birthday."

"How courteous of him, son of a —"

"Ma! I still have a check. I still have a check! I better get to the bank," I resounded.

Mom said, "The bank will be closed by now."

"I'll call customer service; they can tell me what's left in the account. Maybe I can transfer something, or use the check at the teller machine."

As I looked up the number and made the call, the rest of my family arrived. Loud greetings dropped to low chatter and murmurs as Mark and my Mom explained what had just happened. My Dad peeked in as I started to communicate on the phone about the status of the checking account. My father's concern was deep within his hazel eyes. The bank representative delivered the news that Josh had closed his account yesterday. The account balance had been over $15,000.

In shock, I hung up the phone. Words spilled out of my mouth: "He outsmarted me. I can't use a check if there is no account attached to it." Mark's mouth dropped open as he too turned into a believer.

"Wait – there is still the joint account! It's at a different bank because we had to open it for the second mortgage. There's like, $3000 in there. We never use it. It's like a safety net. That would help cover a mortgage payment. Josh probably didn't even think of it."

Quickly I called that bank while some of my family members started preparing to feed all six kids: my three, plus my adorable niece's. The bank service representative informed me that our account had been closed yesterday. Almost pleading with the representative, I asked: "How can it be closed? The account is in both of our names. How can he close it without my signature?"

It turns out a spouse can totally do that. *Boom*... It all hits me. Turning to face my brother, my father, and my mother I confessed, "Josh wrote a mortgage check the other day, but he didn't mail it. He wanted me to think he put it in the mailbox, but I caught that he put it in his work bag. I mailed it, but it won't matter. He closed the account; the check won't clear. He didn't just stick me with the next mortgage bill... He is putting me under the previous bill too."

Sadness crept past rage, traveled up my throat and set anchor as I tried to talk. "I defended him. I knew he did awful things, but I defended him. I took the view that he was addicted, or even mentally ill. I stood by him as a harmed man trying to do well. But this is what an asshole does. He didn't leave making sure his family was okay... He left us to burn." Adding salt to this gaping wound was the embarrassment of having to admit this in front of the caring hearts and eyes of my family.

Greg and my father immediately discussed the added complications of not paying a mortgage on time. Fees and credit issues would arise quickly, affecting my ability to buy another house. They asked for my payment details, which I looked up, fumbling through our paper files. We had about six days to pay the bill on time. My dad immediately offered to cover the next payment; he insisted upon it. I had little choice but to accept, knowing full well that my dad would have to tap into his retirement monies. There was the comfort and hope that our house would soon sell, and I could pay him back. We mulled around, and then slowly joined the kids. My bubbly nieces helped disguise the mood. However, Connor approached me and whispered, "What's wrong with everyone?"

"What do you mean?" I asked.

"Everyone is acting like somebody died." Connor was completely serious, and rather perceptive.

I didn't want to fabricate. "Everyone did receive some bad news. If you don't mind, I would rather not talk about it right now."

"Okay, but Mom —"

"It's not a good time, Connor. Grandma and CJ are bringing out dessert. They love it when a young man offers to help. Ask them what you can do, please." Connor walked over to my mom, gave her an unsolicited hug, and offered his assistance.

Perhaps calling Josh's family would be of some use, though

they were probably all in a fog of false information. We still kept all our phone numbers in a Rolodex. Thumbing through the Rolodex, I found that Josh had taken out all the cards with the phone numbers of his family and his friends, including those in Canada. Obviously he was headed there, and did not want me to reaching out. This was not a "walkabout". This was setting the house on fire with piss and gasoline. I could already picture Josh telling future women in his life that we all died in a fire, and they would say, "Poor Josh. Poor, poor, Josh."

Only Connor noticed his dad's absence. Later that day, while the rest of the kids were swimming, Connor asked where he was. I decided to tell Connor that his dad had chosen to go on a motorcycle ride. Connor was satisfied with this answer.

George, the leader of our intervention pack, returned my call, and was very understanding of the situation. George said he would try to get hold of Josh, as well as inform the other two therapists and Mary of the intervention cancellation. The remainder of the day droned on hour by hour as my family and I thawed out from our shock and disbelief, and jelled together. They were all completely there for me, and I loved them. They remained unwilling to be bitter or belittling. They problem-solved, and they respected me as a capable person. The world was going to keep spinning, even if my kids were joining the club of abandoned children. I still had time to unfold the story of their dad, as if he had left in a manageable, non-dramatic way.

MOPPING UP THE MESS

The next day, I checked and read Josh's emails, an underground link I was still able to access. Indeed, I read an email Josh had sent to his mom informing her that he had safely arrived in Canada. Other emails were addressed to professional colleagues explaining that he was going to visit his sick parents, and wasn't sure when he would be back since he had to help take care of them. This clandestine method of checking reality via emails was a game changer, allowing me to behave with additional, measured patience.

George got back to me, saying that Josh was ignoring him as well, and that Josh had not given notice to anyone at work about his departure. If Josh didn't show up by the following Tuesday, his employer would be forced to address his absence. George then dropped two bombs on me. First, that Josh had parked his other car, an old TR-6, at his house the week before, and now he understood why. George thought that Josh would want him to sell the car, or at least hide it from me. George suggested we wait; Josh would probably address the car issue soon enough. George mentioned he was not comfortable doing anything about the car—such as bringing it to me—until he heard from Josh on the issue. If that did not make me feel like I was working with a double agent, the following news nailed it.

George dropped the second bomb. "I think you should know something... Mary thought Josh should know we were planning an intervention. She told him about it. Mary told him it was going to be sometime this weekend. I'm sorry. She didn't check with any of us."

Josh must have thought the family party was the intervention. That was why he had left that particular morning, and had been sure to be gone before noon.

"How could Mary unilaterally make that decision? We're talking about mental health treatment. Mary's somehow above consulting any of the four therapists involved, you three in particular?"

"I know. She never had to take someone to rehab. It was out of my control."

"We had an addiction facility on board – they do this all the time! Mary knows better than them?"

George was ready to get off the phone. His hands were obviously tied with Josh needing to sign off on some things, or possibly provide future recommendations. The three of them had their own professional coverage worries. George also had a new baby; he was not in a position to be a hard-hitting team player, though I wished I had one of those.

AFTER EVERYONE LEFT and my clueless kiddos were playing a board game before bed at the kitchen table, I called Mary. Oh, did I call Mary. From the front lawn, I literally screamed into the phone so loudly that a neighbor came out of his house, saw me, and went back inside. Mary's excuse was that Josh was going to Canada anyway, and that our marriage was the problem causing so much chaos. Josh telling Mary our marriage was the problem was his attempt to smokescreen the drinking problem. I realized Mary, who viewed Josh like a son, was caught up in a web of stories. Nevertheless, I jammed the point down her throat that she had been completely duped, that she was untrained to unilaterally mess with an addiction treatment plan, and that she did not get to make this kind of decision for my family. I yelled that she had robbed my children's father of a choice he could not make unless he was sober, and he wasn't going to get sober without help. Eventually, Mary hung up on me. It was a surprise she listened to my venting as long as she did, which in and of itself was a gift since I could not yell at Josh. Obviously, I needed to unleash some serious wrath at someone who had the balls to face me. Returning to the kitchen, I met with three pairs of wide eyes, all stunned and amused.

Collectively, my kids hurled questions and comments. "Mom! Who were you talking to?" "Mom, you dropped the F bomb!" "Ma, is the other person dead? I think you killed 'em through the phone!" "What did they do?" "Don't mess with Mom!"

"Show's over, kids. Yes, the other person still has a pulse, I think. No one messes with our family, especially you guys."

After the kids went to bed, I made two more calls and proceeded to get hung-up on two more times by Josh's mom and dad, although, I did not yell at them. His mom answered the phone only to say she couldn't talk to me...then click. His dad acted clueless that Josh was even there, and hung up when I asked how he thought this affected our kids. What I gathered in emails was that his family was told I had some conspiracy plan against him, and had hired a private investigator. The investigator was Josh's own conclusion, since he could not figure out how I knew so many details about his cheating. He could not recall that some nights he had passed out with the computer screen still on live email chats with another woman, right there for me to receive like the morning paper. Nor did Josh fathom I had been reading his emails, despite the fact that he was checking my emails. I know he checked mine because I found copies Josh had made of my emails to Brendan. In any case, Josh's family did not want a full picture, that much was clear.

THE RETURN OF MERYL STREEP

It took two days for the kids to notice their dad hadn't been around. They casually asked his whereabouts. Gently I told them that their father had decided to take a vacation and gone to Canada. They were surprised, but then, as kids do, they asked: "How come we didn't get to go?" *Well, my darlings, you're not a motorcycle.*

"Because school is starting and that is where you all need to be." I felt an Oscar nod coming.

Connor asked, "Mom, did you know he was going?"

"No. I did not," spoken in a flat, dry tone. "He made that decision on his own."

Connor continued, "Are you okay that he went?" Oh goodie, a child is recognizing this affects me too.

Laying out seeds of truth, "I am not okay with his decision-making process. I was not included. You guys were not included. However, I think traveling and visiting family and friends has value. I understand your dad was feeling stressed and wanted to be with the people who love him, and who have known him for a very long time."

Jolie asked, "How long will he be gone?"

"I do not know." *Smack* – there's the seed of understanding that their dad has gone. That seed will grow; they will ask again, and I will add water and light.

THAT WEEK WAS full of tying up loose ends, for example, un-enrolling Jolie and Nicky from the Waldorf school. After explaining my situation, they returned my $2500 deposit which was a total blessing. Combining those funds with an encore Oscar performance at the bank, I managed to reopen our joint account; otherwise, I would not have been able to cash or deposit any future joint checks. My diligent father paid our mortgage bill on time. I canceled our cushy cable channels, although in order to do that, my brother had to pretend on the phone that he was Josh, and add my name to the account.

My husband finally contacted George. Josh had a buyer for the car who was going to pick it up ASAP. George was instructed to mail the purchase check to Josh. I tried to prevent George from helping, as the sale represented not only a month of bill payments, but we lived in a 50/50 divorce law state. George said if I showed up to his house, he would have to let Josh know, and Josh would call the police because the car was in his name. George conceded that if I produced something legal he could throw at Josh, he would not partake in this plan. George did not indicate that Josh had threatened to make completing his professional pursuits difficult, but George simply fearing it was enough.

Conversations with two different police stations resulted in the same information: there was nothing the police could do because the car was in Josh's name, and there were no divorce papers. *Poof!* the car was gone, and so was the $5000 Josh got from the sale. Fortunately, because of my due diligence, I already had copies of all car and motorcycle titles, registration, and price information to submit for court to prove his equity. The more equity Josh had, the greater the percentage of funds I would get from the house sale—the house with no offers.

Since the kids were back in school, I requested to be assigned five more Early Intervention cases, bumping me up to the next pay grade. Closing up our pool cut the electric bill by half, and the fall weather automatically cut the air conditioning costs.

Many of Josh's clothes were still hanging in the closet. I couldn't get angry enough to toss them all because part of me liked touching them...smelling them. Not because I missed him, because it reminded me that once upon a time, I had a husband...shared a closet. Trying to mourn someone or something you did not really have in the first place was weird. At least the closet could be a place to feel sorry for myself. Besides, when prospective house buyers came touring through, it was better to have some male clothes in there.

MANAGING THE PIECES

Jolie and Nicholas were very understanding about changing back to our town school. In some ways, they preferred to be with their old town friends, and discontinue the back and forth living. I considered having Jolie remain at Waldorf by staying with a host family, but decided wholeheartedly that I no longer wanted to split up my kids, and that our relationships with each other needed to last a lifetime. In fact, I wanted their sibling relationships to outlast me. Financially, keeping Jolie in private school was a pipe dream. And besides, I wanted my daughter with me; she's awesome.

Meanwhile, Josh was not responding to some of his private clients, or his weekend employer. Upon seeing the distress in their emails, helped tie up those loose ends. Regarding his main job, George informed me that he got Josh to talk with their CEO, but Josh had very little to say. They gave him a week's deadline to turn things around. Josh never called them back.

They still owed Josh a final check, which would be mailed to the house since direct deposit was no longer available. Heh – guess he did not think of that detail. *And the Oscar goes to... The joint account.*

Grey clouds did part. Finally, I got a full price offer on the house. The buyers were a couple living in town. They were willing to go the 'For Sale by Owner', route. Woohoo!

"Girl, you know how to step in it," said CJ, my dad's partner of thirteen years, in her lovely Kentucky accent.

"Step in what?" I asked while jumping up and down in front of my dad and CJ with the good news.

"In the south, when someone is really lucky and resourceful, we say, 'That fella can step in a pile of pig manure and turn it into gold.' You are making it gold, honey." I love CJ. We all do. My dad landed a true southern belle. CJ, a former beauty pageant queen back in the day, is a decade older than my dad, and a retired school teacher like my mom. CJ said, besides my dad being very handsome, she was drawn to his sweet, old-fashioned gentlemanly style, and that he is 'most unpretentious'. The latter is the source for a majority of our jokes about my dad. CJ can eat the finest food with the finest silverware, as if she were royalty. My dad will eat tuna from a can, or steak with a melted slice of cheap cheese from a wrapper on top and call it gourmet. He has a specific meal per restaurant. Whether breakfast or dinner; he never needs the menu. Half the time the waitresses confirm his order before he tells them, because he has been getting the same entree for years. Even his ice cream sundaes are always the same: vanilla ice cream, butterscotch topping, wet nuts, and "loads of whipped cream". He always puts out his hands to indicate the expected mound he hopes to receive on his sundae treat.

I enjoyed grossing my dad out by mixing wacky flavors of ice cream together such as a scoop of chocolate marshmallow with a scoop of blueberry cheesecake topped with caramel and hot fudge. With a jovial wink, I would often tell the cashiers to swipe some whipped cream from my dad's sundae pile to put on mine. Dad and I also had a history of discreetly stealing each other's maraschino cherry off the whipped cream piles by using a clever distraction... *Hey, look at that dog with three legs!* Swoosh, cherry's gone. It's been our game since I was a little girl. Hence, in our tried and true tradition, my dad and CJ were taking the kids and I out for ice cream to celebrate the house.

MOVING FORWARD

The bliss of having a buyer carried me through attending our town's annual Fall Music Night at the lake. This talented night was taken very seriously in our town. A stage was constructed with lights and a full sound production on the basketball court. All singers performed with a live band of town musicians, ranging from serious drummers to multiple guitars to a full horn section, depending on the song. Singers and band members practiced all summer long to culminate on this epic performance: an evening at the lake complete with picnic dinners, dancing, and plenty of BYOB.

The first time I saw the mild-mannered school janitor belt out a throaty AC/DC song, and a school teacher pull off a Cher number wearing ass-less chaps, I was blown away. I cannot really sing, but the idea of being a rock star for one moment seemed pretty cool. The uproarious town crowd is always supportive, dancing up against the stage under the colored lights...the later the night, the drunker the crowd, the better the music.

That year, the first set was the slowest, with ballads and obscure songs. The second set was more entertaining: classic songs mixed with some dance tunes, which the crowd loved. One guy with a strong voice, and filling out a white T-shirt rather nicely, was singing a Nickelback song. I happen to love this band. That's right, I said it, I love Nickelback. My dancing body grooved closer to the stage, until I noticed that the singer was... Sharky! He was smashing it up there. Of course, Sharky was more than just a lawyer, as I was more than Josh's wife. And the beat went on.

As a crescent moon glinted in the lake, Josh's song came up to cue. He had been slated to play his guitar and perform with a few other singers. Josh had an enjoyable, folk-type voice, but it did not carry strongly, so they had arranged back up singers. When they announced his name, the MC said to the energetic crowd, "Josh is on vacation in Canada. Unfortunately, he won't be joining us. Let's give Josh a toast!" The crowd held their drinks up in the air and all shouted, "Cheers!", somewhat ironically drinking to Josh.

A group of six guys, all playing different instruments, performed the Billy Joel song, The Downeaster 'Alexa' without him, which no doubt had commiserating lyrics for Josh. As the full band played, I moved further back to wallow. I chose not to tarnish his name. I did not announce what he did around town. I didn't post it out on social media. Josh was in charge of his integrity, not me. As a result, this gave Josh a safe space to begin reaching out to a few friends via Facebook. He told them he was on vacation. Sara and Liam received his feed. As Josh began to emerge more on Facebook with photos of himself and his motor-cycle road trips, I got a sense of his new life. Liam told me he would love to blast Josh, but since that may not help me, Liam held back. Other than Sara, I was slow to tell my close friends, because I did not want to be 'that woman'—the kind of woman these things happened to, whatever that meant.

The band took a short break and Fall Music Night headed into the last set of the evening. The snack bar had been converted into a dressing room for the performers. Inside, I retrieved my big white box, sat next to my friend Shelly, and showed her what was inside: a pair of red vinyl, knee-high, lace-up boots with platform bottoms. It was bucket list time.

Shelley hollered, "Girl, you are gonna be smoking hot in those kinky boots! Ooh, and I love your skirt, matching red belt, and that denim bustier."

"Thanks," I said while tugging on the laces. There was more racy polyvinyl than leg.

"Hey, you okay, Jess? Don't be nervous, you'll do great. Do it like we did in rehearsal." Despite everything that went down, I had kept my rehearsal commitment.

"Easy for you to say, Shelley. Rehearsal did not have 300 shouting people watching me," I said with the jitters. "These boots are taking so long. Our number is next."

Shelley knelt down to help with the laces. "This crowd needs a good pop song. Let's get them on their feet, pretty momma!" My glamorous, curvaceous, red-headed friend was up and ready to join me on stage. Determination swelled as I channeled the Lady of the Gaga.

For the first time in my life, someone handed me a microphone and pointed to a stage. The keyboardist and drummer were jamming the intro of *Telephone* by Lady Gaga, featuring Beyoncé. Shelley, a true trained singer covering the smaller Beyoncé part, was already on stage giving me a welcomed smile. The MC announced my name, I summoned my sass and strutted out, rocking my five-inch platform, candy-apple red boots. Despite the song beginning in a conversational manner, the crowd was already pushing up to the front of the stage – a pair of sexy legs can do that. It was a shaky opening on the vocals, but then the pounding dance beat kicked in. I ripped off my glamour shades, and started jumping with bass beat. The crowd went nuts! Drunk dancing moms, dads, janitors, teachers, councilmen, and maybe even a lawyer, all formed a bouncing mosh pit. I belted out Lady Gaga, and my friend killed the Beyoncé part in full diva mode. The crowd chimed in to the chorus...

"Stop callin'! Stop callin'! I don't want to think anymore! I left my head and my heart on the dance floor."

For a brief wrinkle in time, I was a rock star. *Thanks, Lady Gaga. You always deliver.*

INSIDER TRADING

The following week brought disappointing news: my buyers for the house were backing out. They had kids nearing college age; when they broke down the cost of running a big old house, it was not a wise purchase. They did not want the house at any price. This was a pretty big blow. *Stay positive. Another buyer will come.* In the meantime, we had a garage sale. This endeavor raked in a few hundred dollars, plus, a local guy ended up buying our pop-up camper. The loss of the camper disappointed the kids, but they understood that $2100 was a big help. The kids and I camped for one final night in the driveway before the new owners took it away.

Though Josh's parents continued to ignore me, I gained an insider: Caleb's third wife, Jacque. Jacque had a good head on her shoulders and was willing to correspond via email with me. Jacque was unable to rationally talk to Caleb about Josh's current behavior because, as she wrote, "Caleb thinks his boys are perfect and never wants to hear if they do anything wrong. But, he is willing to put down my kids." Jacque had five grown children. Years ago, she had lost her husband, and almost her twins, in a fatal car accident. Jacque told me, after that, she didn't argue anymore; nothing was worth it. When Caleb got mad at Jacque, she didn't fight back. All he could do was ignore her for a few days. Caleb no longer drank like he used to, and wine gave him migraines. Caleb has always been a loving and jovial grandfather. Along the way, he had started to repay his dues.

Through emails I made sure were private with Jacque, I set up a phone call with Josh, who had been living with them since he left us. This situation was ridiculous... The kids had to speak with their dad. When I called their house as arranged, Jacque barely said hello, handing the phone right to Josh without a word it was me. Josh was very cold and short. He was evasive during our conversation, answering questions with questions. Josh accused me of having a plan to put him away, and that would not have helped him. Listening to him, I felt as if he wanted to put on a show for anyone within earshot; find an excuse to be the victim. I quickly commanded, "*You* tell the kids... I'm not doing it for you." I put them on speaker phone. The kids displayed a mix of happiness and confusion while talking to their dad. Straight from the soul-crushing Harry Chapin song, "Cats in the Cradle", the kids asked, "When are you coming home, Dad?"

"I don't know when," he said. Their dad got to be elusive, and then sprinkle out how he missed them so much before he swiftly ended the call. Dumped in my lap was the job of explaining how some people face their problems, while others choose to run.

I had to bite the bullet and educate the kids on the choices their dad had made. The icebreaker consisted of telling them their dad chose not to stop drinking, not to try AA meetings, nor rehab, and that he would not listen to people in recovery. I explained addiction as a disease, and the power of addiction in causing addicts to lie, lose their jobs, hurt their families, etc. The focus was kept on addiction behaviors.

I summed it up with: "There's no room left for your dad to think like a parent. He can't and he isn't." Surveying somber faces, big eyes and motionless bodies, I assured them, "This has nothing to do with anything you did. There is nothing you could have said or done to stop the situation. Your dad was drinking morning, noon, and night. He wasn't listening to his workers; no one could get through. He made up stories about me to cover his actions – it's part of the package. If you hear anything or are told anything, you can talk to me, okay? I will be straight with you."

Connor asked, "Why can't we just drive Dad to rehab?"

"I tried pumpkin. He won't go."

"We'll make him go! Drop him off, and leave him there!" Connor insisted.

"You cannot drop someone off. A patient has the right to refuse treatment and leave at any time. I tried to get him there... had a big meeting planned with his friends and Pop-pop and Grandma. We were going to try and convince him to go. There was even a rehab bed waiting for him. Your dad found out about it, and left. The day I was mad and cursing on the phone... That was about his leaving."

"Daddy would keep alcohol in his water bottle. He told me it was 'special water'," Nicky said.

"I saw him grab a beer can from a bush once," Jolie solemnly added. "I asked him about it. He said that you would get mad. He said it was just a beer."

"Mommy does not get upset over a can of beer, and our lives were not turned upside down because of a few beers. His drinking kept getting worse, and we deserve to be safe. This is a serious problem, and it does not belong in our house anymore. We are going to be okay. We'll get a smaller, wonderful house in this same town." The kids' expressions looked as if someone had taken away their favorite toy and told them, *Don't ask for it back. You can't have it back, and that's just the way it is.*

Far away in my mind was a disgust...a disgust I hid from them because it was for grown-ups. Josh got to say, "I don't know" and hang up the phone, never looking into their eyes, never answering their questions, and certainly never wiping away a single tear.

ABANDONMENT SINKS IN

Absorption of shocking news takes time. It was difficult for me to read a pulse on how the kids were processing their dad's leaving. Over the next few weeks, acceptance of abandonment – even though they couldn't label it – gripped my children at each one's particular and precious developmental stage.

EARLY ONE EVENING, I heard my eleven-year-old Jolie and her little brother fighting over a toy in her room. She appeared to be the bully in this instance. Jolie had a doll collection of miniature animal-critter families. We often created magical worlds playing with the Critter houses, the Tot School, and the families of bunnies, kitties, and puppies wearing overalls and plaid dresses.

"Nicky won't leave my stuff alone! I had them all just the way I wanted it!" Jolie scowled, dropping in defeat to her knees on the bedroom floor.

"Aww, you always play with the village together," I reminded her. "Nicky's seven. He likes making their homes and setting them up with you."

"Why do I always have to share with him? He always gets his way!" Jolie was grabbing parent bunnies with static smiles, pups and kittens, and these hoarding the fuzzy refugees by her lap.

Nicky hovered over the decimated world. I sat down beside my daughter. "Nicky, make sure you ask next time. They're Jolie's special Critter families."

I gave my deflated Nicky a hand squeeze and suggested he play in his room for a while. Nicky crouched down and placed a forgotten pup in the refugee camp. "I'm sorry, Jolie," he said standing back up, his arms a dangly pair of noodles. Subordinately he walked back to his room.

Jolie's agitation lingered. She fidgeted with the crashed miniature world around her. "It doesn't matter anymore," spoken as the loving big sister once again. "Nicky can play with them."

The air in the room felt heavy, as if the ceiling was pressing down on us. Jolie seemed unable to articulate her own turmoil. We remained sitting crossed legged on the floor, side by side. Through a moment of grace, I spoke to her from left field. "Sweetie, I am so, so sorry your daddy left you."

As if her heart had dropped a great burden, my daughter bursted into a deep sob over my lap. My arms wrapped around my little girl, validating her pain without further words. Her long blonde hair cascaded onto a sea of violet carpet. I loved my daughter so much. It was painful knowing I could not protect her from this inevitable ruin of emptiness.

Soon enough, Jolie rose up, her sweet face with five freckles brightening. "I'm okay," and she left to go hug her sibling sidekick. Spent, but not overdrawn, I entered into a divine dialogue: "Please put the odds in my favor that the moments I reach my kids outweigh the times I don't." I too ascended from the ruins, acknowledging that bravery was not within their father's parenting skill set.

COPING with abandonment emerged more indirectly for Nicholas. Nicky had a particular handful of irreplaceable *Stuffies*. This pack included a friendly tiger named Toby; Peanut Butter, a caramel-colored plush lion; Jam-jam, a powder-blue teddy bear; and last but never least, Hammy. Everybody loves Hammy! Hammy was a palm-sized, pink and white Beanie hamster. Understand, I had spent years making Stuffies come to life, especially at bedtime. They communicated with the kids, as well as with each other. Our elaborate Stuffie-adventures had been the finest examples of what therapist's label 'floor-time play'– an interaction between parents and their kids where they get down on the floor for imaginative, creative, and communicative play at each child's assessed developmental level. For my kids, this activity created an emotional backup system. If one of my kids could not tell me about his bad day, or confide her woes, an attentive Stuffie would understand everything, despite the fact Mom was holding it out at arm's length. Stuffies give good hugs too, right under the neck in a tickly spot.

Nicky had other Stuffies that sat on the sidelines, such as Hammy's Beanie hamster parents. They arrived way after Hammy, without fanfare. The couple never got much play action, and somewhere along the way, those parents went missing. I don't know what happened to them... Maybe the dog. Finding them did not seem to matter, until the day that it was all that mattered.

IT HAD BEEN a couple of months since their dad left. By the time my kids got to bed, I was as exhausted as most parents, especially with a three-to-one child-to-parent ratio. As bedtime approached, I clung to the anticipation of quiet solitude and decreased responsibility. Kissing the last of my three cubs good-night, I turned off Nicky's bedroom light—door knob in hand—and stepped one slipper into the hall across the parental finish line. All of a sudden, Nicky cried out, "Mom! Hammy lost his parents!" This literally erupted out of nowhere. *So close. Step away from the finish line.*

Turning to face him in the semi-darkness, I whispered, "We will totally search and rescue tomorrow. Good-night, sweetie." Stepping back towards the hall...

"They're not anywhere... I looked. We have to find his parents! I lost them!" He began to cry, hard. Walking towards the bed... I returned to his side. "No, you didn't lose them. They got lost. It happens. It's not your fault," I reassured him, brushed his hair to the side and proceeded to walk back towards the door...

Nicholas screamed out like he wasn't even talking to me. "Hammy can't be without his parents! What's he going to do?" He escalated. "Poor Hammieee... He need**s** them!" Nicky struggled to catch his breath. "I-I have to-to-to find them for him. Poor Hammieee!" His voice trailed off as he covered himself under his blankets and settled into a meditative sob.

He was crushing my heart, and I was unable to find his MIA hamster parents. Adding salt to the wounds were Peanut Butter and Jam-jam, staring at me with detestation reflected in their coal-y eyes. *Traitors!* I argued at them. *What do you want from me?* Jam-jam gave me the silent treatment while Peanut Butter flicked me the tail.

This "door knob moment" of unexpected crying over Hammy's lost parents became Nicky's ritual every few days, week after week. All the Dollar Stores had run out of Hammy parents and I couldn't risk ordering a pair of stunt doubles because I couldn't recollect the exact color of their stupid fuzz. A horde reunification was not going to happen. Our only option was to help Hammy handle his missing parents.

Nicky and I began educating Hammy on some coping mechanisms, such as helping Hammy draw pictures or pound clay to get out his frustrations. This gentle emotional dissociation allowed my son to step out of being a victim because Hammy was now the victim. Thus, Nicky evolved along with Hammy as Nicky and I identified all of Hammy's feelings, and what we could do about them. Peanut Butter and Jam-jam explained to Hammy that his mommy and daddy were healthy and okay. They were still a part of him and they loved him. Our brave Peanut Butter the plush lion performed a moving soliloquy, pronouncing to all the Stuffies in attendance on Nicky's bedroom floor that Hammy had a big heart, and was a strong and brave little dude. It was declared that Hammy was also crafty, smart and capable of handling these difficult circumstances. Brave Sir Hammy could and would grow up a bit, alongside Nicholas who subconsciously took in these messages and lessons.

Hammy steadily became our new champion and the tears ceased to fall when the lights went out. Many a time I thought, *I owe you one, Hammy.* If I could give one piece of advice to a new parent, I would say: any *Stuffie* or *Blankie* or *Woobie* that you know in your gut will form a unique attachment with your child, for the love of grass-fed butter, buy two. If have to use the back-up, take it to your grave.

———

NOW THIRTEEN, Connor was starting eighth grade. He was finally taller than me and close to beating me in arm wrestling. He could win with his left arm, but I continued to slap down that right arm. I did whatever it took to maintain my alpha status and protect his ego from over inflating too soon. The journey of raising a teenager was quite a roller coaster ride, complete with the following hills and drops: Entitlement Hill, Anger Hill, Annoyance Hill, Feeling Hurt Falls, and of course, Peers Only Tunnel, where parents were supposed to remain in the dark.

Josh caused structural damage to this amusement ride with his divisiveness and belittlement. My relationship with Connor was also complicated because sometimes his words or tone mirrored his dad's. Penitently, this situation created a defensive landmine within me, and I would converse harshly with Connor, as if he were a grown man with selfish intentions. No parent escapes the inevitable: how you talk to your kids will eventually be how they talk to you. But my son and I were in this together. We had safety belts on, and all the structural nuts and bolts of Connor's upbringing were strong and tight, ready to hold, no matter what. Parents learn to navigate whatever lay ahead. I was not going to abandon him.

Steve Harvey handed out some parenting advice on his radio show. Summarizing Mr. Harvey, he said, "Your job is not to be your kids' friend. They got plenty of friends, and they probably like their friends better than you most days, so don't worry about it. Your job is to be their parent. Your job is to make the decisions that are safest and best for your child, not decisions that make them like you. Friends come and go, parents are forever." When I found myself without backup, his philosophy helped me set that tough boundary. *Thanks, Mr. Harvey*

Despite our struggles, Connor was adored by many parents for being such a courteous kid who could always hold a rather thoughtful conversation. Now that he attended junior high with students from three other towns, he was meeting many kids with divorced parents who alternated between two households. Connor said he was glad he didn't have to do that.

Of my three cubs, Connor was the one who asked the most about the details of his dad's absence. "When might he come back? Can he still work? How do we pay the bills? Do you think he will stop drinking?"

I would tell him, "I do not know" with regard to that last question, but Connor was persistent – he wanted an answer. I remember when Connor was four years old, he would constantly ask me on the drive to preschool, "Mommy, how many buckets of water do you think it would take to put out the sun?" He would demand a number. "Just guess, Mom. How many buckets?" My fabricated numerical answers were not good enough: his keen senses could tell I was not being forthright. Eventually auguring a white flag in the ground, I insisted to Lord Connor, reigning from his booster seat in the back, that I could not compute the mathematics necessary to answer his query, and furthermore, buckets were an unacceptable form of measurement for extinguishing the center of the universe. *Kibosh on the sun.*

It took less than two minutes before Connor's innocent voice of sincerity rose up from his booster seat to ask, "Well, how many fire trucks would it take?"

CONNOR NEEDED FACTS, and he needed to feel reassured. Hearing a mother bitterly call his father a narcissistic drunk was not reassuring to a child. I know... Eh-hem, I tried. Objectively explaining how the mental health field described personality types and associated thinking patterns seemed to quell some of Connor's concerns. I told Connor, "We all have faults, and strengths, and talents. How we handle our faults, and the faults of others, is part of building our character. Nobody is perfect. There is an old adage: fall down seven times, get up eight." King Dad was becoming a mere man, and a man, a person, any person will always have faults.

Another focus of our conversations was the behavior and thought patterns of active addicts. Imagine living your life from drink to drink, from hit to hit...focusing only on the security of the next fix. Such dependence builds consuming and selfish thought patterns. I pointed out to Connor that his dad parented well from the behind the scenes, where he was comfortable, but as the alcoholism progressed, his job and the next drink had edged out his family. This was not okay on my end; the time had come to pull the plug. "Your dad is not choosing treatment. I know that's tough to understand."

"Couldn't you make him go to rehab? Can't a doctor just stick him in there?"

"No. I already explained that I tried. My trying to force him is why he would call me 'controlling', and lots of other things. I became an enemy in a way."

"But you were just trying to help him."

Snickering, "I think he viewed me as trying to take away his fun and his best friend and blah, blah, blah. Addicts have to take some of the lead in going to rehab. But, if your life hangs so tightly onto that next drink or that next fix, it's tough. We can offer your dad compassion. Compassion is strength, plus clarity and understanding."

Through self-education and shared feelings of anger, frustration, and compassion, Connor and I created common ground as my son dealt with abandonment and embarrassment issues related to his dad, as well as frustrations or disappointments with me. Connor mentioned a surprising number of kids in his school with a parent who had been, or currently was an addict of some sort. He even had one friend with a father in jail. Connor mentioned that he was glad to not have a father in jail. If only he knew.

"I like our house. I don't want to leave our town," he said.

"I know; don't worry. This house will sell at a good price, and we will have a nice home and you will have your own room."

"Good. Can I have my own bathroom?"

"I cannot put that on the promise list, but we can try."

"Try really hard on that one." Connor appeared to zone out a bit with no particular emotion; he was just lost in thought. His eyes turned sad, then he confided, "You know, Mom, I carve tally marks on my bed frame. I use my pocket knife. Every night Dad doesn't come home, I carve a notch."

"Oh, Connor!" My heart sank, then dug beneath the ocean floor like a clam. Gazing at his somber face, "I-I never saw them."

"I know. I etched them where you wouldn't see."

"Connor, I am sorry your dad left. You have always been a son that brightens our day, our life."

"You don't have to say sorry. He's the one who screwed everything up. It's on Dad if he doesn't get that he has a good family, and a good home."

"Well, you deserve an apology that the adults in your life did not meet better standards. I know I'm not perfect. I will always try to up my game." Connor flashed that contagious smile I love. "I'm coming in for the bear hug. I love you, pumpkin."

With a tight squeeze, he whispered into my ear, "I love you too, Mom."

Pulling back to look at him, "By the way, you have a pretty special job and hold a lot of weight being an older brother. Your attention and kindness are meaningful to your sister and brother. That also means your negative comments are extra hurtful."

"But they can be so annoying." Connor straightened up.

Speaking in a mom-like tone, "Why? Because they act like little kids?"

Traces of a smile emerged at the corners of his mouth. "I guess. I don't know what it is."

"Perhaps if you appreciate them a little more and accept their age, you will find two of your biggest fans." He seemed good with that.

NEW NORMAL

After Thanksgiving, Josh communicated with the kids every couple of weeks, sometimes only because we called him. Meanwhile he posted on-line photos of places he went with his motorcycle. Per Jacque, Josh's family was becoming more aware of the situation Josh had created, as well as his drinking issues. Janelle, who is Josh's sister-in-law and a therapeutic counselor, lived with his brother, David, in Austria. Janelle was trying to form an alliance with Josh over the phone.

Janelle was supportive and informed me that she was trying to get Josh to acknowledge the position he had put me and his family in, and to handle things more appropriately. Janelle was also therapeutic with me. She explained that the interpersonal connections in Josh's family did not carry much weight. Janelle shared that one time, she had asked Josh's mom to explain some peculiar things about her son, David. Janelle was David's third wife. Ingrid's answer was, 'I know my boys don't make good husbands.' That was it, the most validation any of the daughters-in-law were going to get. Ingrid offered no explanation. Janelle suggested that Josh send support money, but that task would take more groundwork.

WINTER NEWS: we had another offer on the house, just in time for Christmas. They were the cutest couple. They owned a flower distribution center that dealt directly with Holland. Despite lowering the price fifty grand, not using a realtor was saving me a lot of money. The buyers requested a second tour of the house with their visiting family members before finalizing the sale of intent. They gave me a deposit to take the house off the market. "Guess what kids?" I was able to say… "We're getting a tree!" Turns out, if you bought a Christmas tree on December 23rd, you got it for half off.

We visited the local tree farm, famous for their tractor rides around decorated evergreens which included a cup hot cocoa with marshmallows. The owner traditionally set up a raised six foot by twelve foot platform train set for visitors to enjoy. We were the only ones in the whole lot buying a tree; the owner ran his trains just for us. No room for gloom. *We're gonna be okay, kids.*

We had a wonderful Christmas with my family. The kids chatted with Josh, Caleb, and Jacques over the holiday. Josh and I spoke amicably with him saying that once he found work, he would send money. I was not holding my breath, but those words were a start. Our divorce court date was set for the following month. I would meet the judge without a lawyer, without a spouse, and without two signatures on the divorce agreement. Interesting, yes, but I was sure it would all work out.

Rest in peace 2011.

The only time drinking isn't good for you is when you write or when you fight. But it always helps my shooting. - Ernest Hemingway

Despite certified mailings, strained phone conversations and fruitless e-mails, Josh still hadn't signed the divorce agreement. I assumed Josh thought this tactic would stall everything. Once the contentious topic was dropped, our communication improved. Our focus became the kids, which started the ball rolling for a visit. I imagined Josh's family had put pressure on him to see the kids over their winter break. We agreed on a visit after the holidays, which happened to be a week before our divorce court date. At least the kids were thrilled.

Thrilling was not the theme for the sale of our house. A letter arrived from the buyers politely stating they were backing out of the contract, foregoing their deposit of good faith. They had concluded, after consulting with their family, that they could not handle the demands of such a house, and despite the appeal of the property, they wanted a more modern house. The contract was cancelled without any hard feelings, only disappointments. *That's it. I want a realtor.* Turns out, it was pretty darn awesome having a partner to take over the leg work. Her name was Missy and she was my super realtor.

SUGAR DADDY

Josh made the two-day drive to visit us without incident. He said he had his drinking under control. I expected that if he could make the drive to get here, it had to be true. All three kids greeted him at the door with hugs and squeals. After almost four months apart, they were very happy to see and touch their dad. Personally, I had three goals for the visit: 1) make it safe and engaging for the kids 2) not halt the divorce for any reason 3) get money towards this sinking house, as promised.

Right away, Josh exhibited a degree of remorse for his actions. He was helpful with the yard and cooking meals, and made bread with the kids. His mood was a bit despondent. He seemed to be processing a delayed goodbye to his former life – a world he had worked so hard to build. After days without harsh judgement from me, he finally talked about things from my perspective. Josh agreed that paying me some support money seemed reasonable. He was willing to write a check for $3000. However, "willing it" was not the same as "writing it".

Was he drinking? I could tell within a half hour of his arrival: Josh still lugged a vodka bottle in his grey backpack. Josh admitted that he didn't want the kids to see a ton of beer cans, so he was trying to sip vodka discreetly. "Less embarrassing...," he had claimed.

I respected his right to choose, and did not go around and around with him. Josh offered a generic apology, stating: "I screwed up. I can be better, and I do love you." He made advances to sleep with me in a playful manner. I imagined he wanted to wake up in a bed with a woman, and a fixed life. I turned him down nicely, so as not to bruise his ego. As the days went by, he harmlessly persisted by wrapping his arms around me, or turning a mutual hug into kissing my turned away face.

The day before he was scheduled to drive back, I still did not have a signed, $3000 check. An unspoken arrangement was emerging that would solidify me getting that check. I formulated two viewpoints: one from a business side, and one from a personal side. Technically, Josh was still my husband; earning $3000 for fifteen minutes was not a bad rate. On the other hand, would I feel too morally compromised? As a single mother, was I selling myself out? What to do? What to do? Oh, whatever should I do?

Uh, cha-ching! The next day that check was cashed before he even started the car. Josh drove back, safe and sound.

DIVORCE COURT

As I walked from the parking garage to the judicial complex building, rigid blades of grass from the evening's frost cracked beneath my shoes. A leather attaché full of prepared documents for court was in hand. My mom and Sara met me at the metal detector line. I wore black dress pants and a white blouse to symbolize death and rebirth all at once. The courtroom was full of people in suits, representing those with glum faces. The prestigious bearded man wearing the pressed robe made eye contact with everyone. The judge diligently listened and asked fair questions during the eight divorce cases that preceded mine. Those clients had lawyers. Only myself and a gentleman across the pew from us did not have legal representation. The judge called my case next to last.

At the podium, my nerves vibrating, I informed the judge, "Your honor, I am representing myself." The judge spoke with me as seriously as he had the other clients, but unlike clients with lawyers, I got to talk to him directly. He asked about the absent party, and requested to see the certified mailings proving that Josh had been properly notified. I readily provided those receipts. The judge also asked about the attempts to get Josh to sign the divorce agreement. I concisely explained that my husband would not sign. The judge paused to mention that it would be very difficult to prove the equitable distribution portion, and that it should be done with the utmost care. The judge used that point to revisit the idea of my retaining a lawyer.

I mentioned that I had receipts and papers for everything. The judge seemed to waiver slightly, but told me to proceed. There was no point in explaining our particular story, but I did produce my receipts for various items, plus my numerical tallies of equity. The judge focused on the house and asked for the appraisal. *Huh.* I told him what I was selling it for, and what we had originally paid. For that, I had proof. Apparently, my selling price did not count as an indicator of the current value of the house, nor did what we had paid for it. I needed a current appraisal. The judge indicated politely that he had heard enough. He put up his hand and explained that what I was presenting was not working, and that there were several things missing. I listened and tried to piece together what he was talking about, but it was confusing.

I was able to ask the judge questions, and he answered with patience, explaining the need for more cohesion of supporting documents. The judge talked about future provisions...future this...future that... Emotionally, I could not muster enthusiasm for all the provisions I was entitled to receive. I could not envision Josh ever being capable to provide anything. I just wanted the divorce. The judge, however, did not want me to suffer future consequences because of matters not being dealt with properly. I stopped talking as a sign of appreciating what he was saying, but it hurt. The judge postponed the hearing for one month so that I could be more prepared. He suggested that I try again to get Josh's signature, otherwise there was a lot to cover. He repeated my right to have an attorney present when I returned to his courtroom. Gavel drop. Court dismissed. Nothing had changed.

Gripping my attaché case with sweaty palms, I turned to see that final gentleman in the courtroom pew, waiting his turn.

Walking down the aisle, I mouthed, "Sorry you had to wait." To my surprise, his face illuminated with a smile and he said, "You did good, kid. Hang in there; you'll get it," and enthusiastically shook my hand.

Maybe it was only a small sign, but I would take it. This stranger had made my attempt seem less desperate—perhaps even brave—yet naïve at the same time. Many people become powerless during the divorce process; I was trying to remain in the driver's seat. I would get a lawyer, but I'd also keep the navigation rights. Sara and my mom both commented that they thought the judge had been very understanding; however, we were all disheartened the divorce was not over. It seemed never ending.

HOMESTRETCH

Twenty-eight days remained until my second court date. Once again, I had sent a copy of the divorce agreement through certified mail, and emailed a copy to Josh's work account. This was a big deal since Josh did not know I was aware he had found employment; the acceptance offer was in his personal emails. His Human Resource department was very helpful in obtaining my husband's professional contact information. An email correspondence from me in his work inbox would be quite the shock-a-rooner. I gave him a day – no response back. My patience was about the size of a jelly bean. Since Josh did not eat lunch, what better time to reach into his double-life. His phone was answered on the second ring.

"Hello, Dr. Josh here," politely stated. Dr. Josh waited for a response. "Hello?" he repeated.

"Hi, Dr. Josh. It's your wife."

Long pause, his breath was audible through the receiver. He asked with a hushed voice, "How did you get this number?" Perhaps an effort not to be heard by others.

"Come again? I couldn't quite hear you," I pressed.

"Never mind. I know you are very resourceful. What do you want?" he curtly asked.

"I sent you an email containing a copy of the divorce agreement. I need you to sign it and send it back."

"I did not get any email. I do not know what you are talking about."

"Then look for it. I'll wait." I gave him a few seconds to respond. "Josh, don't tell me there isn't a computer at your desk, because half of your job is writing reports."

"I cannot check my emails right now," Josh responded. "I will do it later."

"Yeah – but you won't. I can call back and leave messages with various department heads that I, your wife, am having a hard time getting a hold of you, or you can choose to handle this now. Your co-workers do know you're married, right?" As they say, the sound of crickets a.k.a. nothing came over the phone. "I need a response, Josh."

"I am checking now, Jess-i-ca."

"Let me know the headline of the email I sent, so I'm sure you have the right one."

"Why do you have to be—?" Josh stopped mid-way through his sentence. I heard fingers banging on a keyboard. "I do not see anything, Jessica. I am checking my emails...it is not here. You cannot call me at work."

"Did you check your work email? I'm sure it's there."

"My work email!" He put the phone down; I heard rapid typing. In a deep tone, he snapped: "I see it. It has the headline 'El Divorce – snap'. What do you want me to do?"

"I need you to print it out and sign it today. I'm sure someone in your medical facility is a notary."

"I-I cannot open the document. I am literally trying, and it will not open. This stupid computer won't print. I am hitting print and nothing is happening. I cannot do this Jess-i-ca. I cannot read it now. I am at work."

"This is like the fourth time I sent it to you. You have already read it. We already agreed on it. I wrote it like a fifth-grade book report, so you would not decompensate when you saw it."

Joshua reprimanded, "You – you cannot expect me to read a legal document. Legal documents take forever."

"It's literally two pages! Allow me to jog your memory... Nobody wins! I sell the house to pay off two mortgages, which barely leaves enough for us to stay in this town. You pay a third of what you have been earning towards child support – it should be half your pay. No alimony payments, so you can feel vindicated, and I will continue to work two jobs, raise three kids and manage a home by myself. You get to do whatever you want, and see the kids whenever you would like as long as I'm around. Bottom line, every day, you can wake up and think about only yourself, except when you send food money. Is that too much to ask, Josh-i-wa? Any man would kill for two pages like that, but you run."

I heard a mighty sigh, then he spoke, "You're not staying in the house?"

"What? How can I stay in the house? It took both our salaries."

"When you sell it, you'll be fine."

"The house isn't selling—two deals fell through. I've lowered the price now eighty grand. It's winter; the oil bills alone are over $500. How am I paying bills if the house is not sold? How do I stop the bills from coming, if this house is not sold? I tried to avoid spending money on lawyers by doing this divorce myself, thank you very much."

"You don't have a lawyer?" sounding surprised.

"Read the divorce agreement! Does it look like a lawyer who passed the bar exam wrote it? It's a disservice I didn't write it in crayon. I'm not kidding, it's two pages. This never had to be complicated. I tried a mediator, remember? You stopped going."

Josh sounded distracted. "The printer...is not working. The printer – it is literally not working. This place sucks! They are so incompetent here." He was stammering, and curt. "I am trying another printer and...it is not working. Nothing works here." His voice faded in and out.

Entering super calm mode, I spoke with an even tone. "Josh, you mean to tell me that in an entire medical center there is not a single working printer?"

"Yes, Jessica – they do have working printers. I cannot seem to get the computer to print."

Deep breath. "Okay Josh, so what you are telling me is, as a man who holds a doctorate degree, actively treats medical patients, and writes formal reports all day—you are incapable of printing an email?"

"Yes that is what I am fucking telling you!"

Keeping' my chill... "If you prefer, I can forward the divorce email to your human resource department, and ask them to print it out for you. They gave me your work email. I'm sure they would be delighted to assist us. They could put the printed divorce pages right there on your desk." How the high and mighty Dr. Josh appeared in front of others was of great importance.

"The computer is working," Josh stated blandly. "I got it – it is printing both pages right now." His tone was softer, less articulated.

"I knew you could do it. You're amazing." What had just happened was not supposed to have been the hardest part of the phone call. I bit my tongue, then let it fly. "This needs to be signed and mailed by tomorrow afternoon. I'm asking that you send me a picture of it notarized, so I know you followed through. Then send a picture of the addressed envelope after the post markings are on it, so I know it's coming."

"You want what? I am not—"

"This is a court-ordered deadline. All you have done is stall and cause complete mistrust. Providing proof is the consequence. If I do not hear back from you, or you do not handle this by tomorrow afternoon, then I have to take other measures. I'm not waiting around to get dragged through some head game.

You are either going to man up, or you're not. Either way, I need to know."

"You have a great way of asking someone to help you," Josh stated point blank.

Flashback: same argument, different topic. Shock stole my voice. How should I have asked a man who abandoned his family to live in another country to avoid getting divorced so he could hold onto wealth he was blowing away faster than he could make it, with a preference to drink himself into oblivion? What is the etiquette on that one?

"I look forward to hearing from you, Josh. Have a nice day." *Snap.*

THE FOLLOWING DAY AT NOON, a formally written email arrived in my inbox from Josh's personal email account. In business format, Josh informed me that he did not feel comfortable signing any documents before having a lawyer look them over. He did not know how long it would take to obtain a lawyer as he had recently started working, and it would be sometime before he could afford one. He signed the email professionally, with sincere regards. At least, I knew the status.

Upon printing out the email, I added it to my folder of proof and correspondences. I wanted to cry, but wasn't sad enough. Wanted to scream, but I was being too rational. I wanted to say, "I'm fine", but the glue holding me together was disintegrating. Afraid to jostle my thoughts, I sat in the eye of the storm until my mind drifted to the dearest people in the world to me: my aunt and uncle in California. They had always brought out the best in me, and I'd always admired their strong humanitarian views. They had no children of their own, so when my brother and I stayed over at their house as kids, we had received unwavering attention. My uncle, whom I often thought looked like Clint Eastwood, seemed like the most down to earth person that to call. My Aunt Rain, a beautiful artist, answered the phone, and listened to my plight. 'Rainy' as I affectionately called her, cheerfully replied, "Hold on... This is a job for your unc." Uncle Clint got an earful as to my current situation. He did not disappoint.

"Jessie, I am writing you a check right now. I am sticking it in the mail today. Get a lawyer, and get this shit done." I heard the check rip away from the card stock.

This Clint Eastwood quote, from *The Outlaw Josey Wales* seemed fitting:

> "Now remember, when things look bad and it looks like you're not gonna make it, then you gotta get mean. I mean plumb mean, mad-dog mean. Cause if you lose your head and you give up, then you neither live, nor win. That's just the way it is."

LAWYERED UP

Through search and recommendation, I found a great lawyer for $500 an hour. *No can do.* However, his assistant, Gina, who was also present during my interview, charged $350 an hour; I liked her as well. Gina did not belittle my situation; in fact, she seemed determined to make it work the best way possible in a short amount of time. Gina and I took an afternoon and between the two of us, we made it all come together.

Gina's goal was to clearly demonstrate that Josh's equity was equal to half the value of the house. This would mean an even split, and I would get the proceeds from the sale. This was not as glorious as it sounded because I had two equal mortgages to pay off. Josh would receive equity credit for the commercial building, but I would have to pay off. That equated to about half the bittersweet falling equity in the house. Gina had me get the house re-appraised ASAP. Apparently, the market was quite unkind: the low appraisal sent dreams of college funds and a future turn-key house sailing away. My realtor dropped the price, however, my positive thinking remained: the sale of the house would wipe everything clean, and allow a fresh start. Gina and I were ready for court.

By now, I could have gotten to the courthouse with my vision occluded. My mom sat next to me on the plaintiff side of the courtroom. The judge called up my docket case. I left our pew to join Gina up front. From behind the podium, the first words spoken out of the judge's mouth were directed at my lawyer, "Am I glad to see you." The judge and the lawyer were unified in making this a solid divorce, and in addressing alimony and child support as the law allowed, versus my limited faith in Josh to support us.

Things in the courtroom progressed in a slow whirl. Using documented information, Gina answered all the mandatory questions. Then came the first order of business: equity assessments. The decision came down... I got the house free and clear. Josh got his cars, motorcycle, trailer, shares in the empty commercial building, half the money he took when he left, and his retirement monies. Added relief to me was that I could sell the house without having to deal with Josh. The judge progressed through the proceedings, leaving no stone unturned with fairness to both parties. Last was the issue of custody.

"Your honor, my client is requesting sole custody of their three children." Those words... They were finally out there, spoken on behalf of what my heart would never, ever, ever, EVER surrender.

The judge announced: "He has abandoned his children, and has made no efforts on their behalf. Full custody shall be awarded to their mother. Any visitation by their father, shall be at the sole discretion of their mother."

Sole discretion... No one had ever mentioned... I never even thought... It was an order of complete trust, reverence, and recognition of me... *Me.*

It was an appropriate legal decision to protect the children. There was also a judgement on my legal fees, child support and alimony. The support was significantly more than I had requested in my two-page, crayon-document Joshua refused to sign. Handling a divorce proceeding was really out of my league. But, had I turned the matter over to someone else earlier, the outcome would not have been the divorce I needed, or deserved, and that had been worth fighting for 'til the very end. *Thank you, judge. Mahalo Nui aloha.*

To get that kind of legal decision, I was fortunate to be a white woman living in suburbia with a just-crazy enough white husband. The legal system was and still is an awful hurdle. I hope judges everywhere will carve paths and provide common sense protection for desperate and exhausted women fighting without resources. And justice is not served by capable women with ample resources tearing down their counter-part men just to be excused from carrying more responsibility. A divorce tests one's integrity and the ability to withstand and make changes. In the words spoken by a beloved rapper and tough guy actor, Ice Cube: "Check yo self, before you wreck yo self."

My mom was in the courtroom that day, just as she was always there for me, always believing in me, and always my cheerleader. After the divorce was final, we hugged. Unlike last time, we made no after plans; we didn't want to jinx anything. "No thanks on the lunch offer Mom. I just want to go home."

"You were fair and you were strong. This whole time you were never afraid to grow. Give it some time honey, there is more waiting for you."

Wandering alone in the concrete parking garage, I came to terms with the divorce being over. For posterity's sake, I asked myself, "What do I feel?"

Here is Jessica's divorce analogy... Imagine sitting in a fine restaurant about to eat. On the plate is a delicious, hearty, wholesome meal. As flavorful aromas entwine with piping hot steam from this incredible dish placed before you, the waiter takes away your fork and spoon. Turns out, the meal is just for show. The waiter proceeds to smash everything up, and place it all in a vastly overpriced, sterile, Styrofoam container, and tucks that into a plastic bag with a generic smileyface logo using a loosely tied knot... Bon appetit!

In my mind, our marriage was that fancy meal on a plate, now converted to leftovers. My divorce was like taking home leftovers wrapped in a bogus reality with a generic smileyface. There was the promise of child support and alimony packed in my container, but I wasn't going to get any. Josh would likely never make a payment, nor be capable of maintaining a job for any significant length of time. An appetite without the ability to taste or swallow is no appetite at all. I had full custody of abandoned children. I won a house I couldn't afford, nor sell. My retirement money was used up, and we had no health insurance. There would be no victory lap today.

I dug out the car keys from the bottom of my purse and held them in my hand. I wanted some kind of message – a simple burning bush would do. Officially, I had just become a single mom to three of the most precious, sweet, loving kids in the whole wide world... that was my meal. No matter where the kids and I went, we would have a home filled with love. In time, the house would sell. I had a great career that impacted many lives, and I was free of playing the blame game. As the soot of my emotional abuse caked off, I caught a glimpse of myself smiling in the rearview mirror.

PROTECTING THE CUBS

The day my divorce papers with the gold seal arrived, I followed up on a safety task and visited my kids' elementary school. The principal, swiveling in a chair behind his desk, was a gregarious man, dedicated to his job. He was capable of naming all 247 students and their parents, and he volunteered to sit in the dunk tank every year for the annual Ice Cream Social. He never held it against me that I dunked him with my pitching arm—the arm that had taught my Connor how to pitch.

Reaching across his desk, I presented the official page from our divorce packet, declaring that I had full custody of the kids. Also included was the final page bearing the judge's name, date, and official court seal. The principal, who resembled a tall glass of water at six feet, seven inches, rose from his chair and approached me with the gentlest expression on his face. "Thank you for this – I'm sure it wasn't easy. I will speak to my staff right away, in confidence, of course." He called for his secretary to come and take the pages to be photocopied. She was in and out of his office with efficiency.

"My ex-husband is never to leave this school with any of my children. He can never visit, never call, and never pick them up, unless you see me standing next to him."

"All I needed was that paper. The kids here are like my own." The principal's eyes deepened with emotion. "He'll have to go through me first."

"We're good then?" I asked, standing under his protective shadow.

"We're good," he said, pushing his wire rims back up to the bridge of his nose.

SOMEONE HAS MOVED ON

Ever since I had moved back to the mainland from Hawaii, I was in awe of spring flowers spontaneously sprouting where the ground had been vacant of life for months. This surprise out of the earth had given me a particular love of planting bulbs: tulips, crocus, irises, narcissus, grape hyacinth – and of creating freshly cut bulb arrangements combined with ornamental grasses. Jolie and I had just finished cleaning up all the clippings from a productive gardening session when I received an unrecognizable international call. I sent Jolie off to join her brothers on the trampoline.

"Hello," I greeted the caller.

"Hello. Who is this?" asked the female on the other end. Her voice sounded non-threatening and without confidence, yet I didn't care to respond. Before I could hang up on her, she hooked me. "Oh, do you know Joshua?"

"Y-yes I do."

"Yah, I was wondering whose number this was," said the female caller with the Canadian accent. *Ah-ha. It's "the call."*

"I see. Let me guess: you're checking Josh's phone numbers because you are suspicious, and think he may not be playing by the rules."

"Um yes-s-s. How did you know, ay?"

"Because I've done exactly the same thing. Don't worry dear, I'm his ex-wife." Her gasp was audible.

"My name is Jess, perhaps you've heard. Nice to meet you. So, how long have you and Josh been together?"

"Yah, he's mentioned you. You've had to check on him about dating too?" She spoke in a whisper.

"Is Josh there, somewhere?"

"He's out taking a walk. He likes to do that, ya know. He tells me these other numbers are just friends, but I have my doubts. We met before Christmas, but I think he may have been seeing someone else at the time. I caught him going on a date, yah. We decided to go out and ah, he was supposed to stop all this."

"Well, Josh will say the things you want to hear. Generally speaking, he is not a cheater, but Josh has not made any good decisions for quite some time. Did he mention he has children?"

"Oh yah, he loves them very much!"

"Ri-i-ght...that's why he doesn't send child support." *Throw you into his pit of despair over miss'n his children, yah.* "Is he still drinking every night?"

"Oh, he does drink quite a bit." Her voice sounded high-pitched, and she talked with a slow cadence – homegrown Canadian for sure. "I have a kid too, ay. I didn't know he wasn't sending any child support for his kids."

"Well, feel free to mention what you think a standup guy should do."

"I'll see what I can do. He just started working; he doesn't have much. I should go. Don't tell Josh I called you. I don't want him to get upset."

"It's fine. I don't have a reason to tell him."

"Would it be okay if I call you again sometime? I don't want to cause any trouble, ay. But I might have some questions." *That would be totally fun, yah.*

Josh had forgotten to put away a bottle of nail polish one-time while Skyping with the kids. The bright fuchsia bottle came into the screen shot, so I had definitely suspected Josh was right back on the dating horse.

"It's okay if you need to call. I guess you've seen his new apartment? Josh showed the kids on a video chat."

"I live there too. We decided to get the place a month ago, yah, when he got his new job. He was tired of living in his dad's basement apartment." *O-o-kay...that was more than I had bargained.*

"I better be gettin'," she whispered. "Talk later to you."

CHAKRA CHECK... I was not bothered by this like the ole days. I didn't care anymore, echoing a sentiment that Phil Collins had belted out in a song many moons ago. Coincidently, that song had recently gone into my playlist. It was frustrating Josh got to move on so quickly with his life, though I did not regret making the "grown-up" decisions. Josh told me that he would send money once he had some paychecks coming in, and was living independently. I had taken him at face value. On the flip side, unbeknownst to Josh, I was working with child support services to garnish his wages. Despite logical thinking, the taste in my mouth after that phone call kinda sucked, yah.

GOT A BUYER

What did not suck was finally having a buyer for the house. Yahoo! It was a young couple looking to start a family. I had lowered the price another $10,000, but as I looked for new places to move, other listing prices were dropping too. I could still buy a decent four-bedroom, two bath home; in fact, a charming white Cape Cod had lowered to a reasonable price, and my bid was accepted – contingent upon my house selling. This had been the only home, so far, that we all liked; the yard was spacious since it was a corner lot. We could all envision a new future.

My realtor, Missy, and I were becoming close buds during this process. She went all out for me. Being a realtor was such a difficult job: lots of legwork before getting any pay. Missy informed me that my third potential buyers needed to push the settlement date further out by a week. The couple were closing a lawsuit with a hospital for a large settlement from which they planned to buy the house. The delay was fine by me. The kids and I donated a couple car loads of stuff to a local charity, which decreased enough clutter to organize the packing.

The sellers of our potential next house had already given their basement furniture to their son, whom had recently moved out. In the spirit of honoring the changes involved with raising kids, I dropped off a lucky bamboo plant to them with a note wishing them luck and letting them know we loved the house, and hoped to fill it with many new memories. The wife called to thank me, and like good town neighbors, we had a lovely conversation. She said it was okay for the kids and I to stop by for one more quick look so we could decide which kid got which room, etc. A week later, on a nice spring day, we were given a tour of our future home. This included managing tips about the house, such as where to find the fuse box, shut off valves and all the appliance manuals. That tour was given to me by the husband. It did not escape me that these responsibilities were normally handled by *the husband*. My new job description was covering for two.

A FEW DAYS LATER, Missy called me while at work, luckily while

I was between clients. We talked almost every other day. Missy said in her no-nonsense voice, "Hey, you're not going to like this."

"Not like what? I have to move the closing date again? It's annoying, but fine. I'm procrastinating on packing anyway."

"No, it's not about the date. Your buyers went to court this morning. They didn't get the settlement: some new kind of delay. I didn't get all the details, but they are devastated. They have been dealing with this lawsuit for a longtime. They cannot handle having a house waiting in the wings; they're backing out. I told them we can be flexible, but their realtor said they cannot cope with anything else. They feel bad, but this is what it is. I'm sorry, Jess. I really wanted this to work out for you."

"Thanks Missy; so, did I. This messes up the other couple too – we just toured their house again. This is a mess for everyone."

"Jess, I see it all the time. You never know until it is actually closing day and the ink is dry. But I am going to stick a "House Sold" sign in your front lawn. We are going to get there!"

"When that day comes, I want two sold signs in my lawn."

"I will make you and Jolie matching sashes from sold stickers."

COUGAR TIME

As spring continued to unfold, I decided to partake in the crap-piest part-time job I knew - internet dating. No more self-pity and whining. I wanted to bring out those tucked away parts of me. After a few sparks of profile interest here and there, I began to hit it off with a chiropractor around my age, in his early forties. Communication was very upfront in our chats. He admitted that once a relationship started, he was looking to engage in sex sooner rather than later. I volleyed back the complete and utter opposite: strangers and sheets don't mix. He appeared to understand. Our rapport grew. Despite the seventy miles between us, we decided to meet for an equidistant dinner.

Meanwhile, in an effort to get the house sold, I was having the outside trim work repainted, and some minor repairs done to improve the curb appeal. The painter/carpenter I hired had impressed me with his courteousness and work skills. In addition, when the kids asked him never ending questions, he was genuinely attentive to them. Bonus feature: he had a nice body. Over several conversations, the kids and I learned that our contractor man practiced martial arts.

He also shared that at age fourteen he entered the foster care system because of his mom's drug habit; he never knew his dad. He preferred to keep to himself, was not materialistic, and has been supporting himself while climbing out of a challenging past. I gathered all this information because he and I had tea one morning on the patio. Initially, our conversation was awkward, but we kept pushing through until we reached a pleasant and more comfortable interface. He referenced his high school days quite a bit, because high school had been less than a decade ago for him. It slipped my mind to mention I already had my twenty-year high school reunion, a "senior moment" on my part.

FRIDAY MORNING ARRIVED, the day of my internet date. The chiropractor had not contacted me in recent days. I sent a note requesting that if he had changed his mind, it was okay, but for common courtesy sake please let me know. As my departure time of 3:00 p.m. approached, I conceded to having been stood-up, and messaged him: "As a chiropractor, you really should grow a spine."

A sitter was still lined up to watch my kids. I would take myself to the movies, unless...

Outside working in the front yard was the contractor guy or, as my kids liked to call him, "the Ninja painter". Ninja walked over as soon as he saw me approach; we small talked a bit. Ninja had a couple more days of work, then he would be gone.

I managed to slide into our conversation: "I'm going to see a movie tonight. Thought I'd take myself out."

Ninja: "That's cool. You're going by yourself?"

"Yes—actually, I had sort of a blind date planned, but I got stood-up. It happens."

Ninja sounded surprised. "Somebody stood you up? That doesn't make sense."

Aww. That soothed my stood-up sting. Ninja looked at the sky for a moment, then responded, "Sorry to hear about that."

"It's fine. I didn't know him... Some chiropractor I met online: a whole dating scenario I hate, but thought I'd give it a try. Anyway, I told him to grow a spine and now I have the night off."

Ninja arched his back. "No – you didn't say that? That's awesome! He deserves it." Ninja flashed a sly smile and pondered for a moment. "Well, if you would be interested, I'd like to go to the movies with you." His six-foot frame was right next to me. He had brown hair, brown eyes and a well-defined nose I was getting used to...and a pretty boy face with perfect white teeth. His muscular shoulders were much broader than his hips...at least I think they were—I mean, I hardly noticed.

"Uh-hem, really?" I said. Of course, I was hoping he'd want to join me, but I did not assume the odds were in my favor.

Ninja squinted his eyes at me. "Yes, I would like to go with you. Why?" he asked with candor, "you didn't think I'd want to?"

"I did not have a sense of confidence about it, but yes, I'd like you to come to the movies with me." My face flushed; my chest felt warm. Was it hot out here, or was it just...?

AS PER THE details we worked out, Ninja met me at the movie theater after he went home to shower. I tried to buy the tickets... After all, I had started it. But he insisted on paying and would not have it any other way. The movie was a comedy, which we both enjoyed. There wasn't any hand holding, however, our elbows and knees touched half-way through the film, and remained so until it ended.

Back in the parking lot, we sat in his truck for a while and talked. The conversation had our best flow thus far. He showed me some funny videos on his phone, and pictures of him going through obstacle courses in mud-run races. Ninja stated almost everything he owned, except for his tools and his weights, would fit in one huge suitcase and he liked it that way. We touched a little on the subject of spirituality. We were both in agreement there was something bigger than ourselves out there, and that our lives should strive towards emanating that source, no matter what the circumstances. Eventually, it was time to admit...

"It's getting late. I go to bed fairly early when my days are physically demanding," Ninja explained, resting his hands on the steering wheel.

"Yeah, I'm due to get home too." I grabbed my purse and put it on my lap.

"I'll walk you to your car," he offered. The lot area was empty except for our two vehicles and the moon.

"Sounds good to me," I said, opening the truck door to exit. *Wonder if he'll kiss me.* It had been over a year since I had genuinely kissed someone...felt a caress through my hair. I squeezed my purse under my arm with anticipation.

Walking side by side, we stopped at the driver's side door of my SUV and faced one another. Under the moonlight, I saw him glance at me, then the ground, then back to me. He was wearing black sneakers, jeans, an aqua blue t-shirt, and a denim jacket. Slowly, my eyes met his smile, and our bodies moved toward each other. I caught a brief glimpse of his lips before I closed my eyes, and felt the press of his kiss. His lips did not part as he lingered. My arms floated up and around his neck; I wanted more. A few little kisses turned into one long, gentle, entwining kiss. His hands slid across my lower back and up my shoulders.

Our kiss dwindled as our bodies, pressing together, melted into a tight hug. We broke free, easing back in a way that mimicked an ocean wave rhythmically receding from the shore.

He leaned over placing his chin against the skin of my neck, and whispered in a deep, raspy voice, "Mm, good-night."

"Good-night," I whispered back. A cool breeze moved a strand of hair across my face. Ninja tucked it behind my ear with his finger.

I eased into my car, playing it cool, and drove out of the parking lot. Once a few blocks away, I pulled over, shook my head and repeated, "Wow, wow, wow. Wow! Wow, wow." Finally I had my turn up to bat and hit the fountain of youth.

The next day, I woke up to a text message, the first of its kind for me. The text read: "Good morning, beautiful!" Yeah, baby – I'll take that 'cloud in my coffee' as Carly Simon used to sing in her song, You're So Vain.

OUR MESSAGES quickly upgraded to cute emojis and flirtatious comments. We planned to meet again the following Sunday. This date entailed a walk in the woods, complete with a picnic of hoagies and water bottles. It took a couple miles of walking and talking for the awkward barriers to come down again. Once we found a grassy spot by a stream and set a blanket out, the hoagies went one way and we rolled the other. Our bodies and lips suctioned onto each other until the seal got broken by our laughter. We found a groove of short and long kisses mixed with subtle nuances of touch, such as interlacing our fingers, his brushing the hair off my neck, or my tugging on a belt loop from his jeans. Remaining fully clothed, we were more playful than passionate. It was a fun novelty to lie on top of him, or flip over to feel the weight of his body on mine. After all our surface areas had been tantalized in some way, we took a sandwich break, along with a side dish of *'Tell me what you're thinking...'*

Ninja began. "What do you think about us starting something?"

"Isn't the girl supposed to ask that kind of question?" I teased.

"Not today. I want to know what you think." Ninja rested his sandwich on his lap.

"Okay, I can be serious. I don't date just to date. I want something genuine and intimate – something I look forward to each day. It's great if that happens with us, and it's okay if it doesn't."

"Was it okay I kissed you the other night? I wasn't sure, but then you made it seem very okay."

"If you're going to impress a gal, then do it." We exchanged a smooch. "I love making out. Wait, let me rephrase: there is an art to making out that should not be overlooked. Also, having a physical chemistry has become very important to me."

"So, did I impress you?" he asked while his arms put a great squeeze on me and his teeth bit my neck. I responded with the squeal he was probably seeking.

"Yes. You don't kiss too much, or too little. Honestly, you impress me every day. Whether it's the skill of something you are working on at the house, or how you view life, you have my interest." I squeezed within his squeeze. "And the kissing is very good." My teeth went for his neck to get the moan I was seeking.

My turn to probe his thoughts. "What do you think about me? I'm a package deal, with kids."

"I don't mind the kids – I don't. They're a part of your life. Don't feel you have to worry about that."

"Thanks. I'm not worried, but I don't have a lot of time, or much of myself to share. Usually, it will be easier if you come to my house so I can be with them or near them."

"That's fine. If you don't mind my asking," with utmost sincerity, "does their dad see them much?"

"Not unless he uses a telescope," I said, shaking my head.

"He is pretty far away, like a country away. It's not worth explaining. I'm not seeking a father replacement; the kids and I just want to heal from the effects of a recent divorce."

Ninja nodded his head. He took a sip of water from his bottle and offered me one. The water tasted especially refreshing under a canopy of tree branches and the sun's warmth. Ninja caressed my free hand and said, "I think you're beautiful. Your eyes are amazing: sometimes they turn really green." *Aww.* Ninja cupped my hand in his. "You have this light about you that I'm attracted to. I don't like or need a lot of people around me. So, when I do, I want it to be a good person."

"You just got yourself another kiss. Come here, muscles!" We rolled some more, roaming our hands over back pockets, caressing waistlines, and intertwining our legs. Coming up for air I asked, "What about our age difference?"

"What about it?" Ninja asked, then took a sip of water.

I said in a deadpan tone, "You know... I'm way younger than you."

Water sprayed out his mouth, followed by an uproarious cough. With a quick recovery and a well-placed kiss on my open palm, he stated, "I don't care about our age difference. There are many other things in a relationship." He looked for my reaction; I nodded in reassurance. "What do you think about our age difference?" he asked.

"Seriously?" He waited. I looked him right in the eye. "Well, I think it's cool as shit!" I laughed, but Ninja laughed harder. "It's like an extra bonus, but not in some profound way. The stream of energy emitting from this package of you stirs my energy in reverse; it's youthful. May as well put it out there it, baby." Though feeling slightly embarrassed, a weight was lifted through our honesty. Underneath, I felt a sense of responsibility towards him, towards his youth. I did not want to rob him of any life experiences by having him meet me at my age, or even our median age. In the back of my mind sat my aged wisdom; if push came to shove, it would be my responsibility to be fair, and protect him. I also sensed this relationship would run its course. It did not hold longterm relationship ingredients for either of us; nevertheless, we were thankful for it.

Ninja smiled. "Since it doesn't matter, what exactly is the age difference between us?" Obviously, he had given thought towards delicately asking this question. Typically, I am mistaken for someone six to ten years younger than my actual age; it's a curse.

My response was a bit whiny. "Who wants to talk about math on a romantic picnic?"

Ninja chuckled, "It's okay, Jess. You probably have a good guess as to my age, so the difference is probably—"

"Let's save that question for another day. Algebra is so confusing with the whole X factor this, and if Y equals that... Who cares what X equals?" I pulled my hair over to one side and whispered, "We could study biology...or chemistry...," I snuggled in closer, my lips brushing against his jawline, "or anatomy... So many subjects, muscles. What do you want an 'A' in? Is it really...math?"

GOTTA SPILL THE TEA

I was dating! I had to tell a girlfriend. I decided to call Moss. He wasn't a girl, but his favorite topic was dirty stuff. As soon as he answered the phone, I blabbed, "Moss, I have news!"

"Aren't we excited this morning?" Moss replied. "Shall I get my coffee first?"

"Yes, I am excited; no, on the coffee. This is your jolt," I spilled enticingly.

"Do tell, I'm all ears," he crooned.

"I had a date."

"You had some dried fruit?" Moss loved to be annoying. "You know, dates are considered a delicacy in the Mediterranean."

"Can you stop amusing yourself for a change and pay attention to me," I barked without bite.

"Jessi-kins, you know I love you."

"Yeah, yeah," I said as I briskly walked in circles around my house. The kids were making play dough creations out on the porch table.

"Tell-tell, where did you two meet? And more important, have you seen him with his shirt off?" Moss always goes right for the juice.

"We met at my front door," I said flatly. "He is doing some painting and repair jobs around the house; and he happens to work while wearing a shirt."

"Hold up... How did y'all go from 'fix my house' to 'start my engine'?" Moss dove into a southern accent to mock me. "Did you happen to twirl around in a towel saying... *Oh, Mr. Contractor, my shower water is running way too cold fer me. Would you mind turning up the heat fer me? It's just so hard fer me to do it all by myself. Ya know what I mean by 'hard', don't you Mr. Contractor?*"

"Yes Moss, that is exactly what I said, and how I said it."

Putting Moss on speaker phone, I began to sort laundry, and shove a white load into the washer. "We got to know each other over many conversation; he's been painting this house that won't sell. Anyway, I had a date scheduled with a guy from an online dating site and that guy canceled – stood me up was more like it. With kid sitting already arranged for the night, I decided to put on my brave-girl pants. I went right over to him, mentioned I was going to the movies alone, and waited to see if that went anywhere before embarrassing myself."

"Good move, good move. That must have been when you started twirling around in your towel... '*I have some overtime work fer ya Mr. Contractor. The list is right here in my hand fer ya. Yes sir, I have a nasz-ty little job in my hand fer ya. Know what I mean by a 'job in my hand' Mr. Contractor? Do ya?*"

Just like my snooze alarm, I ignored him. "Well, Ninja— the kids call him Ninja— seized the opportunity. It was next to his last day of working for me. Anyway, we went to the movies together, and afterwards, we hung out in the parking lot and then we called it a night."

"Actually Jess, that sounds kind of nice. You certainly got to see his work ethic and got to know him in person. You saw how he acts around your kids and most important, you got to see him wearing a tool belt – indeedie-doo. Now, let's back-it-up to the parking lot moment. What were y'all doing in the parking lot, hmm? And don't you hush me."

"After the movie, Ninja and I chatted for quite a while in his truck about all sorts of stuff. He showed me pictures of races he was training for; I had never heard of a mud run. Have you heard of those?"

"Yes. Those races have rope climbs, traverse obstacles and lots of mud. You come out all sweaty and dirty. A lot of people find it fun; workplaces will make mud-run teams. It's not for me;I prefer sweating without the dirt. I like my mountain bike and I like being clean. Hey, wait... How old is this handyman if he's doing mud runs?"

"Uh, I'm not really sure. Maybe slightly older than me?" I squeaked. "Or maybe he is way, way younger than me."

"You cougar!"

"I know, right!" slamming the washer lid down.

"Hey, Jessikins, my wife is a cougar and that's okay. My true-love is eleven years older than me and she rocks my world. It's a nice little high for both of us, but that's only one ingredient on a long list of things we enjoy about each other. I hope that is not all this is for you, unless you want that."

"Moss, I haven't dated in a long time. I dedicate myself all day to kids at work and home. Dating is a tight fit. But this guy already had lunch with my kids and my mom, he laughed at my jokes when he didn't have to – he's a simple guy. He had a rough start, so he doesn't like people who are fake. He's trying to master a trade and watch his own back. It feels like we're a genuine complement to each at this phase in our lives. It's flattering to me, of course, that someone younger and attractive like him is interested in me. It wakes you up inside."

Moss spoke with elation. "You deserve a trip around the moon. I am thrilled for you."

"Thank you. Perhaps the universe is sending me some bells and whistles."

"Is he a good kisser? I know that is important to you."

"Yes, Ninja man is a good kisser and I will tell you why: because he knows you don't just kiss with your mouth – use the hands. One can grab your waist, one can caress your hair or your neck, or reach for your fingers. Oh, today I got a wake-up text that read, 'Good morning, beautiful.' Never, has anyone said that to me first thing in the morning."

"You are beautiful, and one of my favorite people," Moss said as he descended into his farewell. "Keep me posted on the new guy."

"Oh, I will. Talk to you later, Moss."

"Adios, Senorita Cougita... Meow!" Moss hung up, giggling at his own hilarity.

OTHER REALITIES

My tax refund came in to help keep me afloat another month. Though it was my first time filing separately, the check was made out to both Josh and I. Fortunately, I still had the joint account, otherwise I would not have been able to deposit it.

Other due diligence: contacting Josh's human resource department to get the name, address, and fax number of the person who handled "wage garnishment". Time to get those automatic support deductions rolling. During the call, I may have given the impression I was from the child support agency to more easily obtain this information which I hand deliver to my caseworker. Mr. Grey was a senior guy, given my case specifically because he had experience with international situations. Mr. Grey was rather impressed with my data collection, stating it usually took them a while to obtain and verify. That said, he informed me things would still take a few weeks because of the mailing time, waiting for responses, etc. *Uh, momma don't like plan A. How 'bout plan B.* Since I provided them with the direct numbers, I implored that perhaps faxing and phone calls would be more appropriate. The caseworker agreed, stating he would start confirmation of Josh's employment the next day. Child support was on the horizon.

THE KIDS MET Josh's girlfriend on a Skype session. Josh had asked if he could introduce her. He kind of had to since showing them his new dog, a white poodle about the size of a roll of toilet paper. Josh would never have bought himself that kind of dog. Obviously, someone was living with him. During their Skype session, I peeked from a spot out of camera view. Josh's girlfriend was around my age, with dark curly hair and bright pink lipstick. I watched long enough to conclude I was prettier, even if it wasn't true. The kids seemed happy to meet Miss Rebound and their fluff puff dog; however, after the session, they admitted their discomfort.

Connor put it out there first. "It's weird seeing Dad with a girlfriend. He has an apartment; that means he is going to stay up there."

"Maybe we can go up there and visit him?" asked Nicky tentatively.

"Why couldn't he get a job down here? That is so messed up. Are you okay, Mom? That must be weird – Dad living with some-body else," Jolie inquired.

"We have separate lives now," I said, "comes with the territory."

Jolie snapped her fingers across her face. "You're much pret-tier than her, Mom."

"Right!" I started to tickle Jolie and said, "That's because I am so happy to be living with you guys!" I hugged Nicky and grabbed Connor's hand.

"Is he at least paying child support?" Connor asked.

"It's all in the works. Your dad needs a nudge, but we have a caseworker handling it who seems very competent."

"Good," said Connor.

Jolie mentioned, "Their dog, Bella, is really cute."

"They have a dog? I thought it was a rescue cat." *Hiss, meow, scratch.*

NOODLE TALK

Moss and I had agreed to meet for lunch at The Ramen Noodle-Doodle House. The tables were covered in reams of white paper and each center piece was a tin can full of crayons so patrons could doodle while....

We hugged outside the noodle house. Moss always picked me up and spun me around which was easy enough to do at his height. Moss liked to joke that he was five foot, twelve inches tall. We went inside, chose our ramen ingredients at the buffet counter, then took our steaming bowls to the most private booth. Embellishing the top of every booth were tropical planter boxes filled with stunning orchids, anthuriums, and indoor ivy plants.

Feeling like a balloon about to burst I said, "Moss, I can't wait to see the expression on your face."

"Whoa, Cougita. Let me sit down. I want to savor my noodles, not wear them." We slid into our cafe booth. Moss was loosely up to date on my relationship progression with hombre Ninja.

Mimicking an authority type figure such as a principal, Moss began an interrogation while tapping his fingernails on the table. "Did you two have a slumber party?"

"Yes, we did. I cannot lie."

"Did we slumber, or did we par-tay between the sheets?" His fingers interlaced together in front of his face, except for an index, which lingered on his bottom lip.

"Well, I think we need to talk off the record."

Moss splayed his hands out on the paper-white table. "Okay, did you two do the wanka-wanka, or what?"

"Yes, it was so fun! We would laugh and chat, then things would get all heated and touchy. There was a lot of rolling around. Wow, he has a nice body. Full on washboard abs, shoulders out to here, his deltoids are perfect handles to grip onto when you need it." My hands provided a quick, visual demonstration. "Oh, before we started anything, Ninja picked me up and tossed me way up high onto the bed. It was so cool. That will never get old."

"No, it doesn't. Neither does getting thrown over someone's shoulder like a sack of potatoes. So, is he covered in hair? I like hairy men...the hairier the better. Front, back—I like it all."

Okay, Moss was bisexual, in case that was not made extremely clear. With me and his gay friends, Moss could turn up the heat with his at-rest homosexual core. When with his wife, he turned it down. It was a beautiful component of their relationship. What Moss felt for her, and who they were together, represented a monogamous choice. Sexual orientation is not an on/off switch, and in Moss's case, there was a dial. Outside of their marriage, Moss was simply all talk and flirtatiousness, expressing his full self.

I responded, "Ninja has no hair. He was a canvas of contours and I was paint on a brush. Ninja said that 'I kept myself up well'."

"Did Ninja add: 'for an old lady'?" Moss dove his chopsticks deep into his ceramic bowl and lifted out a wet blob of long, wiggly noodles. He shoved the drippy ramen into his mouth, and sucked up all the noodle-tails with puckered fish lips. "Get it? Kept yourself up well, for an old lady."

"No, bitch. He omitted that part." I stabbed a chunk of hard-boiled egg and held it up as I spoke. "Mr. Muscles and I poke fun at our age difference so it doesn't get the best of us." I popped the egg chunk in my mouth, chewing it up quick. "After we finished rolling around, I told Ninja: 'I am never going over the age of thirty again.' He cracked up."

Moss leaned back, "Listen, honey, a cougita meal is like crack: always leaves you want'n more. You a crack hussy," he said with a crooked smile.

Imitating his sly-fox smile, "Guess what else? And you can't tell anyone." Our faces zoomed together over a tiny bottle of soy sauce. "This is delicate news... Ready? I have a hickey – on my ass." We zoomed out as our backbones sprang straight up.

"O-o-oh!" exclaimed Moss.

Our faces boomeranged back, and we were once again whispering over soy sauce. "It's purple. The kind of purple you'd find on the neck of a Jersey-diner waitress, except this one, is on my ass! I'm sorry," placing a hand over my heart. "I never imagined that coming in my forties."

My high school friend leaned back, brought his hands up and proceeded to clap. Yes—a little applause for the single mom. Moss nodded and said: "Wise move, Miss Hussy. You're too old to have a hickey on your neck." Sage advice. As old friends do over bowls of ramen, our delightful conversation went back and forth with varying levels of questionable maturity.

SUMMER SURPRISE

Food shopping was a task I usually did biweekly. Our meals were not planned ahead, too much organization. Meal decisions were based on sale specials and what I imagined myself making while shopping, which then may or may not actually happen. There was a sense of pleasurable solitude meandering up and down the aisles while snacking shamelessly on a bag of cookies due to be half-empty by register time. On this particular shopping day, Connor called me as I neared the pet food aisle. He sounded in a near panic, asking if I had heard anything about dad's Facebook.

"Connor, you know I don't have a Facebook account? What is it?"

"Dad posted an announcement. They got engaged. There's a picture of Shelley wearing an engagement ring."

"Wh-what? Was this announcement to you directly? Or did he put it out there for everyone to see, and this is how you are finding out?"

"I was looking at his feed and it was there today. He may not even know I know."

"He didn't bother to—" I bit my lip, finding this unbelievably rude. Yet, there it was.

"Connor, I'm sorry this is the way you found out."

"Mom, did you know?"

"No, Connor, I did not know." My son went silent for a while. I had the wherewithal to put my own feelings on hold and asked Connor how he felt. Assuming how a child feels is never the same as asking.

"I feel sad."

"Why do you feel sad?"

"Because it means you and dad won't be getting back together." I had not been expecting that. "I feel bad cause you're alone."

"Oh Connor, I'm fine. Life is going to hand you struggles. You can face them, or you can avoid them. I don't mind facing them: that's me. I think your dad rushed into this, uh, engagement. He is still drinking and he is not on solid footing, but these are his decisions to make. Your dad and I were not bringing out the best in each other. That's not going to change. Do you really want us back together?"

"No. I know he's a drunk and he wasn't nice to you. It's strange to think of you guys marrying someone else. I was surprised he did it so soon."

"Yeah, me too, pumpkin."

"I don't really want you marrying someone else. I don't want someone else thinking they can tell me what to do, and try to be my dad."

"Connor, if I ever brought someone else into our family, don't you think I'd pick someone awesome? Someone who adds to our lives... Not some fly-by-dad replacement. Ninja is a new friend. We enjoy each other's company, but we're not looking at anything more serious."

"I can live with that. It's fun to play Nerf dart wars with Ninja. He jumps over furniture and stuff."

"Thanks for calling me about your dad. I'm glad we talked about this."

"When will you be home?"

"I'm checking out as soon as I load up on ice cream."

"O-o-o, get chocolate mint. Don't forget whipped cream for when Pop-pop and CJ come over." My dad and his legendary whipped cream...

"I bought a can of whipped cream like a week ago," I pointed out to Connor, slightly annoyed. "We should still have, like half a can."

"Jolie and Nicky used it up squirting streams of whipped cream in each other's mouth."

"Really?" I said sarcastically. "And you simply watched as a complete, innocent bystander?"

Connor said in his sneaky voice, "I didn't say, 'I didn't do it too'. I only said, 'I saw them doing it.'"

"Uh-huh. See you at home, son."

I TRIED NOT to dwell on the disregard of the kids finding out like second class acquaintances. Josh certainly did not have a playbook helping him navigate interpersonal parent to child behaviors. Buying an engagement ring instead of providing child support was one scream going off in my head as the world revolved around me. My case manager had informed me that almost everything was in place to begin international wage garnishment. The human resource person at Josh's employment has been on vacation causing the delay. Ugh, this was taking forever.

PROTECTING WILLIE

A more pressing matter beyond everything else was the dog. Our young Willie continued to escape out of our fenced-in yard. We had a wire fence and dang if he couldn't jump and clear it at certain spots. Other times, we thought the front door was shut, when it wasn't, and Willie managed to get out. Neighbors had called me after witnessing Willie nearly get hit by a car. Putting him on a wire leash attached to a yard stick helped a bit, but he usually got tangled around something. Willie was a high energy breed. I took care of him, walked him, set up doggie play dates, etc. The kids played with him at random short periods of time. They absolutely adored him and vice versa, but the responsibility was all on me. Added stress was that Willie ate the cat's food, hence he disliked his own and was always hungry.

Willie's breeder came to mind. I called and asked if she would border Willie until we could keep him safe in a new house with a proper fence. She spoke as an angel answering my prayers, "Yes, I'd be happy to take Willie." The kids did not take the news well at all. Each one became very emotional over this decision. The timing sucked after everything they had been through. They feared I would either give Willie away, or not take him back.

"We're an ohana!" said Jolie, which meant "family" in Hawaiian.

"Yeah! Willie's part of it!" echoed Nicky.

Explaining my stance, "Willie deserves to be taken care of properly and as his family, we need to admit when we're not doing it right. What's going to happen when one of you forgets to lock the gate again? He runs out, gets hit by a car, and then you'll be against each other in blame and pain. I've had three calls over the last couple months from people witnessing Willie almost get struck by a car. How are any of you going to feel about that? His breeder not only lives on farmland, but she has many other dogs for Willie to play with. He will thrive being active all day, every day."

This decision was up for discussion, but not for changing. The kids could learn the difference between being a proper dog owner and doing a disservice. The tough part was admitting it; the humane part was fixing it. I was at my limit, and was not going to dump a responsibility on them that they couldn't handle. Willie was going to get hurt, or worse, and that would split them apart.

Eventually the kids conceded that this plan was geared towards Willie's best safety. We dropped Willie off at the breeder's expansive property, and he was immediately greeted by three adult Border collies. We threw the tennis ball that we brought, and all four of them went after it, returning in unison. These dogs were comfortable being with other dogs. It was one big play fest.

Before leaving, I huddled with the kids. "Willie doesn't love you any less, but he does love this kind of life. I am really, really sorry. This is not easy for me either." In fact, the hardest part was whispering to Willie how sorry I was. Willie only panted for more ear scratches. I sniffled my emotions back and kept scratching. "Thank you, Willie, for loving me and my kids every day, no matter what. I'm sorry I can't take care of you anymore. I tried, I really tried. In our next house, we'll get a fence."

Perhaps from either seeing me get choked up, or from seeing Willie's new life, or a bit of both, the kids didn't seem so mad at me anymore. Before leaving, we spent time in the puppy barn. There were eleven, chubby-bellied puppies all yipping and tripping over each other. The kids got on the ground and received puppy kisses, a pretty nice salve for their wounds.

"They're eating my socks." Jolie laughed out loud from her seated spot on the ground.

"Watch what happens when I lay down," said Nicky as he lay face down on the ground. Immediately, five puppies climbed all over him, biting and tugging at his clothes from every direction.

Connor was walking in small circles, holding one calm, pink-bellied puppy in his arms.

"Ow! They're biting my butt," yelled Nicky.

"Roll over," yelled Connor.

"No! They'll bite my wee-wee!" squealed Nicky, which stirred us into a more jovial mood.

I helped my Nicky cub back on his feet, and fixed his chewed-up hair. We left for home, minus one. Bye, Willie.

IT CAN GET WORSE

The latest news from the family support case manager arrived. Turned out, the human resource person got back from vacation just in time to handle Josh losing his job. Yup, and literally, his very next paycheck would have been garnished for child support. Guess my lesson of learning to stand on my own two feet was far from over.

My behind the scenes prayer dialogue churned with frustration. Whatever lessons were still there for me to learn, I didn't want them anymore. My life had to be more than this; there was so much to appreciate. By day, I worked with kids who could not zip a coat at age nine, and by night, I helped adults who could not get out of a wheelchair or go to the bathroom by themselves. When I needed to pull myself together, I wrote. I had been doing that ever since my mother gave me my first diary at age eleven. I wrote to receive, and I wrote to rethink. Some of my writing has led to daydreams that these times in my life would become a book that pulls others out of the muck, or better yet, helps them to avoid it. Regardless, the writing process was therapeutic. At the mercy of the monthly cost of staying in the house, Missy and I lowered the price, yet again.

SUMMER LOVIN'

Romance led to summer fun with Ninja man. A friend loaned us her beach house for a week. (Disclaimer: the first couple of days were without kids.) Then, Sara came up with all our combined family to spend the day. Sitting in beach chairs with our toes in the sand, Sara and I took in the coastal view of the kids building sandcastles from the giant hole Ninja was digging, shirtless. We were pretty content watching Ninja work that shovel.

Ninja had bought the kids a huge Orca whale raft to float around in the calmer waters. The kids loved flopping all over it. Our family playtime at the beach gave me the sense that we were whole. Ninja was not a dad replacement, but he gave me hope that I would find a true partner someday. Ninja and I were not in love: the feelings were not there.

The inevitable shelf-life of our romance faded to an end after summer. His phase of life and mine were so different; the age difference... It was what it was. He did not like to hold hands; he wasn't affectionate. He lived a rather isolated life, unintegrated with any community, or even the world at large. When we occasionally got stoned together, he did not like that I started using "big words". Ninja and I parted ways as friends without benefits. One of his white undershirts still rested, neatly folded in my pajama drawer. He said I could keep it, which added more meaning on the nights I wore it as a way of remembering that part of myself.

TAKING ONE STEP FORWARD

Do I not destroy my enemies when I make them my friends? - Abraham Lincoln

Josh was back to living with his dad, and had been looking for work everywhere. He had used up all his savings and his retirement monies. His family—aware of his drinking problem—was not willing to loan him any money. His relationship with his fiancée seemed to be going well, though she had stopped working when Josh got the new job, assuming he was going to take care of her. My daughter called it, out of the blue, when she said: "Mom, Shelley's a gold digger." Where had she even learned that phrase?

Josh had secured another job offer in the Midwest section of the United States. He and I had maintained open communication with each other through texting, and he demonstrated some humbleness by asking to visit with the kids before moving out West. I wanted to bridge the gap between father and child. Connor had begun high school, Jolie junior high, and Nicky, third grade. I knew Josh wanted his children to have a healthy life, and not suffer anything he went through. I knew that mental illness and addiction were diseases that inhibited one's good intentions. So, I agreed he could come for a visit, but he had to stay with Roger. He could not drink in our house, and he was not allowed to bring the fiancée to my home.

SPEAKING OF BENEFICIAL FOR EVERYONE, I had another buyer: hopefully the fifth one would be a charm. Nobody actually says that, because fifth buyers turn out to be nightmares. The husband was an uppity good-looking businessman and he talked with charm, but behind closed doors, he bullied the real estate agents. Missy limited what she told me about him, usually resorting to exasperated sighs. We got through the haggling, once I lowered the price another ten grand; Mister Uppity had requested thirty. My bluff that he could walk was not a bluff. We signed a contract pending inspection, loan approval, etc. I gave them an extra look at the house so their designer could come in and get some ideas. They did not need to sell their house since his company owned it. Our projected settlement was just before New Year's Eve.

Per Mister Uppity's request, I began the tedious process of providing my monthly cost for heat, water, electric, yard maintenance, etc. I seriously considered providing my therapy bill information as well – to his wife – just in case.

My most recent visits with Dr. Phoenix had occurred on an as needed basis: a "tune up" she had called it. Dr. Phoenix had helped me reach a safe plateau; now it was up to me to do my thing. It had felt good to cut the cord. Endless thanks to Dr. Rachel Phoenix.

DAD'S HOMECOMING

When Josh arrived, it was big hugs all around. With the divorce behind us and spousal expectations at the wayside, it was nice to see him appreciating the home and family he had helped to create. Josh made no comment about the missing dog. He already knew through the kids, and had nothing to contribute, at least not out loud. Josh went right to asking what he could make everyone for dinner. Focaccia bread with fresh rosemary from the garden was top of the list. As the kids pulled out the ingredients for dinner, Josh pulled me aside, hugged me, and whispered a sincere thank you. He mentioned that I looked great and said he was going to financially support me as soon as the new job came through. I had verification of this new job out west, so things were looking good.

That night, we were to eat in the dining room, an elegant room with regal pineapple wallpaper, a small chandelier, and a rosewood dining table. Josh was slicing the focaccia on the cutting board and placing it in the familiar bread basket. The kids were back and forth, setting the table and filling water glasses. I went over to Josh from the side, and gave his ribs a squeeze.

"Thanks for making all our favorites. It's nice to give the kids a big family dinner."

"It's great to be making a family dinner. Does the bread look okay? I think it turned out pretty good."

"It looks delicious. The crust is a nice golden brown, the olive oil fills in the finger divots nicely, and what's more...fresh rosemary and sea salt on top."

"Thank you. I made a dipping sauce too."

"Gotta have the dipping sauce."

"Gotta have the dipping sauce," he repeated while chewing his gum.

Josh pleasantly carried off the bread and accoutrements to the dining room. Who chews gum while cooking, and right before they're about to eat? NOT Josh. He obviously wanted to cover up his breath.

"Mom, come on! It's time to eat!"

"I'm coming. I-I need to use the bathroom real fast. Go ahead and load up your plates." I walked past the dining room entrance towards the bathroom and then kept going, briskly walking around the first floor and scanning...scanning... I scanned the corners, behind sofas...nothing. Then I thought of the closet: he'd had a jacket on when he arrived. Josh's jacket was on the floor in the closet. I lifted up his jacket, which was resting on top of that grey backpack that never dies. I unzipped it, and saw the vodka bottle. A third of it was gone. A pair of leather gloves I had gotten him for Christmas were in there too, along with a Lego keychain, a soccer player figurine.

I couldn't believe that the drinking hadn't lessened, or that he couldn't skip a few hours. As always, I had a choice about how I handled it. Everyone else was fine; they were waiting to eat a family meal made with great effort. Bringing up how I felt would disturb the peace, and I would be coming from a place of judgement. Josh had a separate life from me, and he was making choices that worked for him. It behooved us all, if I could turn myself down a notch. I knew he could not stop unless he welcomed assistance. Josh might never learn about the world of options for a healthier, sober way of living. I wished him the chance to see what he was missing, while understanding that his fears blocked the way. Compassion was the path I chose upon entering the dining room. A bowl of roasted chickpeas and tomato slices was being passed across the table, and a gravy boat was pouring a delicious sauce over slices of pork tenderloin plated next to chunky applesauce.

"Everything looks so good," I said to my family.

"Everything okay?" Josh asked as I sat down.

"Everything is fine, Josh." Nothing good, nothing bad...no labels. After dinner clean-up, Josh left to stay at Roger's house. We both knew to keep the evenings short.

THE NEXT DAY, we tackled cleaning out the basement and the small garage while the kids were at school. The roof was under repair due to a significant leak − another payment for the credit card. The bonus of this misfortune was a dumpster in the driveway. We cut the sentiment and threw out anything and everything we did not need.

It was nice to have the physical and emotional assistance to deconstruct and essentially toss out our former lives, a process we should have done before. Our divorce could have honored our past and paid tribute; instead, he had left me to burn. The label on my back now read "fireproof".

Josh noticed that many of his textbooks were missing. That was because I had set fire to a majority of them. It had been a rather significant bonfire, I must say. Never claimed to be an angel, though I only burned his old school books. None of his treasured or relevant clinical books were turned to ash. The bonfire had burned for a couple hours while my friends drank wine and watched my I'm-so-done-with-you purge of clothes and textbooks go to their fiery end. Admittedly, it had been a bit therapeutic to say, "I think we need more gasoline." All the while, Josh's Hemingway, Steinbach, and Freud had been spared, safely nestled on bookshelves.

The dumpster was slowly filling with stuff we no longer needed in our simpler, future lives. In the spirit of being productive, Josh asked would I mind if he had a beer. He said he had brought two. I appreciated his asking—it was an exchange of openness, and trust. I let Josh know that I was aware that he was drinking more than a couple of beers. "I only mention it because I care about you; the kids care about you. I would encourage you to recognize that other people have faced this, and when they got help, things got better. All the deceit, the covering up, the shame: it all has no place in a recovered life. I wish you would allow yourself to experience that mindset, and make decisions from that headspace."

Josh paused. "It doesn't matter if I quit. It's too late for me."

"What does that mean?"

"I mean it's too late. I went to see a doctor. I was bleeding when I went to the bathroom. No surprise – it's my liver. It's not good," he said.

"What does *not good* mean?" Josh got teary-eyed, and gave me a hug. Stunned and unsure I asked, "Josh, what exactly did the doctor say?"

"It spread to my pancreas. All my years of drinking has caught up with me. There isn't much they can do. I want to spend time with you and the kids. That's all I want."

"Are you at some final stage of something?"

"Yes. It may have even spread further into my lungs. They need to run more tests. I don't want to know anymore."

"Do your father and Jacque know?"

"Yes, they know, but not all of it. Dad took me to the hospital when I was initially sick."

"What hospital was that?"

"What hospital?"

"Yes, what hospital is treating your diagnosis. Obviously, you've been there a few times by now."

"Yes, it's a good place." He gave me the name.

"And your doctor... I hope he is giving you some of the best options you can take."

"Yes. They all seem to know what they're doing."

"Who's your doctor?" Josh didn't respond. "I assume you have a relationship with a specialist by now, I would hope," I said with concern.

Josh agreed and told me his doctor's name. "Can I just spend time with you and the kids?" he asked. "I don't want to argue. I want to be useful."

"Of course." We hugged for a long time. He kissed the top of my head, but it didn't get weird.

We finished excavating our stuff and trekking it to the dumpster, at least for that day. "What shall we have for dinner?" I said, staring into the abyss that was my refrigerator. "Not much selection."

"I can go get groceries, if you want; pick up stuff for dinner," my ex-husband offered.

"Works for me." Totally.

Josh solemnly added, "I want to bring this up. I am going to need something for later. Can I get some wine to have with dinner?"

"Josh, I hate being in a position like I am the one controlling your intake."

"I know. Shelley lets me do my own thing. Without anybody coming at me, I am actually fine with drinking beers throughout the day. She can even see how many beers I have in a day, and it's fine." *I'll go out on a limb – it's because Shelley doesn't know you're tapping a hidden bottle of Jack.*

Josh brushed his coat smooth, pulled out his car keys and said, "If somebody tells me I have to do something, then I want to do the opposite. To be honest, if I stick to drinking beer here, I will need a beer, like, every hour and I don't want the kids to see a bunch of beer cans piling up. But if I have vodka, I can take a sip when I need it and I feel like I can control it better. I don't need to drink as much, and I don't get the shakes. Also, I won't smell like some drunk dad and embarrass the kids."

Upon taking this all in I respond, "How about a bottle of wine and a six pack? You'll know it's here; you can pace yourself. Leave early if you need to, but save the hard stuff for outside the house," I said as the ex-wife wearing overalls, a plaid shirt, and a ponytail.

"Okay, that's fair enough." Josh laughed a little at me. "You're so cute."

"I'm glad you think my concerns are cute."

"No, that's not what I mean. You really are cute. I don't know why I didn't see it before," Josh put his arms around me.

"Probably because you were being an asshole," I said, patting his chest, which put my arm between us.

"Ouch! Yes, you're right," dropping his arms flaccid and stepping back. "I'm so sorry. You are balancing a lot, I know. And here I come, back into your life, and I am still a mess and I want to visit and be helpful and you're being very accommodating, but you're probably thinking: when is this guy going to leave and stop touching me? I want to be helpful, and as soon as I start making some money, I'll send it. I'll work for as long as I'm still healthy. As long as I'm able to work to help you and the kids, I will."

"Thanks Josh. I appreciate it," bowing in gratitude with a namaste prayer posture. "The kids are almost done school. How about we go pick up Nicky together? He will be very happy to see both his parents in the school yard."

"Okay, that sounds nice." In his soft smile, I could see the resemblance of my kids to their dad.

ONCE ALL THE kids got home, we headed out to the trampoline. The kids liked to play a game they had made up called "Smelly", a trampoline version of the game "Marco Polo". Whoever is "IT", closes his eyes and crawls around the trampoline, trying to catch everyone else who randomly calls out "smelly". Connor always made it extra fun because he rolled all over the tramp so fast that the other two were forced to bounce and trip and dive. Nicky was usually caught with a full body slam as Connor loved to wrestle him. Jolie liked to grapple with Nicky too, but they were more of an equal match. No doubt, Connor peeked during the game; then again, we all did after a while.

When the game changed to double bouncing and back flips, Josh and I got off, for their safety as well as our own bone integrity. A few weeks prior, Connor had begged me to attempt a backflip on the trampoline. I had never done a backflip in my life, but I wanted to be a cool mom. In conjunction with Connor's coaching, I tried and tried until one day, I did two backflips in a row! Connor captured this pathetic miracle on his phone. During the first flip, I had screamed and landed on my butt; however, on the second flip, I stuck the landing. We both joyously freaked out in the video, which was the best part for me.

Josh left the jumping zone, and headed out to buy groceries. With the kids occupied, I internet searched liver and pancreas diseases related to alcoholism. Once the pancreas was involved, the statistics were not pretty. Upon gaining a general sense of the various symptoms and treatment approaches, I explored my other curiosities: namely, the hospital Josh had mentioned. It did exist; however, it was a medical center that specialized in addiction treatment. The doctor was also legit and worked there, but he did not specialize in cancer. I hypothesized that Josh probably overdid the drinking and went to this hospital for some kind of acute treatment or assessment. It had probably scared him enough to get functionally sober for a while, but without insurance coverage... Same story, different day.

Hmm, what would he gain if I believed he had a terminal illness? Sympathy perhaps? Maybe he wanted to stay with us. Did he think I would consider a reconciliation knowing that we faced the same unresolved issues that neither of us liked? What the heck? Josh was pretending to have a medical death sentence.

I remembered a psychiatrist I had worked with telling me that he always approached his patients by believing them. These were patients he was called to see for pain management. When there was an agitated patient bugging a nurse every twenty minutes for pain meds, that nurse needed back up, and a quick decision. "First," he said, "I believe their pain, then I try to uncover what they are after. Is it relief from pain at an injury site, or relief from pain in general? I can believe them, while recommending no pain meds." His specific way of connecting with a patient when a quick decision or recommendation was needed had stuck with me. It was no skin off my back to give Josh the benefit of the doubt while he was telling me about his morbid ailments. I was still going to follow my intuition.

Josh would have to accept that he was relocating somewhere he did not want to go because that was the only job he could get. He would have to work to hold onto his fiancée, who was immature, but loved to coddle him. He was not going to attract a wiser woman at this phase, and he was too old to land a naïve, twenty-something-year-old anymore. Shelley was a special needle in a haystack at forty. She had a sixteen-year-old daughter who lived with her boyfriend. Shelley was prepared to leave that daughter to follow Josh, a guy she barely knew, into another country; she would be dependent on him. Shelley knew that Josh had a drinking problem, and already lost a job. They had quite the future lined up. No wonder he was playing me.

AGAIN, we had another nice family dinner. Josh seemed to be drinking only wine. The kids dispersed to their playful ways after we all cleaned up. I asked Josh to sit and talk in the dining room. I explained that I had researched the hospital and the doctor he mentioned; clearly, neither specialized in oncology. "We are going to back up from the claim that you are dying, and get to the real issue. Did you receive any treatment for drinking, and is your family trying to support you?"

Josh got really mad and accused me of being invasive. I waited him out and did not respond to his short rant. Eventually, he admitted that he did not have any insurance, so he was out of options for going to rehab. He said he'd had a scare, but he seemed better now, and that was that. He was not happy explaining anything, but that was the opposite of lying, and I appreciated it. Josh headed back to Roger's place in a low-key huff. At least his mortality rate was up, and we would live to see another day together.

BUY THE HOUSE ALREADY

The roof was repaired in time for the home inspection. Naturally, the uppity buyer joined the inspector. They looked over every nook and cranny, which was to be expected. Our contract stated: "As is condition"; however, it was a ninety-year-old house. They were bound to find things, and they did: mold.

They found evidence of black mold in two places, and brought up the disclosed knob and tube wiring as a potential liability for home insurance. Our response was to have a formal mold inspection, and we recommended they use our current home insurance company. Missy had a guy for the mold inspection; every realtor has "a guy", if they ever want to get a house sold.

It was confirmed: mold was in one of the bathrooms and the basement ceiling. It would cost over $4000 to get it remediated. I booked the appointment ASAP to get it done. Another credit card bill racked up, but with this out of the way, we should be good to go.

Mister Uppity went to the re-inspection of the mold remediation. He was not happy about something, and wanted the company to address the issue. At least now, it was between Mister and the mold guy, who guaranteed a certain level of workmanship. The mold guy indicated not to worry and did whatever was necessary, which meant more contract time. The holidays were coming with winter's chill. I called the oil company and changed my payment plan. Instead of enduring another $400-600 oil bill, I requested, "Give me whatever two hundred bucks will buy."

"Yo, kids! Sweaters are the new pajamas."

WITH JOSH LINGERING AROUND because he had not been given an official start date for his job, I worked some extra hours on the weekend, skipping soccer games and forgoing supervision of everyone at every moment in order to bring home a paycheck. My brother, who ran a mortgage loan department, was consulting with my realtor, offering her any support he could, since the buyer was such a bully. Then, the bully escalated to the thug.

Missy said over the phone, "We have a new problem. The buyers said the home inspection found possible evidence of asbestos. They want it addressed."

"What are they talking about? You mean, the covering on the duct work?"

"Yeah. They want that removed before they move into the house."

"I personally talked with the inspector on the phone regarding that issue. He said it was "likely" that in an old home, the covering on ductwork "may have asbestos". The inspector said it was usually wrapped up so tight that disturbing it could be worse than leaving it. He said most of it was replaced when the house had upgrades."

"Yes, I know," said Missy. "I asked what it would cost, just so we know. He said it would be around $3000."

"There was no asbestos detected in the air or the vents!" I reiterated.

"I know. I'm just the messenger. What do you want to do?"

"Missy, ask me what I am NOT going to do because I am NOT going to replace the freaking ductwork in this house! Hence, what I am actually going to do is nothing."

"Okay. I'll call his agent. This is not going to be pretty."

EX IS A MESS

Back on the front lines, I was getting text messages from Josh's fiancée saying that Josh was not responding, and she wanted to know if everything was okay; ah, the dream relationship triangle: me, my ex, and the new girl - not. Actually, the kids and I had not seen Josh in a couple of days—a wellness check was definitely in order. After work, and after dropping Nicky off to Sara's house and Jolie to Kate's house, I got a chicken in the oven, switched a load of laundry, wiped up some cat barf, and then drove over to Roger's place because I had nothing better to do.

Josh was staying in an add-on room down the hall from an open garage. Since no one answered the front door, it was an easy walk from the garage to Josh's bedroom. Behold, on a mattress on the floor, there was Josh, curled up under a blanket. Roger had only bare-bone accommodations. There were beer cans about the room, and an empty vodka bottle. It smelled like cigarettes.

"Josh, Josh! Are you awake?" *You better not be dead.*

He opened an available eyelid, the one not smushed into his pillow. *Holy Bloodshot Mary!* Josh's monocular stare fixated on me for a moment, then he lit up. "Hey. You came to see me."

"Indeed, here I am. You don't seem okay, big guy. In fact, all curled up, I think you're smaller than me."

Josh grinned. "Yeah, it's fucking cold down here. I'm sleeping with my boots on. All night, I have my boots on my feet. They are on my feet all night long, so my feet stay warm."

"Well sweetie, it's not night time. Maybe moving around would help you warm up."

"It's not night time? It's daytime; that's right." My ex, the cyclops, closed his mono-eye and he was out again. Unzipping my old army coat, I squatted down in my burgundy jeans and black Doc Martin boots. I tugged at the shabby blanket covering this disheveled, inebriated corpse that was the father of my children.

"Josh, sit up. Josh! Sit – up."

"What?"

"Sit up, man! Get up! You can't lie in a ball all day. Hasn't Roger checked on you? Some friend... Come on, get up!" I pulled the blanket off his adult/fetus-body.

Josh squealed, "No! No-o-o! Not my blanket. You're so m-ean-n-n."

"I am not mean. I'm being very caring. Nobody is making me check on you, and certainly, nobody is paying me."

"Ha-ha Jessica, you're pretty funny. I was only joking. Actually, you are being really nice to me. You are being really, really nice to me. You know, I still love you. I actually really, really do love you."

"Show me the love, Josh. Get-t up-p!" Josh slowly moved himself out of park, and into a sitting crossed leg position. He smiled at me, and I took in the yellow-red eyes, the greasy hair sticking-up on one side, and the fact that he was still wearing the same mustard yellow sweatshirt from three days before, which now reeked of ashtray. His face had whiskers all over and—

"What happened to your face?"

"What? I didn't shave?" He started rubbing his face like he had forgotten it was there.

"The side of your eye is black and blue. And you have a cut on your eyebrow." Josh reached up, touched his eyebrow, and winced.

"Oh yeah, that. Does it look bad?"

"Well, it looks like it probably hurt when it happened."

"Jessica, you look so pretty. I'm such a mess! You must think I'm such a mess."

"Josh, what happened to your face?" I was not smiling.

"I fell." Josh frowned.

"You fell?"

"I fell."

"You're telling me you fell – on your face?"

"Roger and I were standing around a bonfire. One of his friends was there. This guy is such a jerk! I don't know what his problem is. Roger says he's like that all the time. Anyway, this guy gets mad at me for saying something about his truck, or something. I don't know. He goes to leave; he pushes me and I fall down."

"Hmm. So, you upset this guy by offending his truck, he pushes you and you land on your eyebrow. Well, I'm sorry to see you got hurt."

"It's no big deal. Guys shove each other all the time. I can take a shove."

I bet you could take a punch too. If a guy threw a right hook, it would hit square in the left eye; and if that punching fist had a ring on it, that would explain the cut on your eyebrow. Moving on.

"Thank you," my-ex continued. "I tried to clean it up. Roger didn't have any bandages. I think I might have a concussion. That's why I haven't been able to get out of bed."

"Uh-huh. Your head certainly does need to get looked at; I've been saying that for years," I said, flashing him an alluring smile. "Would you like to come over for dinner? I'll cook."

At this, my ex-husband lit up. He turned his head real slow to the right, then with an equally retarded motion to the left. "Yes, that would be lovely," he said.

"Great! First, you have to shower."

"Do I look that bad?"

"I know you can look better. Let the water run over your cut. If it opens up a little, I can put on a Steri-Strip, and close it back up."

"Jessica-a-a, you're so pretty."

"And you're pretty stinky. Let's go, cowboy."

"Am I showering at your place?"

"No, you are going to shower here. I will wait for you. If you let me, I will help you."

"I'm a mess, I know."

"I believe the correct term is 'hot mess'. May I help you detox? Then we get Shelley here, you two head off to the new job, you'll get some structure to your day, get yourself some health insurance... You'll have options. That can all start with a shower."

Standing up, Josh declared, "I can handle starting with a shower." Appearing to have experienced some dizziness, he sat back down.

"We won't go cold turkey; we'll do a weaning process. You will know when another drink is coming. Are you good with that?" Josh nodded.

"Don't mess with me, Josh." A simple head-nod was not good enough. I let my concerns fly out on a broomstick. "I do not need anymore shit right now. I have three kids at home, two demanding jobs, and this whole family has zero health insurance. I had to borrow money from my dad's retirement and now my brother has to chip in too. I have a buyer trying to bully me at every turn to sell this house, if it even sells. I've already had four different buyers bail out. Poor Jolie is wearing a scarf and a hat inside the house so I can keep our heating bill down, and now I have to babysit your sorry ass taking a shower, otherwise you'll finish off a vodka bottle because you can't help yourself. I get it, Josh. I am bleeding compassion for you, but do not come into my home and give me any shit!"

"Okay. No-o-o shit." Josh stood up. "No shit. I'm shitting no shit. I am not shitting a shit." He started spinning in a circle then stopped, almost falling over. The superman before me asked, "Uh, what do I do?"

I responded very slowly: "Pick out some clothes, and grab a towel." Josh followed these basic guidelines with minimal stumbling and fumbling. He grabbed his toiletries, which were all in one bag, and a fresh sweatshirt.

He paused, looked at his vodka bottle, and asked, "Can I have just a sip before I get in the shower. I don't want to get the shakes."

"You can have a sip *after* you shower, I promise. Let's go." I stepped behind him and started pushing on his back to get him out of the room.

I stood outside the bathroom door until I heard the water running and could tell he was under it. Dashing back to his room, it was operation detox. Any signs of alcohol were immediately tossed into the outside trash can. Unopened beer went into the trunk of my car for the weaning process. The half empty vodka bottle got poured out until there was about four inches on the bottom. I went upstairs into the kitchen, filled the bottle halfway with water and shook, not stirred.

Darting back to the bathroom, my ear to the door, the water was still going. Nope, wait, he's turning it off. I bee-lined it back to his room for one more quick check everywhere... Ahh: a bottle of white wine was actually *under* the mattress. That one I would keep for myself.

I made his bed and put his dirty clothes in a pile. Grabbing his wallet and his keys, I locked them in my trunk with my new wine bottle. The watered-down vodka bottle was still in my hand. I held it behind my back. We met in the bedroom.

"You look better," I said, out of breath.

"You cleaned up the room."

"Yup. I'm making it easier for you. Why don't you grab your computer, phone – any chargers you need. If we work together, you can stay with us and get out of the woods."

"Thank you. I think I have a concussion. I am having symptoms that match a concussion. I am being very serious, Jessica."

"Okay. We will take that seriously. That means you should not drive, nor attempt to buy any alcohol. I have your wallet and your keys which will be returned when you are back to your sweet, charming, good-looking self."

"You still find me attractive?"

"Doesn't everybody?'

"I am asking if you do?"

"I find a man who can keep his shit together attractive. Do you think you can pull that off?"

"You're avoiding the question; that's all right. I do love you, and you want me to fly straight. I don't care if you have my keys. You can keep my wallet." Josh gathered all his things, this time, with some actual thought behind it. He even grabbed a couple of files and his grandfather's watch. He was ready to go.

"Look what I have for you," holding out the vodka bottle.

"You added water to it, I can tell."

"Yes, I did."

Our history of animosity was replaced by humor and beaten down egos. Neither of us were looking for the other to come out a loser in this situation. Once his hands were free, and he was in the car, Josh took a sip from the bottle, and then immediately opened the door to spit it out.

"You added a lot of water!"

"I didn't think you'd notice." We peered at each other, two chameleons on a log. "See, that's funny cuz you of all people *would* notice. You would totally be laughing right now, if it weren't for your concussion."

Josh shook his head and shut the car door. I backed out the long gravel driveway, ignoring his drama. Josh managed to palate sipping his aqua-cocktail.

OPERATION DETOX

Back home, we put his bottle in the back pantry so Josh could have access; however, I continued titrating more water over the rest of the evening. Once that bottle was gone, a beer would be handed out with increasing hours between doses. Dinner went smoothly. The kids accepted that their dad's eyebrow injury was from a fall, though he later admitted to Connor that he got punched in a fight; a father to son bonding with brawl stories.

After dinner, Josh incessantly hovered around me. He mentioned that this was an opportunity for us to get back together, and he needed to know if that was possible before Shelley flew out. Most taxing was that he didn't get tired when he was like this, and nothing registered with him. Finally, a break occurred from his obsessive behavior when he went upstairs to call his fiancée for some much-needed attention. Outside the door, I listened for a little while to get a pulse on Josh's thinking.

Josh professed how much he missed her and that he couldn't wait to see her again. Then he focused on detailing what led to the "gash" on his head, the concussion, and how nobody seemed to care. He repeated himself and continually revisited how much he was ignored. That earful was enough for me. I had already texted Shelley about the one inch cut across his left eyebrow and that I would be detoxing him. I gave her warning that in my opinion, he was pretending to have a concussion to hide his level of intoxication. Shelley had responded appreciatively, and understood his need for attention.

An evening can really drag on when someone is off-the-chain, cuckoo nuts. Josh did not seem to be getting sleepy. "Enough!" I yelled. Josh was denied any more beer until he drank half a bottle of Benadryl, which he reluctantly did. Once Josh was set up in the TV room with a beer, a snack, a blanket, and the remote, I decided to go to bed. I told him there was one more beer in the fridge to help him get through the night; how quickly that disappeared was up to him. Josh was willing to go with the plan. Since his dramatic pleas had received no rise from me, he pretty much had to do as I said.

THE NEXT MORNING, Josh joined us for breakfast. He was quiet and polite; his sole interest was coffee. I avoided moments alone with him, since I knew he would ask for a morning beer. Josh cleaned up the kids' breakfast dishes; they went upstairs to get dressed for soccer. This was a good moment to deliver my newly-harvested thought for the day.

"Josh, you made it through the night. It has been over six hours since you had a beer, and one to two hours from the one before that. Since we have a goal to achieve, I think it would only take you backwards to have another beer."

"What is the goal?" he asked in a flat tone.

"You tell me, Josh, because I do not have a goal of wasting my time."

"To get me past the cravings, so I can function again, and be of service."

"You are a team player. If it helps, I feel bad this is not easy for you. I know it's very difficult, but you were days, if not hours, from urinating blood or worse when I found you. I know you can do this, even if you hate it." I put my arm around him.

"You smell good," he said.

Boy, give a guy an inch. "Thank you. Let's take our kids to soccer. You can come with us."

"I don't think I should go. I don't feel well and—".

"Yeah, how you feel isn't going to change, no matter where you sit. The soccer game will be a distraction for you, and besides, the kids deserve to see two parents on the sidelines for a change. Jolie and I are working the snack bar. We leave in thirty minutes. Why don't you check your emails? You've probably ignored many people by now."

Josh could not seem to problem-solve anything to do with his time, or his body. It appeared as if I was treating Josh like a kid, but really, I was treating a grown-ass man like he had a poorly functioning brain. Welcome to chronic alcoholism: this is exactly what you get. Josh's cognitive functioning was way down; in addition, he was manipulative at every turn, and emotionally immature. I was sensitive to not inadvertently destroy him, so I politely turned down any sexual advances. He was in no way sexually aggressive or crude, nor had he ever been, but as a drunk, he was annoyingly persistent. Perhaps I was too polite, but I expected a man to put the brakes on after he hears you're not interested. I wish someone had told me: if a guy is drunk, he will not stop. At best, he will only tap the brakes.

THE SOCCER GAME turns out to be a success. Josh talked with a few guys he knew, our sons played well, and Jolie was a wiz at making corn dogs and hot cocoa. Once we got home and I had turned down another plea for a beer, Josh slumped his way upstairs to the attic and stayed in bed – all day. By early evening, he was having sweats and weird visions. He said that a blue cat lady came to talk to him; he did not recall what she said. I supplied him with cool washcloths and water, and left him alone. I gave him a bell to ring if he needed me. I knew that there was about a twenty percent chance of seizures and/or death during this withdrawal period.

THE NEXT DAY, my mom came over to babysit Josh while I did things with the kids, and went to work. We were in the background if he needed us; we let him know he was cared about. By day three, Josh re-emerged from his attic cocoon looking and sounding like the power got turned back on in his head. He ate some crackers, took a shower, and sat at his computer with a blanket wrapped around him. Luckily, he responded to his upcoming employer before anything went awry. They had a fixed start date, and they needed him to fill out some human resource paperwork. Josh completed the paperwork; I faxed it over for him. Josh was pulling his life forward. He searched online for apartments, and handled 'Dr. Josh things' again.

Josh opened up about what the three-day detox experience had been like for him. "It was rough. Detoxing is one of the most awful things to go through. Your body is so hypersensitive to everything. I mean, my skin actually hurt. And my mind went to this alternate reality. It was really weird."

"A blue cat lady sounds pretty weird."

His eyes opened wide. "How did you know about the cat lady?"

"Uh, you told me."

Josh ran his fingers through his dirty blonde hair. "I did? I do not remember."

Being genuinely curious I asked, "Do you know how many days have gone by since I got you from Roger's house?"

"I don't know, like two days?"

"Four days. I found you curled up in your bed, in the middle of the day, and we had not seen you two days prior to that. That is six days total. You looked and smelled like a homeless person, and I do not mean to put down the homeless. I want you to understand how quickly you go down a rabbit hole and can't function, especially when you keep starting and stopping. This is progressive, Josh. There is no bouncing back like the ole days."

"Every time, I think: 'I'll just have a wine or a six pack'. It gets embarrassing going back to the store, so I think if I buy vodka, then I don't have to go back as much. Then I start buying a bigger bottle of vodka because what I drink doesn't even faze me."

"Oh, it fazes you. That's when the rest of us start paying for it."

"I am sorry. Thank you for coming to get me, and thank you for letting me stay here. It is nice to be around you and the kids, and be comfortable and in a warm bed."

"You're welcome. I'm glad you're feeling better."

JOSH WAS HELPFUL ONCE AGAIN. Together, we finished cleaning out the basement and he picked out a few tools he wanted to keep. He helped with yard clean up, and chopped wood for the fireplace. That night, he and Connor got a really good fire going in the TV room. The kids and I roasted marshmallows and made s'mores. Jolie loved to stake out her blanket right in front of the fire's heat, and drink hot cocoa. Nicky joined his sister, as always. They were both wearing footie-pajamas, making them two of the cutest peas in a pod.

TEAMWORK MAKES DREAMWORK

Missy heard back from Mister Uppity's realtor via a faxed letter written by him and his wife. Missy attempted neutrality as she read their request over the phone. They felt that the duct work should be removed as a precaution for the health of their children, and that I should understand their concerns having kids myself, blah, blah, blah. Their suggested compromise was that I merely lower the sale price $3000, and they would handle the issue for me.

Missy asked, "What do you want to do Jess? I know it's $3000 more off the price, but then it's a done deal. They said everything is a go."

"We don't even know if they will have the duct work removed, but they get the price lowered again. No. First, he bullies, then he plays a 'you have kids too, card'. This guy is used to getting his way. I'm not doing it. No."

"You're willing to let the sale go for $3,000 dollars? Jessie, I know you want out of that house."

"I have already let go of college money, and lowered the price below any sense of a comfortable ride. I'll be lucky if we can stay in this town. Another three grand is the loss of a bathroom we'd use every day. Nobody knows my contract price; I will take the risk of staying on the market. I am also willing to risk they don't back out. Go make some magic happen, Missy!"

"I'm going to need a bigger wand."

I INFORMED my dad and brother of the bargaining situation.

They understood; however, my Dad wanted to talk to me about it in person. My dad and I had a thing of jogging together around his neighborhood, then going back to his house to chat over oatmeal, which I made while he showered. Sitting at his circular kitchen table on chairs with wheels, my dad passed the raisins, along with a dash of persuasion.

"It's been a long-haul, honey. Maybe it's better to get the deal signed. A lot of offers have fallen through."

"I know, Dad. But life keeps handing me these moments when I need to draw the line for myself. I am not giving a $3000 discount for an A-hole tactic. Do you think his wife will let them lose the house at this point?"

"We shall see tomorrow," my dad kindly replied.

MISSY CALLED me first thing the next morning, speaking in a low calm voice. "We got it done."

"What do you mean, we got it done?"

"I mean the other realtor and I kept going back and forth, and we got it done. We sold your house." Her exhaustion over-powered her excitement.

Still reeling in shock, "I'm not lowering the price? He took the offer?"

"No. That guy's a jackass; he wouldn't budge. I told the other realtor that if we split the three thousand and took it off our commission, we could get this deal done. It's still a good commission."

"She went with it?"

"No. She was like, 'I don't know.' I said to her, 'Ya want noth-in'? Cause that's the option. We will sell this house to someone else!'" Missy laughed. "Then she agreed, but then he still didn't want to agree. I think his wife stood up at that point. I've been up all night, Jess, but it's done. It will come off the commission. It's done."

"Missy, I feel bad. That's not what I wanted to have happen."

"You wanted it sold; I wanted it sold. It's sold! Now, I have to find you another house."

"You're the bomb, Missy – thank you! Oh my gosh, the house is sold!"

Thank you, house, for the childhoods that were nurtured here, and for holding us through our mistakes.

SEPARATE WAYS

Despite the kids being a mix of sad and happy, they were quick to request "must haves" for the new house. Mostly, it was Connor hoping for an entire basement to himself, which was not going to happen, but he was welcome to dream. Plans were made for Josh's fiancée to fly down in a couple days. They would stay at Roger's for a bit, then drive off to the Midwest and start a new life. Josh asked if the kids could meet her. My answer was "hell no." The kids would not be part of a petty meet and greet. I reminded him, should he have forgotten, of faking his impending death, hitting on me, playing both Shelley and I for the better outcome, and good times at Camp-town Detox. Be a standup guy first, introduce our standup kids second.

Josh was riding on tissue paper wings from a weeklong sobriety. With the clock ticking on his new beginnings, he plotted to freeze time. He enjoyed the comforts of being in the house with the familiar hustle and bustle of us around him. He expressed uncertainty around the debacle with Shelley. He frequently mentioned that he thought his concussion was seriously impacting his functioning, and didn't know if he should travel. This stirred no reaction from me except for a quick rebuttal. Josh, determined to plead his case, called one of his former students to come over and evaluate him. When she showed up at my door explaining her purpose, it blew my mind. Politeness urged me to invite her inside. She performed a brief assessment involving asking Josh questions, and checking his pupil reactions. She was very doting as Josh explained his symptoms.

When I got a moment alone with her, I quickly explained his recent detox situation, and hinted at the double play he was making with Shelley and I. Her questions shifted focus to a more alcohol-related cognitive assessment, and Josh had difficulty with problem-solving and working memory. She seemed stunned, and not sure what to do. She stopped everything, told him that traveling might not be a good idea, and quickly left.

Despite Josh hearing what he wanted; this assessment made it painfully clear that he was demonstrating a cognitive decline. Later that evening, after much computer research, Josh told me about Wernicke-Korsakoff syndrome (WKS), often found in chronic alcoholics. He thought maybe he was exhibiting some of the symptoms. With a reduction of alcohol intake, many of the symptoms could improve in acute situations. Cognitive impairment was certainly a scary thing for Josh if he wanted to retain a professional career. Ta-da! His concussion disappeared.

SHELLEY FLEW OUT and stayed with Josh at Roger's house. Through secretly reading email exchanges with his brother, I learned that Josh was planning to leave in two days. I had imagined Josh would share this information with me, but he did not.

ON THE EVENING before he was supposed to leave, Josh came over to make dinner; said he could not stay long. It was understandable that he didn't want Shelley waiting around. I could tell that he had gone back to drinking; he was overly complacent, and aloof. Josh attempted to excuse himself once we sat down for dinner. He told the kids, "See you tomorrow!" as he walked out of the dining room. *But I know you won't be here tomorrow.* I informed the kids that I needed to talk with their dad, and that they should *mangiare.*

I escorted Josh upstairs and requested that we sit on the bed to have an honest conversation. Josh was definitely buzzed. He agreed to talk, but mentioned apologetically that he did need to get home soon.

"I understand. I'm sure it's awkward balancing between Shelley and I."

"Yes, it is. She gets jealous easily, but she likes you."

"Shelley does not need to be my new best friend. That's not why I want to talk to you. When are you planning to leave?"

"I-I'm not sure. We need to find a place, and that will take some time. I found a couple of places online worth checking out. I don't know yet if I can get any relocation assistance."

"I didn't ask you about getting an apartment... I am asking, when do you plan to get in your car and drive away? Which means your kids would not see you again until who knows when."

"We are thinking of leaving pretty soon."

"And when might that be?"

"Maybe tomorrow. I mean, we're not certain. Things may change." He still had a postcard smile on his face; he slouched while looking at me. His head bobbed a little every once in a while.

"If I text Shelley right now and ask when are you planning to leave, is she going to tell me tomorrow, or will she indicate that she has no idea?"

"She will say tomorrow."

"So, when are you leaving Josh?"

"Tomorrow morning."

I confirmed, "You were planning to leave the kids without saying goodbye?" A rage began to surge through every muscle, bone, and fingernail in my body. If a full moon had appeared, I would have transformed into one pissed off werewolf.

Josh did not answer. He put his head down, stating: "The kids already know I'm leaving. They know I am moving out west."

I growled, "They do not know you won't be here tomorrow.

They would wake up and you would be gone—gone without saying good-bye – again. The only reason you are back in their lives is because I apologized for you. I did the explaining for you. I put most of the blame on alcoholism instead of your thoughts. And now you want to raise the dead, and have them feel abandoned all over again?"

Josh had nothing to offer: no gesture, no words, no look of seriousness, and no game plan. Putting his hands on his lap, he made a pleasant face and said, "I'm sorry."

"You're sorry? This is way past sorry. With every ounce of my being, I could literally rip your throat out. You are not fucking up their development while driving away with a cup of coffee in your hand and a vodka bottle under the seat!" My ex-husband went white as a ghost looking as if he had just swallowed his tongue. I spelled out the game plan. "Tonight, you are going to say goodbye to your kids and tell them what they mean to you; that includes telling them you're sorry for whatever truth you can own."

"I'm no good at this. What if I start crying? My kids will hate me. My life has the tendency to fall apart when I'm not strong enough."

I know him. Admitting out loud where he has no structure, no form, is a real voice. A genuine voice, uprising from behind Pandora's box, straining to speak louder than his chronic alcoholism. I swallowed hard and met him with the same genuineness. "I see you. I know you love your kids. I know you want them well. I know you can't hold accepting every misstep you've made. Your kids love you. You are their dad, and you're going to miss that if you don't open up to them. This is as much for you as it is for them. I will help get the ball rolling; you can handle this."

Josh asked, "Do we have to do this now? What if I'm not enough?"

My cheeks filled out as a smile emerged...my green-eyed gaze softening because for once, we were on the same page. "Parents have to wait about twenty years before they know the answer to that question. I think it's a question the good ones ask." Placing a hand on his knee I stated, "I'll get the kids. There's no trust you'll do this later."

OUR KIDS WERE STILL SEATED at the dining room table. I informed them that their dad had something important to share, and that we were going to sit on the bed upstairs as a family and listen. They gathered around their dad who appeared to be very caring, humbled, and solemn at this point. Josh pressed his lips together while he squeezed their small hands. He glanced at each son and daughter with a loving, wide-eyed expression, but no words came out. They waited. They settled into a serious mood.

Providing an intro, I said: "Your dad wants to tell you what is happening tomorrow." I extended my open palms towards him.

Their dad explained that his new job was ready for him to start and that, unfortunately, it was time for him to go. The kids were visibly surprised and taken aback. Josh explained his upcoming tasks of looking for an apartment, the job training procedures, and the timeline he had to follow. Three little faces drooped into sadness, but they seemed to understand. The kids asked some practical questions about the trip, and their dad answered truthfully. I asked Josh if there was anything else he would like to share.

Josh looked at me without any anger, took a deep breath and rested his hands flat on the yellow hibiscus bedspread. "I know I've been drinking a lot, and I'm sorry you had to see that. I know that makes me a bad dad. I know I say and do some stupid things. You guys are so perfect in every way. I love you, Nicky, and Jolie, and Connor," looking at his sons and his daughter while he said this. "I plan to make a good start out there, and I will send your mom money. I know you guys will get a new house and I expect that you will take care of each other and your mom." He gave me an appreciative nod.

Josh was without any bravado. I don't think the kids had ever seen him so visibly emotional or honest. A child to parent love is quite the magnet: all three kids simultaneously hugged their dad, holding him tight. Overwhelmed with pure love and perhaps forgiveness, Josh hugged his children back, and mouthed "thank you" to me. At this point, I left the room allowing them to finish hugging it out on their own. I felt I had done something right. I prayed it might mean fewer therapy sessions when my kids got older.

Joshua came downstairs. We hugged good-bye. My ex-husband softly kissed me on the cheek before walking out the door...down the long, brick path...passing under canopies of giant Sycamore trees whose outstretched branches were still holding on to the golden leaves of autumn. This moment was a reminder that he had once abandoned me too, left without saying good-bye, or saying I mattered. For a moment, I felt sad for that woman left holding the bag. Nevertheless, she persisted. No more coffin. No one stole who I was inside: a beautiful, happy, smart, expansive, and playful woman. Sure, parts of me needed to mature, become more disciplined, more self-reliant, and less exhausted—there's always a to do list. But I was okay. I loved pouring myself into raising my babies, my children. Other chapters were coming; I could sense it in air.

A FEW DAYS LATER, we received two headlines of good news. First, Josh and Shelley arrived safe and sound. Second, Missy had found us a house that had gone on the market only ten days before. It was within our new, slashed budget.

"It's a three-bedroom, one-bathroom rancher built in 1960. Only one level, but there's a basement. I think it's finished."

We visited the house. A workbench, saw table, and coffee cans separating different-sized screws was not a finished basement. This basement had open beams, vents, pipes, and electrical wiring all exposed, not to mention a concrete floor. The limited curb appeal of this white stucco house amounted to three cement steps and three completely different bushes all in a row: that was it. The backyard had a swamp-maple tree. Its roots were exposed all around the base which extended out to the dry, yellow grass. That was the yard. Inside were oak floors stained with dog urine, and carpets worse than the wood. The three bedrooms were not too bad at ten by eleven feet, each with a couple of windows. The layout and the natural lighting did give this home potential. The living room had a small fireplace and view of our neighbor's rusty, dilapidated shed. But the kitchen opened to an add-on family room with a twenty-foot ceiling, creating a heart-space for the home that eventually drew me to sign.

Missy was wise and sent over a contractor who could do the work of renovating the basement, providing us an additional bedroom and bathroom. Had I never moved into that apartment and discovered what I could do, I don't think I would have had the confidence or the vision to take on this house. It was a fixer upper, and too small, but... Hey, we needed to accept the deal. I told the kids point blank that we would learn how to create a home, and we'd do it together. Connor, Jolie and Nicky were willing to roll the dice of acceptance and hope.

———

I DIDN'T TELL anyone about the new job interview. The house sale took enough crossed fingers; besides, this was a stretch, a reach. A recruiter postcard had come in the mail offering a Rehabilitation Director Position at a nearby subacute and long-term care facility. It would provide full benefits for my family, even advance my career. The interview with the regional manager went well; they had planned on making a quick decision.

When the regional manager called me back, she said I didn't get the job. However, she offered something more appropriate.

"We think you would be great as an assistant director. We want to create the position for you. We think with a staff of twenty-three, it's long overdue. The current director position is being offered to a physical therapist already working here, and he's on board with the idea."

Before accepting the position, I had asked for two things. First, to meet Jake, the incoming director, to determine if we'd make a good team. Jake and I did meet, and he was awesome. Jake was very friendly, proud of his staff, and knew his clinical stuff. Although, I have to admit, his height took me by surprise. The top of his black pompadour hair maybe reached my shoulders. His head and trunk were typical size, however, his arms and legs were not. Then I noticed he had the thickest dark-curly eyelashes, chocolate brown eyes, and a warm smile. Jake also wanted us to be a great duo; we joked of becoming the Batman and Robin of geriatric care. Jake made sure to declare in a deep, throaty voice while pointing a thumb at himself, "I'm Batman."

Next, I had asked for a one time, thousand dollars sign-on bonus. My request was denied. I counter offered, asking for a fifty-cent raise; they said yes on the spot. That equated to more than one thousand dollars every year – not a bad first move as the new assistant director. My job would start in the new year when the kids would be back in school, and hopefully, enough boxes would be unpacked for us to move around. My early intervention cases would age out one by one; I'd swing both jobs as long as I could. Then, I would be home by four o'clock every day to be with my cubs. Our future would not have a hamster wheel.

A WEEK prior to closing on the house, Missy called to say, "You're not going to believe this...." Exasperated, she spelled it out: "The bank said Josh has to sign the papers for the house. The divorce papers don't matter to them." She reviewed the multitude of conversations she had engaged in over the issue.

There was no other option. "Do you think he'll sign? We can fax the notarized papers back and forth. He's good now, right?"

"Oh Missy, if you only knew..."

What she did not know was that Josh had already lost his job, and Shelley had left him on a ticket Caleb had to buy to get her out of there. Jacque had told me, Josh was a mess. His family could no longer deny it, but they didn't know what to do. Despite liking him very much and admitting he was a good "kid", Jacque did not want Josh back in their home. He caused Caleb too much worry. I told her Josh's current situation was a ticking time bomb. He would not be able to problem-solve his way out of it. If he didn't have a car accident, he would be homeless within a month when his lease ran out. Jacque felt she couldn't voice these concerns to Caleb.

Stepping in per request, I talked to David and laid out that it was either rescue time or time to watch his brother drown. They could choose to save Josh and give him a chance, or wish they had tried. Turned out, it was a no brainer decision: they wanted to help. David would be able to fly out in a week, followed by his mother. Until then, Josh would have to survive on his own.

JOSH DIDN'T ANSWER my calls, but did respond to my 9-1-1 style text. He was willing to assist with the sale of the house and sign the papers, but couldn't handle the logistics of the task. Worse, when I talked to him the next day, Josh questioned if selling the house to these buyers was such a good idea; up popped a red flag that he might not be able to see this through.

My brother, Greg, stepped in and pulled a rabbit out of a hat. "I'm sending a courier to Josh's apartment. The courier will get all the signatures we need, and FedEx the papers back. Sis, tomorrow at 1:00 p.m., all he needs to do is open the door and hold a pen."

In my other ear Missy said, "Your brother is taking the ball to the goal line, Jess. You better make sure your ex-husband opens the door. My nerves can't handle any more overtime."

"He'll do it Missy. He'll do it."

Josh and I had a simple heart to heart. He wanted us to be okay. I did not have to twist his arm. Josh signed the papers and the courier mailed them. My brother, Missy, and I sat around a conference table, and went through the mechanics of selling our family home. It was a friendly exchange with the new buyers. Our house of ten years officially sold.

Josh's brother and mother flew out and detoxed him cold turkey. Josh said his brother wasn't as nice about detoxing as I had been. On the mend, Josh then flew home with Ingrid. She lived alone and was glad to have help around the house while Josh lived out the consequences of his choices. Sobriety was closing in and waiting for him, when and if he chose it.

LEAVING THE NEST

Moving wasn't easy, but one tough moment stood out. Connor's blonde, maplewood bunk beds were finally away from the wall. What he had shared, never left my mind. Half-heartedly, I had already searched for his tally marks, but none turned up. Before we left, I was determined to find them. After scanning all the railings...there they were, located on the lowest mattress beam. My fingers lightly brushed over the half-inch ridges; no doubt etched night after night with the gifted pocket knife from his father. Diagonal line after diagonal line, Connor had put the tally marks into groups of five. My son had carved one hundred and seven lines into the wood railing of his bunkbed waiting for his dad to come home—a petroglyph of the organic childhood pain of abandonment.

Two moving trucks came to take away our packed-up lives. Left behind were gifts for the next owners' young son and daughter. In each bedroom, holding a brightly colored balloon was a new *Stuffie,* assigned with the special task of looking after the kids and to help make wonderful childhood memories.

I purchased our upcoming house the following morning. Those two moving trucks with all our belongings reappeared at the white rancher bungalow, but only one stopped. We had to send the other truck straight to a storage center: none of its contents would fit. That's alright, with a fresh beginning of resilience, we would adjust.

CHRISTMAS DINNER WAS at my mom's house. She made the traditional Italian fare that Greg and I had enjoyed growing up: homemade manicotti and chicken cacciatore in Grandma Angela's sauce flavored with oxen tail. The grandkids had assisted my mom by rolling the meatballs and flipping the manicotti crepes. There was also sausage lasagna, garlic bread, Caesar salad, roasted Brussel sprouts and stuffed artichokes. Afterwards, to further decimate the waistline of any survivors, dessert was a five-pound cheesecake with dark Bing cherries on top and loads of whipped cream.

This was my first Christmas season as a divorced woman. Under the tree I had financial security, the magic of raising children, career growth, a house in my name, solid friendships, a supportive family, and three incredible kids loved by both their mom and their dad, and they loved us back. One day, what had felt so much like a survival crawl, would become a mere prologue. I had fought for those in my kingdom.

Farewell 2012.

AFTERWORD

Whew, you made it. Good job! This was my story, my percep-
tions, and the choices I made. Sharing it with you was my effort
to encourage compassion, camaraderie, and an awareness of
options and pitfalls in these types of situations that are all too
common among us. Just to clarify, names and some details were
changed in an attempt to provide a protective layer of privacy
for my family. I admire their courage to support me and bear
being uncomfortable when those moments surely come.

I define compassion as thinking of another person's well-
being when you don't want to or even necessarily like it. Being
compassionate only when it's convenient is self-serving, which
misses the point. To generate compassion I suggest consider-
ing the other person's point of view. Understanding another's
perspective can often quiet one's own judgmental noise. After
all, perspective is unique to each of us.

Another emotion that likes to lurk around me is resentment,
ah the creepy bastard. The problem with resentment is that it
hangs out with anger and bitterness, a trio that stays long after
the damage is over. These three stooges cause me to ruminate
and ruminate and ruminate. What's my point? My point, is "the
pointing". To move beyond resentment, one must eventually

point the finger at oneself to ask, *what can I do to take the next step that does less harm? What can I do about me that creates a piece of harmony?* Once those self-reflecting muscles get stronger: lift-up, carry, and then let go of others, supporting them to walk on their own accord. We are all in this together. In the end, we all cross the same never ending finish line.

Society benefits from men and women courageous enough to own their mistakes and make amends for them. To do this means to first admit the mistake(s). That is painful, difficult, embarrassing and not always well received.

I hope to offer a follow-up book to SHOT GLASS because the next several years were more unbelievable and uplifting in different, unexpected ways. Josh returned and cleared his karma with me, because I allowed him. Better than asking what to do, he looked for what needed to be done and did it. My ex-husband finally chose to fight for his sobriety; but, every time he needed rest from the fight, his addiction – as all kinds do - came back swinging. Was his track record perfect moving forward? No, but neither were my actions. Note, there can be no weak link in the chain towards recovery for every link will get tested.

Rooting for our antagonist is symbolic of rooting for anyone to overcome struggles with addiction, family crises, divorce fallout, or fill-in your own blank. We need to strive towards integrity, wellness, healthy detachment, and to make well informed decisions. May we all resolve our treasured differences in peace.

Thank you, reader, for taking the time to sit with me, with us, page after page, and invest in this story. Now I say with all my heart, go invest in yourself. You absolutely deserve it.

With love,
Rochelle

ACKNOWLEDGMENTS

Special thanks to each of my wonderful and adorable sons and daughter. You are each as amazing and precious as a vibrant lotus flower reaching up strong and beautifully from the depth of its' roots. Lotus flowers grow from muddied waters; I am sorry about all the muck. I love you. Always have. Always will. - Momma

To my parents, thank you for always being in my corner – I love you too. Always have. Always will. - your daughter

To my bro and his wonderful wife – We are blessed to have you and your incredible girls in our lives. I love you all.

To my aunts and uncles – thank you for your attention, humor and influence throughout my life. I didn't turn out too bad.

To my fellow occupational therapists – you rock! Keep fixing, mending and retraining our young, our old, our family members, to have more functionally independent lives.

To the world of indie-writing You Tubers – I could not have self-published without your tutorials, empathy and professional tips. Most helpful to me were the following: The Creative Penn, Jericho Writer's, iWriterly, Alexa Dunn, and Derick Murphy just to name a few.

Thanks to the team at Ebook Launch and their editor Ann Robertson. Ann, you went above and beyond the call of duty - thanks so much!

Much gratitude to Vellum, the best for book formatting.

A special thanks to RF who helped bring the cover package of this book across the finish line, more than once.

My core friends from high school NA, JM, BT, TL: thanks for holding onto pieces of who I am, for making me laugh and for supporting my writing journey. Thanks to mi bella DM-V who starred in my first written play, Swimming In Vodka - you're awesome.

And to those we've lost; you are not forgotten.

Indie author, self-publisher and all rights reserved: Rochelle and Rochelle Books

Cover Illustrator: Ron Farina Photography with Rochelle

Cover Art: Ron Farina Photography and gallery stock

Identifiers: Title: SHOT GLASS by Rochelle. NARRATIVE NONFICTION/ ISBN 9781734161403 (paperback) / ISBN 9781734161410 (ebook)

First press Ingram Spark: October 2019; Revised December 2019

Contact and author info: WWW.RochelleBooks.com

CPSIA information can be obtained
at www.ICGtesting.com
Printed in the USA
BVHW031909130220
572330BV00001B/99